JOHN REIBETANZ

The *Lear* World:
A study of *King Lear*
in its dramatic context

HEINEMANN
LONDON

Heinemann Educational Books Ltd.
LONDON EDINBURGH MELBOURNE AUCKLAND KINGSTON
SINGAPORE HONG KONG KUALA LUMPUR IBADAN
NAIROBI JOHANNESBURG LUSAKA NEW DELHI

ISBN 0 435 18770 8
© University of Toronto Press
First published 1977

The drawing on the cover is by Joe Rosenthal,
courtesy of the Sisler Gallery, Toronto.

Published by
Heinemann Educational Books Ltd.
48 Charles Street, London WIX 8AH
Printed in Canada

TO THE MEMORY OF ROSALIE L. COLIE

'One measure of human greatness ... was the capacity to create a vocabulary celebrating humanity in the grip of irremediable suffering.'

Contents

Preface ix

Introduction: The Dramatic Context 3

1
Gateway to the *Lear* World 11

2
Structure: 'The Dramatic Effect of the Great Scenes' 33

3
Structure: Figures and Configurations 56

4
Characterization: Fools and Madmen 81

5
The Rack of This Tough World 108

Notes 123

Index   139

Preface

'It is no great mark of insight to observe that books on Shakespeare tend to be on Shakespeare and that books on Elizabethan and Jacobean drama tend to be on individual figures "exclusive" of Shakespeare (as course descriptions used to read).' So Maurice Charney wrote in 1974, reviewing the previous year's studies in English Renaissance drama. He went on to describe as 'lamentable' this continued 'isolation of the major Elizabethan and Jacobean dramatist from the study of Elizabethan and Jacobean drama.'

This book views *King Lear* as the work of that dramatist, a man more closely and continuously associated with the London theatre than any other playwright of his time. It is my premise that *King Lear* draws much of its power from Shakespeare's creative reinterpretation of the dramatic traditions and conventions that he knew so thoroughly. Consequently, I believe that a fuller understanding of the play's relationship to its dramatic heritage can lead to a deeper, more meaningful experience of *King Lear*. By 'experience,' I am referring not just to the response of the scholar in his study, but to that of the spectator in the theatre, because the conventions that Shakespeare uses to such great advantage in *King Lear* are means of moving audiences, and the modern spectator's response will be a richer one if he can apprehend something of the context in which the play's first audiences experienced it. That, at any rate, is what actors, directors, and audiences keep telling me after our student productions of Shakespeare; if not true, it is at least a charitable fiction.

As Gombrich's *Art and Illusion* has demonstrated, we see largely as we have been taught to see. We have been taught to view Shakespeare's achievement in a Romantic and post-Romantic light, and even though we like to think of ourselves as liberated from the artistic values of our immediate predecessors, those values still help to determine the nature of our critical response. To be sure, in the forty years that have elapsed since M.C. Bradbrook's pioneering work on dramatic conventions, we have come to reject interpretations of Shakespeare that equate genius with a disregard or contempt for convention; but Romantic Shakespeare is certainly not dead and gone. Besides being unconventional, the Romantic and post-Romantic 'genius' works in an extremely solitary and self-conscious manner: as a mature artist, he mines and reinterprets his own earlier achievements, and he often ignores altogether the creations of his immediate contemporaries. That is not how Shakespeare worked, and yet a great deal of criticism implies that he took such an approach to his art. Rather than look at what his fellow dramatists were writing for the same audiences and theatres at the same time, critics of Shakespeare's mature drama often confine their sense of 'context' to works written by Shakespeare ten, fifteen, or even twenty years earlier. Such studies have brought many fine insights, but they underestimate the extent to which Shakespeare – as actor, playwright, and shareholder – appreciated and responded to the changing forms of an art that developed with unprecedented rapidity. They underestimate, too, the essentially *social* nature of that art. Elizabethan and Jacobean dramatists wrote plays to order, for performance under specific conditions. They, more than later playwrights, had to deal with audience expectations that were being shaped by a continuing interaction between plays and audiences. Thus their plays were written for, as well as in, a context, and the variety of that context contributed to the brilliance of their achievements. It is my aim here to explore the role played by that context in *King Lear*.

In writing a book that tries to show something of what Shakespeare gained from the lively community of playwrights and audiences in which he worked, I have benefited greatly from a community of scholars whose vitality constantly renews the life of *King Lear*. I welcome the opportunity to acknowledge some of the larger debts contracted there during the evolution of this book.

I owe most to the late Rosalie L. Colie. She suggested that I begin such a study, and her enthusiasm encouraged me to think that I could finish it. She read and commented extensively on the earliest version of this work, and I deeply regret that the final version could not have the benefit of her kind and stimulating criticism. But as those who knew her will acknowledge, her generosity far exceeded such specific labours: she displayed an energetic interest in the ideas of her colleagues, whether they were masters or novices, and she did her best to help bring those ideas to fruition. The only way I can express my gratitude now is to dedicate to her memory this book on a play she loved so well; in doing so, I take comfort from the fact that Rosalie Colie was always an accomplished rhypologist, and welcomed little things as if they were great.

I must also thank Gerald Eades Bentley, with whom I had the good fortune to study at Princeton, and who laboured cheerfully through my diffuse doctoral dissertation on non-Shakespearean drama, the source of many theories that I hope I have developed better here. Readers of this book will realize how deeply my view of Elizabethan drama has been influenced by Professor Bentley's life-long insistence on the importance of Shakespeare's 'context.' They will also realize how indebted I am to another distinguished scholar, one whom I have met only through print: Maynard Mack's *'King Lear' in Our Time* suggested ways of looking at *King Lear* that are now the common property of all of the play's students; this particular student is especially grateful for his sensitive observations on the relationship between theatrical and pictorial concerns.

Other debts are closer to home. My good friend and colleague, W. David Shaw, gave a detailed and helpful reading to an intermediate version of the book. Another good friend and now also a colleague, John J. O'Connor, checked references and gave my style the scrutiny of his embarrassingly sharp eye. The University of Toronto Press's anonymous Reader A made so many fruitful suggestions and criticisms that I asked the Press to reveal his identity so that I could thank him properly: as a result, I am very happy to acknowledge here the role played by Maurice Charney in giving this study its present shape. Also at the Press, Prudence Tracy has been a shrewd, resourceful, and kind editor.

I am grateful to Victoria College for the grant that enabled me to attend the World Shakespeare Congress in 1971, and for the sabbatical leave during which I completed my final draft. I wish also to thank the Canada Council for the Leave Fellowship that supported me during 1974-5, and for an earlier Research Grant.

My wife, Julie, did not prepare the index, and probably would not have agreed to even if I had asked her. Instead, she has had the less mechanical but far more demanding task of following the progress of virtually every sentence in this book, and of responding critically but comfortingly. She has been happy to do so, but will I suspect be most happy to have me back, once and for all, from the state of total absorption that has marked my many excursions into the *Lear* world.

I should mention that I conceived of my title, and indeed completed my final draft, before I encountered Bernard McElroy's fine discussion of 'the *Lear* world' in *Shakespeare's Mature Tragedies* (Princeton, 1973). After reading his book I thought of changing my title, but I have decided not to because the concept indicated by it is so central to this study; anyway, the fact that another scholar can reach the *Lear* world by a different route is welcome evidence that that place has some objective existence outside of my own theories.

Finally, I am happy to acknowledge that this book has been published with the help of a grant from the Humanities Research Council of Canada, using funds provided by the Canada Council, and a grant to University of Toronto Press from the Andrew W. Mellon Foundation.

Victoria College
September 1976

THE *LEAR* WORLD:
A STUDY OF *KING LEAR* IN ITS DRAMATIC CONTEXT

Introduction:
The Dramatic Context

In Act V of Ben Jonson's *Poetaster*, Caesar asks Horace for his opinion of Virgil's learning. Horace responds with the highest praise: 'His learning labours not the schoole-like glosse,/ That most consists in *ecchoing* wordes, and termes.'[1] Virgil's learning is not something he wears on his sleeve, says Horace; it is deep and well assimilated, the 'summe/ Of all the worth and first effects of artes.' But the encomium does not end here: as if Virgil's learning were inextricably related to the worth and effect of his poetry, Horace at once delivers another opinion:

> And for his *poesie*, 'tis so ramm'd with life,
> That it shall gather strength of life, with being,
> And liue hereafter, more admir'd, then now.

It is easy to see why Yeats believed that the tribute was meant for Shakespeare.[2] Of Jonson's fellow playwrights, Shakespeare carried his learning most lightly – so lightly that later ages were able to view him as an untutored child of nature, a rough but prodigious genius who simply looked in his heart and wrote.[3]

Modern scholarship has done much to dispel this illusion. In the 1940s, T.W. Baldwin demonstrated that Shakespeare's early education provided more than a nodding acquaintance with the classics, and Theodore Spencer made it clear that Shakespeare's plays were alive with a critical knowledge of the philosophical problems of his age.[4] More recently, Kenneth Muir has emphasized that Shakespeare was even more assiduous than his contemporaries in collecting a wide range of source materials, and Muir's claim has been substantiated by studies linking Shakespeare's art to traditions of iconography, folklore, Heliodoran romance, rhetoric, and paradoxy – none of them pursuits of the unsophisticated mind.[5] If this Shakespeare warbled anything, it was probably ayres or madrigals rather than woodnotes wild. Most importantly, we have come to appreciate the vital connection between 'His learning' and 'his *poesie*' that Jonson's statement presupposed. Shakespeare's plays are 'ramm'd with

life' *because* of the traditions and conventions that they incorporate and rein-
terpret, not in spite of them. Such traditions provided him with a means of
incomparably rich compression, a shorthand that could contain, refer to, and
communicate vast areas of human experience. As Rosalie L. Colie has written,
genres and forms were the language of the Renaissance writer.[6] For Shakespeare, a sensitive response to traditions was as much a part of the writing
process as a sensitive response to words, and both these responses were his chief
artistic means of comprehending life.

Ben Jonson's tribute is especially applicable to *King Lear*: more than Shakespeare's other tragedies, this play has 'gather[ed] strength of life, with being.'
Much less popular than the other tragedies during the latter part of the seventeenth century,[7] and banished from the stage for two hundred years by Tate's
'improved' version, Shakespeare's *King Lear* has come into its own in our time.
Numerous productions, film versions, and critical interpretations testify to its
renewed strength of life.[8] It is my contention that the play's richness in forms
is largely responsible for its ability to speak to us so profoundly; and just as the
nature of our modern dramatic traditions and critical emphases have enabled us
to see *King Lear* as a work of 'our contemporary' more easily than (for instance) A.C. Bradley and nineteenth-century audiences were able to do, so I
feel that a greater awareness of Shakespeare's own dramatic heritage can lead us
to a deeper, more meaningful experience of the play.

There is at present no study that approaches *King Lear* by way of the
non-Shakespearean plays of its time, and relates its achievements to the traditions and conventions of Shakespeare's Elizabethan or Jacobean colleagues. In
writing such a study here, I am making two assumptions: that the dramatic
traditions and conventions available to Shakespeare when he wrote *King Lear*
were so rich and varied as to constitute an extremely resonant, complex 'language' that he could use to great advantage; and that Shakespeare would have
taken the trouble to learn this language. The basis for each of these assumptions needs to be set out, before the main part of this study can explore the
nature of particular traditions and conventions, and their reinterpretation in
King Lear. The following few pages are meant to provide readers who are not
specialists in Elizabethan or Jacobean drama with some general sense of Shakespeare's immediate dramatic context and his relationship to it. Readers who
have specialized knowledge in this area may find themselves covering familiar
ground, but I would ask that they take particular notice of my comments on p. 7, since these constitute what I think is a necessary statement on
the method of this study as a whole.

Three factors combined to create a dramatic context of unprecedented range
and variety in the early 1600s: the rapid evolution of English dramatic form
through a multitude of styles; the existence of several different kinds of theatrical venue, each contributing its own traditions and emphases; and the multigeneric nature of Elizabethan drama.

In 1575, there were no playhouses in London. In 1604-5, Shakespeare wrote
King Lear.[9] During the intervening thirty years, English drama had undergone

an extraordinary development. In the late 1570s and 1580s, rambling romantic adventure tales gave way (although never entirely) to the heroic drama of Marlowe and the allegorical court comedies of Lyly – along with the progeny of both – and Senecan tragedy was replaced by the more contemporary forms worked out by Kyd and Marlowe. The 1590s witnessed the evolution of the history play, the development of romantic comedy by Greene and Shakespeare, and the beginnings of humours comedy. The early 1600s saw further refinements in English tragedy by Shakespeare, Chapman, Marston, and Jonson, and the rise of satirical comedy and intrigue comedy. Even such a quick sketch as this presents an awesome array, leaving aside such developments as late moralities, biographical plays, early tragicomedies, domestic dramas, and classical adaptations. For the practising playwright what was most significant about this evolution was that it took place in so short a time that none of the 'older' forms passed from memory – either his own or that of his audience. All were available, and their availability was heightened by a repertory system that assured the frequent revival of older plays in a company's possession. The dramatist had a wide selection of living traditions at his disposal.

The existence of different theatrical auspices made for further diversification in Elizabethan drama. In addition to regular commercial productions, plays were staged at (and sometimes written especially for) the Court and the various Inns of Court;[10] and since these productions often recruited playwrights and acting companies from the established playhouses, there was constant opportunity for mutual enrichment. The commercial theatres exerted pressure towards a drama of action and mimesis,[11] while the traditions of Court and Inns of Court placed a greater emphasis on artifice and pageantry. But one of the most prominent sources of diversification was the presence among the commercial theatres of two distinct kinds of venue. Since this distinction played a significant role in shaping the dramatic environment at the time *King Lear* was written, it merits some attention here.

Elizabethan and Jacobean audiences were able to choose between performances at the public theatres – large, open-air structures situated in the London suburbs – or at the private theatres, fully enclosed buildings located in the centre of the city and accommodating much smaller audiences.[12] Each type of theatre had its devotees: the public theatres attracted a wide audience that was representative of the whole spectrum of Elizabethan society, while the private theatres, which charged six times as much, seem to have catered to a more exclusive upper-class audience.[13] In an age when dramatists wrote plays *for* particular acting companies and playing conditions, it was only to be expected that two such contrasting theatrical environments would foster different styles of dramaturgy.

We might anticipate, for instance, that the more intimate surroundings of the private theatres, where performances were held by candlelight, would favour a more restrained kind of playwriting. There would be less emphasis on violent sound and action, and more on softer gestures and a delicate interplay of voices. Also, the practice of featuring musical performances between the acts of private-theatre plays, so that spent candles could be replaced in the intervals, required a kind of dramatic structure somewhat different from the unbroken performances at the public theatres; and the exclusive use of the private theatres by all-child companies (until shortly after 1608, when the King's Men began regular performances at Blackfriars) would have placed certain mimetic effects beyond the range of private-theatre drama.[14]

For Shakespeare and other Elizabethan dramatists, the presence of these two kinds of theatrical venue provided opportunities for a richer drama: instead of a complete dichotomy between two hostile 'rival traditions,' we may think of the situation more aptly in terms of two streams of dramaturgy, moving generally in the same direction and often feeding into each other. For instance, humours comedy first appeared on the public stage, and was then developed in the private theatres; conversely, the private-theatre practice of dividing plays into acts was widely followed in public-theatre drama after about 1607. And the King's Men seem to have had little difficulty in moving back and forth regularly between the Globe and the Blackfriars theatre after acquiring the latter in 1608. Other kinds of interaction will be noted in the course of this study.

Elizabethan playwrights moved as easily between different generic conventions as they did between theatrical ones. The mingling of kings and clowns that Sidney objected to was only one instance of many incursions that forms and genres made on each other's territory in Elizabethan drama – to the horror of purists and the delight of audiences. When Rosalie L. Colie looks at *King Lear* as a work of *genera mista* (*Resources of Kind*, pp. 123-8), she is emphasizing one of the play's most typically Elizabethan characteristics. Examples of multigeneric works abound, from Marlowe's *Doctor Faustus*, blending tragedy, morality, and comedy, to Greene's *James IV* (history and romance), to Shakespeare's own *As You Like It* (romance, pastoral, and court comedy) or *Henry IV* (history, comedy, and morality). Elizabethan dramatists were well practised in the art of pillaging and combining widely different genres, and this eclecticism was undoubtedly a major source of the rich heterogeneity that Madeleine Doran finds at the heart of Elizabethan dramatic form.[15]

Shakespeare was in a better position to appreciate this wealth of dramatic traditions than any of his contemporaries. Playwright, actor, shareholder, housekeeper at both the Globe and (after 1608) Blackfriars, he was more intimately and continuously involved with the London stage than any other Elizabethan dramatist. His plays provide evidence that he took full advantage of this position throughout his career.

In early comedies such as *Love's Labour's Lost* and *A Midsummer Night's Dream*, he adapts the settings, characters, themes, structures, and verbal artistry of Lyly's court comedy to a new vision of romantic love, resulting in plays that leave Lyly's art behind even as they so unmistakably echo it.[16] Marlowe's popular achievement in *Edward II* (itself dependent on Shakespeare's *Henry VI* plays) is recognized and judiciously transformed in *Richard II*, while *The Merchant of Venice* turns a remarkable variation on Marlowe's *The Jew of Malta*.[17]

Shakespeare builds *Hamlet* on a solid foundation of popular revenge tragedy;[18] a few years later he responds to the (mainly private-theatre) satirical comedies and tragedies of Jonson and Marston by writing such plays as *All's Well That Ends Well, Measure for Measure*, and *Troilus and Cressida* — all marked by the same bitter wit and the legal jokes and jargon that appealed to the Inns of Court men who greatly influenced contemporary dramatic taste.[19] Contrary to what Rosencrantz and Guildenstern thought, Shakespeare made sure that the boys certainly did *not* 'carry it away.' Shakespeare's last plays manifest the same thorough awareness — and reinterpretation — of different dramatic traditions. In *Pericles*, he revives a number of conventions that characterize the popular drama of a much earlier period; while in *Cymbeline, The Winter's Tale*, and *The Tempest* he responds to the latest achievements of private-theatre dramaturgy in the same creative manner by which he had earlier transformed those of Lyly's plays.[20]

The purpose of the following study is to show how Shakespeare responds to some of these various dramatic traditions in *King Lear*. More particularly than in the preceding paragraph, my concern is with his reinterpretation of such traditions, with their re-creation rather than their mere accretion in *King Lear*. I want to observe the results of Shakespeare's working in a context, rather than to track down particular sources. To further this aim, I have given the dates of non-Shakespearean plays after references to them; by thus calling attention to the fact that a number of these plays were written after *King Lear*,[21] I hope to make it clear that the object of attention is not documentary sources but a context of living, evolving traditions, where Shakespeare gave at least as much as he took, anticipated as often as he recalled. Furthermore, I am interested in exploring Shakespeare's use of his dramatic context to shape our response to the play — our reactions to characters and incidents. More than the other major tragedies, *King Lear* concerns itself with *feeling*, and Shakespeare's dramaturgy here is one that makes constant demands on us in accordance with this emphasis. He demands that we as spectators act out that compassion stressed so many times in the play. In this respect, his traditions are still alive, and 'gather strength of life' again whenever *King Lear* is performed. I want to view Shakespeare's dramatic context not as fossil or even as chrysalis, but as a means of moving audiences then and now.

The one chapter that departs somewhat from an emphasis on Shakespeare's *use* of his traditions is Chapter 1. There, I am concerned more frequently with citing parallels than with following at length their creative usage in *King Lear*, and (with Tate's famous description in mind) I ask the reader's tolerance for what he may sometimes feel is a heap of undeveloped allusions. But it is my aim to set up a perspective for the rest of the study, especially for Chapters 2 and 3; the term 'gateway' thus refers to the relationship of the first chapter to what follows, as well as the relationship of *King Lear's* opening scenes to our total experience of the play. The perspective in question pertains to early Jacobean drama.

Critics have noted many kinds of difference between *King Lear* and the

other tragedies. Coleridge wrote that '*Lear* is the only serious performance of
Shakespeare the interest and situations of which are derived from the assumption of a gross improbability.' Bradley wrote that 'with the possible exception
of Lear himself, no one of the characters strikes us as psychologically a *wonderful* creation, like Hamlet or Iago or even Macbeth.' D.G. James felt that 'It is
truer of *King Lear* than of the other tragedies, that we think above all of
certain scenes: the plot is comparatively dim to us.' Maynard Mack observes
that the play 'deviates markedly from the ordinary Shakespearean norms of
probability in tragedy.' And Winifred Nowottny notes 'the absence from *Lear*
of resplendent imagery ... indeed of poetry that survives quotation out of context.'[22] I believe that much of what sets *King Lear* apart from Shakespeare's
other tragedies is what it shares with Jacobean drama, rather than with earlier
Elizabethan drama. The premise behind this belief is a familiar and well-
substantiated one, that Jacobean drama differs noticeably from what came
before it.

Students of this period have shed much light on how its drama reflects the
moral and sociological differences that separate Jacobeans from Elizabethans.[23]
While recognizing the value of their studies, I intend to concentrate more
exclusively on form: particularly in the first three chapters, I want to examine
certain differences between Elizabethan and Jacobean drama through a perspective of changing literary values and dramatic techniques. I am not denying
the relevance of a wider perspective of non-literary changes, but am emphasizing a group of changes that are worth consideration because they were more
immediate to the playwrights' pursuit of their art. The circumstances surrounding these formal changes may be briefly described.

At the beginning of the seventeenth century, a new breed of playwrights
came into prominence: such writers as Jonson, Chapman, and Marston were
avowed men of letters, building or hoping to build literary reputations among
sophisticated readers. Unlike Greene or Dekker, they were more at home with
classical forms than with popular Elizabethan narrative; and unlike Heywood or
Shakespeare, they wrote plays under various auspices, as they chose, instead of
attaching themselves to one dramatic company.[24] Their tastes and background
associated them with Court and with the Inns, rather than with the sources of
popular literature or drama: Marston, Beaumont, and Webster lived at the Inns,
and Jonson had close connections there (Finkelpearl, pp. 78-9); Fletcher and
perhaps Chapman had university backgrounds, and had influential friends at
Court. People with similar backgrounds and tastes, such as Marlowe and Lyly,
had written drama before; but the coming together of so many like minds was
unprecedented in Elizabethan drama. These playwrights were able to effect a
revolution in dramatic form, perhaps because they found strength in numbers.[25] With their arrival, the nature of Elizabethan drama – always changing,
as we have seen – changes even more drastically. As many critics have observed, drama now becomes more self-consciously artificial and philosophical,
more satiric in spirit, more eccentric in its characters and settings.[26] Along with
more subtle formal changes, these developments will be the first object of my

attention. In order to emphasize the point that after about 1600 more pronounced changes occur in a drama that had always been characterized by change, I shall use the term 'Elizabethan' to refer to drama written between 1553 and 1642, and 'Jacobean' to refer to a distinct phase (post-1600) of the larger development and to the dramatists who made their reputations then.

One debt remains to be acknowledged. I have found it helpful to summon up the presence of A.C. Bradley throughout this study. For all its frequently observed limitations, Bradley's essay on *King Lear* is still a masterpiece of sensitive reading. His remarks on the play's opening scenes, structure, characterization, and final scene punctuate the four main areas of my interpretation. I have found Bradley an especially valuable interlocutor because, unlike many later critics, he usually views *King Lear* as a changing dramatic experience rather than as a fixed object of study. In *A.C. Bradley and His Influence in Twentieth-Century Shakespeare Criticism* (Oxford, 1972), Katharine Cooke shows how Bradley has often been censured for failing to take the circumstances of production into account; but I find that he rarely loses sight of one of the most basic 'circumstances,' the moment-to-moment response of one's imagination to what is being presented. His effort to shed light on this experience constitutes an approach that must always be central to any criticism of drama. In the chapters that follow, I turn to Bradley not only to profit from his insight, but also to demonstrate that many of the 'problems' and difficulties that such a fine critical mind encountered in *King Lear* do resolve themselves when one develops the acquaintance with Shakespeare's dramatic context that Bradley lacked.

1

Gateway to the *Lear* World

The opening scenes of *King Lear* have fascinated and disturbed generations of critics – Johnson, Coleridge, and Bradley being only the most eminent of many. If one compares their comments on these scenes, one notices a remarkable similarity in their reactions, despite the great differences of approach: words like 'strange,' 'absurd,' 'improbable,' and 'obscure' form the common vocabulary of a shared response. They also share the opinion that, for good or ill, the scenes are highly uncharacteristic of Shakespearean tragedy. An interpretation of *King Lear* must come to terms with these impressions, if only because they articulate the feelings of unease that the play's opening can still evoke.

What are we to make of an opening scene that, after a quick exchange between three apparently level-headed courtiers, thrusts us into a grotesque world of love-tests and wicked sisters? The courtiers' chatty prose accentuates the formality of the ceremonial setting and patterned dialogue that follow: after fanfare and procession, Lear questions and rewards each daughter in turn, proceeding from eldest to youngest. Yet the love-test itself, biased by the promise of reward, and the inexplicable extremes of conduct to which it gives rise, border on the absurd. This blend of ritualism and unreason is less characteristic of Shakespeare than of the brothers Grimm. We may search in vain for similar incidents in *Hamlet* or *Macbeth*, for instance, which confine the grotesque to the supernatural, and which set their main characters on a far more comprehensible course of action. The subplot of *King Lear* gets off to an equally curious start in scene ii, presenting without apology one of the most tenuous intrigues in Shakespearean tragedy: 'and pat he comes,' notes Edmund, calling our attention to the situation's implausibility.

These radical departures from the norm of Shakespearean tragedy were called 'defects' by Bradley, who found them representative of greater lapses, flaws in the play's overall design. Such flaws suggest, he wrote, 'that in *King Lear* Shakespeare was less concerned than usual with dramatic fitness; improbabilities, inconsistencies, sayings and doings which suggest questions only to be answered by conjecture.'[1] Bradley was right in finding the initial effects typical of *King Lear*. The opening scenes form an appropriate gateway to a whole structure of equally bizarre and incongruous incidents, just as remote from the world of common sense. But Bradley was perhaps too quick to censure the structure for violating the canons of that commonsense world. For *King Lear* sets up its own realities and exhibits its own logic.

Undeniably, each of the major tragedies takes us into a distinct world that encourages and satisfies its own different expectations. Each offers its own world where language and action depart from the language and action of the real world primarily by displaying an internal coherence; the outlines of the play-world are familiar enough (except where they make clear departures into the supernatural) to identify with readily, but we are conscious of a shaped unity that creates a more singular atmosphere in each play. But the *Lear* world makes further demands on its audience. Like many of his contemporaries, Shakespeare here creates a play-world where events seem to unfold and characters to present themselves at a much greater remove from real life.

The opening of *King Lear* is as much a preparation for this world as the 'vilest, out-of-tune music' that leads us into the disharmonious world of Marston's *The Malcontent* (1603).[2] A brief exploration of this aspect of Jacobean dramaturgy, the extreme play-world, can place the *Lear* world in an illuminating perspective, and should clarify the nature of the action that unfolds from those first scenes. The second part of this chapter will show how the lack of exposition in the opening scenes provides a significant entrance to the *Lear* world; and the last part will explore some of the intricate relationships between those opening scenes and the rest of *King Lear*.

I

When John Day placed his characters on a well-guarded island at the start of *The Isle of Gulls* (1606), he was being literal about what other Jacobean playwrights were undertaking figuratively: the creation of a special, isolated world that would elicit extreme and entertaining reactions from their protagonists. The dramatist sets up a play-world where settings, time sequences, and behavioural patterns exhibit notable departures from the logic of the real world. Such departures, consistent and mutually supporting, give the writer greater opportunity for the intense, exclusive development of situation and theme than a more naturalistic framework would allow.

For many of these playwrights, a 'French' or 'Italian' court became the ideal artificial environment, yielding the extreme *données* that would provoke equally extreme reactions from characters and audience. Describing the milieu of *The Malcontent*, for instance, Malevole calls the court a pigeon house that is 'smooth, round, and white without, and full of holes and stink within' (I.iv.84-5). The metaphor may lack fastidiousness, but it accurately conveys the range of theatrical effects that Marston and other Jacobean playwrights could evoke from their court atmospheres: exhibitions of grotesquerie provided by such products of the court as Bilioso (whose ambition makes him pimp for his wife and his daughter-in-law) or Maquerelle (who takes bribes for bringing lovers to the Duke's faithless wife), ample opportunities for raillery like Mendoza's or for radical poses like Malevole's, and the chaotic scenes that result when numerous intrigues and counter-intrigues collide with each other.

Particularly in tragic drama, the court is often a place of inverted ideals, in which policy can face more noble virtues in a series of exaggerated confrontations; policy always wins the individual encounters, and nobility either remains tragically untarnished or is warped by the trial. So the nobility of Marston's heroine, Sophonisba, undergoes a series of trials in the court of Carthage. Carthago describes the hostile world of *Sophonisba* (1605) when he says, 'The only dew that makes men sprout in Courtes, is use.'[3] Sophonisba refuses to compromise, and is consequently destroyed by the play's distorted environment. Marston's play seems to have been written almost simultaneously with *King Lear*, and many parallels may be drawn between Sophonisba's uncompromising virtue and Cordelia's. Both heroines, depicted in a remote, stylized manner, endure the trials of an evil and scheming world (itself depicted more concretely), and each emerges as – in the words of Marston's subtitle – a 'wonder of women.' Philip Finkelpearl has described the world of *Sophonisba* as very close to that of *King Lear*, observing that 'the fundamental conflict in the play is between those who have personal integrity and honor, and those who follow policy and utility. Though we ultimately see the politic creatures punished, evil is certainly shown to be the dominant force in this world. The good retreat from one defense position to the next.'[4]

Similarly, the French court in which Chapman's Bussy D'Ambois plays out his tragic career is described by King Henry as a 'mirror of confusion.'[5] Bussy searches for the chance to express his heroic nature, but the only opportunities that this court provides are sordid ones: duels arising from trifles, the acquisition of a 'brave' wardrobe, an adulterous affair, and a number of shabby subterfuges. The hero takes on the colour of his surroundings, and finally succumbs to them.

Chapman, Marston and their colleagues seek to create a unique 'topsy-turvy world'[6] in each play, whether tragedy or comedy, and the court setting is only the most popular of many imaginary locales. Other examples of the extreme play-world may readily be found in the various conformations that Jonson and Middleton build from the city milieu of their comedies,[7] or that Beaumont and Fletcher create from Arcadian romance settings. They are all self-enclosed, despite the satiric applications to the real world that some of them encourage. Each dramatic world brings its own standards of probability: actions that would be incongruous in any other play, or that are unthinkably grotesque in the real world, are felt to be perfectly appropriate in their proper context. The statuesque posing of Bussy as he is dying, the 'trial' of Oriana in Beaumont and Fletcher's *The Woman Hater* (1606), and the absurd marriages in so many of Middleton's comedies, are all acceptable products of their respective environments.

The world of *King Lear* is similarly integral and exclusive, and similarly extreme.[8] Bradley perceived the unity of the *Lear* world when he made this sensitive appraisal of Gloucester's attempted suicide at Dover:

> Imagine this incident transferred to *Othello* ... In *Othello* it would be a shocking or a ludicrous dissonance, but it is in harmony with the spirit of *King Lear*. And not only is this so, but, contrary to expectation, it is not, if properly acted, in the least absurd on the stage. The imagination and the feelings have been worked upon with such effect ... that we are unconscious of the grotesqueness of the incident for common sense. (pp. 248-9)

We have intuitively accepted the peculiar logic of the *Lear* world, and recognize the incident as belonging to it. The same might be said of the love-test in the first scene, or of many of the 'defects' that Bradley cited. We feel that they all grow in the same garden, and we usually tend to accept them because we have entered into it. We would not accept other kinds of action, though, because the world of this play is also an exclusive one. In Act IV of Nahum Tate's version, for instance, an officer enters and tells Regan that the peasants have been outraged by Gloucester's blinding and are staging a rebellion; and in the second scene of Act III, Edmund has informed us that the people are crying out against the unjust rule of Regan and Goneril. These incidents do not ring true to Shakespeare's play. There, the thoughts and activities of the common people never enter the picture, even peripherally. Power plays and outrages occur within a select circle, and their effects are confined to it. A more national scope would, paradoxically, render the action of *King Lear* less cataclysmic, for Shakespeare's characters share their primitive world only with the elements, like the pagan gods they invoke so frequently.

Similarly, the battle that takes place in Act V is just what we expect. Like Edgar, we hear the beaten drum from afar, and are witness not to the meetings of opposed armies but to their strangely unenthusiastic movements across the stage. Skirmishes such as the meeting of Prince Hal and Hotspur, or of Macbeth and Macduff, are absent here. The stage does not become a corner of the battlefield, nor are any of the combatants directed to enter 'wounded' or 'bleeding.' The battle is never more than a distant background for the speeches of Edmund, Gloucester, and Edgar, and the soldiers' actions seem irrelevant to the hollow victory that is achieved. It is a conflict closer to Tennyson's 'last, dim, weird battle of the west,' than to anything out of the Henriad.

Finally, *King Lear* is 'the greatest anti-pastoral ever penned,' as Maynard Mack has put it (*'King Lear' in Our Time*, p. 65), primarily because its world will not permit the conventional Arcadian solution. Lear must experience the nightmare of the heath, rather than the sympathetic countryside, and is not 'able to return to the everyday world, restored to serenity and ... to temporal felicity' (p. 64). Not here; 'serenity' and 'felicity' are not to be achieved here. Nor will this play even sustain a real-world ontology, Christian or otherwise, in the way that Chapman's private-theatre plays echo the tenets of Stoicism. The world of *King Lear* is *sui generis*.

An exploratory survey of the *Lear* world discloses, first of all, that it is

almost placeless. One reason Edgar's description of the Dover cliffs (where 'The
crows and choughs that wing the midway air/ Show scarce so gross as beetles')
is so powerful is that the cliffs loom up out of nowhere. The other places —
where Lear holds court, where Gloucester and Cornwall live, and the routes
taken by those innumerable messengers — are as vague as the ubiquitous
'plaine' of *The Faerie Queene*. With the suggestive amplitude of allegory, *King
Lear* moves us from Court to Heath. We find no memorable details that partic-
ularize either place, nothing comparable to the craggy seascape around Elsinore
or the nests in Macbeth's walls; the term 'heath' itself was an eighteenth-
century interpolation, added by Rowe in 1709. The first storm scene (III.i)
directs us simply to 'there' (line 1) and 'That way' (54). The Fool in III.ii
informs us only that we are 'out o' door' (11); at line 61, Kent says 'hard by
here is a hovel' — still without particularization, as is his later 'Here is the place,
my Lord' (III.iv.1). The locale shifts, but remains undelineated until all the
characters begin to come together at Dover. There is a complete absence of the
kind of seemingly irrelevant specifics that provide reassurance.

  This impression is fostered right from the opening scene. No editor dares give
a more specific scene direction than 'King Lear's Palace,' and even the map
Lear uses is apparently unlocalized, being without specific geographical references. He gives Goneril 'all these bounds, even from this line to this,' and
Regan's portion is 'No less in space, validity, and pleasure.' Although Bradley
was sceptical of the theatre's ability to transmit this vagueness of locale, he
realized that it imparted 'the feeling of vastness, the feeling not of a scene or
particular place, but of a world' (p. 261). The various nebulous locations reinforce our sense of the self-contained yet all-encompassing nature of the *Lear*
world. One thinks of Sir Thomas Browne's favourite image of the circle whose
centre was everywhere and circumference nowhere.

  Within this vague arena a series of suitably improbable incidents occurs: the
love-test and its outcome, the tenuous intrigue by which Edmund hoodwinks
his father and brother, the famous suicide attempt, the donning and the puzz-
ling retention of real disguises (as opposed to the antic disposition that Hamlet
puts on) for the only time in Shakespearean tragedy, and a plethora of less
fabulous but similar actions. Critics have probed each of them in detail, but it is
enough for our purposes to note how well the incidents complement each
other. All of them break upon us in a rather inchoate manner; their unfolding is
as nebulous as the localities that contain them; and progression from one
incident to the next is often marked by the kind of sequential discontinuity
that characterizes our dreams rather than our waking moments. People and
things keep taking us by surprise. One feels that there could be no better
introduction to this world than the first scene of *King Lear.*

  As in the first scene, too, the incidents and characters in the rest of the play
present a somewhat impenetrable surface to us. We sense an absence of intimate conversations and situations. Rarely alone on stage, the characters make
only oversized gestures, because they are constantly thrust into situations that
demand such gestures. The *Lear* world unfolds at such a breakneck speed that

there is no time for more familiar views. This perspective stands in contrast to that of *Hamlet*, or even to that of the intensely concentrated *Othello*, both of which proceed at a leisurely enough pace to show us what their characters are like in moments of relaxation. There are no such moments in *King Lear*. We never see the intimacies between Edmund and his two queens, or between *any* of the characters. We never see them off guard. After Edmund's proclamation of villainy the long, ruminative soliloquy disappears, and Lear and his daughters share no soliloquies at all with us. Johnson marvelled at the play's 'quick succession of events' that 'fill the mind with a perpetual tumult.'[9] Shakespeare sets the pace in Act I, and from then on the tempo precludes polite conversation.

Not that these characters would exchange any, even if they had the time. There are more instances of unexpected or indifferent acts of physical violence in *King Lear* than in any other Shakespearean tragedy. Kent beats and trips Oswald, Lear strikes his own head, Edmund stabs himself, Kent beats Oswald again, Regan plucks Gloucester's beard, Cornwall gouges out his eyes, the First Servant stabs Cornwall and is stabbed by Regan, Oswald attacks Edgar and is bludgeoned by him, a Gentleman runs in carrying the bloody knife with which Goneril has stabbed herself, Lear kills the man who hanged Cordelia. Brutality seems to be the common mode of discourse in *King Lear*. These 'most savage and unnatural' acts are the shock waves of a world hurtling out of control. We can never hope that a character's assertion of himself (as in *Hamlet*) or a change of heart (as in *Othello*) will right the situation. Actions and characters in the *Lear* world define themselves at irreversible extremes. When they are good, they are very good, and when they are bad they are unspeakable. Cordelia 'redeems nature from the general curse,' while Goneril has a 'marble-hearted fiend' within her; Gloucester and Lear undergo the absurdities of the thwarted suicide and the Fool's antics, along with the unsufferable atrocities of the blinding and Cordelia's hanging.

Bradley objects to these improbable and extreme aspects of *King Lear*, and the nature of his objections provides a hint as to why he finds the first scenes dramatically defective:

> The influence of all this on imagination as we read *King Lear* is very great; and it combines with other influences to convey to us ... the wider or universal significance of the spectacle presented to the inward eye. But the effect of theatrical exhibition is precisely the reverse. There the poetic atmosphere is dissipated; the meaning of the very words which create it passes half-realised; in obedience to the tyranny of the eye we conceive the characters as mere particular men and women. (p. 269)

Bradley feels that no stage can hold *King Lear*, that its titanic world is irreconcilable with the demands of theatrical production. The actors will presumably be unable to convey the play's extreme 'poetic atmosphere' to us because we know that they are only 'mere particular men and women.' What the real eye sees must negate the vision of the inward eye. This view shows that Bradley

shares the late nineteenth-century conception of the stage as a faithful repro-
duction of physical reality. Bradley's stage is that of Shaw, with its real rugs,
furniture, drapes, and 'particular men and women,' beheld through the wide
proscenium window. His Ibsen is the author of *A Doll's House*, rather than of
Peer Gynt. He consequently finds the vagueness of place in *King Lear* dramatically disadvantageous (p. 259), and can say that 'the blinding of Gloster belongs rightly to *King Lear* in its proper world of imagination; [but] it is a blot
upon *King Lear* as a stage-play' (p. 251). He tends to separate the world of the
imagination from that of the stage.

Today we are in a better position to reconcile the two. In the seventy years
since Bradley wrote, we have been conditioned by exposure to such creations
as Noh drama, bare open stages, surrealism, and the theatre of the absurd, to be
more aware of the dramatic experience as one *projected from* the stage rather
than taking place on it. We can therefore appreciate the extremities and
improbabilities of *King Lear* without feeling that they disqualify it as a stage
play, or that its imaginative effects suffer during performance. Perhaps these
changes in expectation help to account for the unprecedented theatrical popu-
larity of *King Lear* in our time.

Like the modern audience, Shakespeare's original spectators were less subject
to 'the tyranny of the eye' than Bradley's generation. As Lear says, 'A man
may see how this world goes with no eyes. Look with thine ears.' One does not
look for exact representational fidelity on a stage where a bed denotes a chamber and a monument a church; and we have Webster's remarkable statement, in
his Overburian character of 'An Excellent Actor,' that the actor is the centre of
'lines drawn from the circumference of so many ears.'[10] This must have been
especially true of private-theatre audiences, who were used to seeing boy actors
play every role, and who were more accustomed to the purely symbolic representation of courtly entertainments. Public-theatre audiences, on the other
hand, were often more interested in seeing 'particular men and women' on the
stage; at least this is the impression that one receives from such commonplace
public-theatre fare as *The Roaring Girl* (1608) or *The Travels of the Three
English Brothers* (1607). [11] This impression is partly substantiated by that
consummate satire of the popular theatre's most sacred cows, Beaumont's *The
Knight of the Burning Pestle* (1607). There, the play-within-a-play context
turns the Citizen and his Wife into parodic exaggerations of popular theatre-
goers, as they watch the 'inner' play. At several points, the Wife even interrupts
the stage action to try to change events, revealing how fully she thinks of the
characters as real people. Beaumont ridicules this suppression of the play's
identity as an artistic projection. Shakespeare, eschewing a completely naturalistic presentation and projecting a unique, self-enclosed vision, seems to have
shared some of Beaumont's convictions when he created the world of *King
Lear.*

But in the main the relationship between life and the world of *King Lear* is
not so antithetical as the above discussion might suggest. While it is true that
the *Lear* world is a self-sustained construct, isolated from many real-world

standards of logic and plausibility, it is a critical commonplace that the play is nevertheless charged with profound meaning for that world. Its indirections find directions out. Unburdened of the need to deal with the accidentals of everyday existence, *King Lear* can present essentials with undiminished intensity. The result is that, as C.S. Lewis once wrote of *The Faerie Queene,* 'The things we read about in it are not like life, but the experience of reading it is like living.'[12] We feel all too deeply that the choices these characters face are our own, and we recognize our own images in their errors. Later chapters in this study will relate these reactions to various traditions and genres of the Elizabethan stage in an effort to show just how Shakespeare draws on them to shape our responses. The remainder of this chapter will turn from the play-world to some of the other fundamentally Jacobean emphases found in the opening scenes. Shakespeare adapts them to form an appropriate introduction to a play-world notable for its thematic and affective concern with man's ability to feel, and as a result they introduce us to a more compelling image of the human condition than was ever achieved by the Jacobean dramatists who more frequently exploited those emphases.

II

A spectator coming to *King Lear* for the first time, after having seen the other great tragedies, would have good reason to expect its first scene to be expository. He would expect the exposition to unfold subtly and indirectly, in the midst of a gripping theatrical opening, but with perfect clarity. It would present immediately the predominant 'atmosphere' of the play, reveal in some detail the events leading up to the present situation, and feed our anticipations of the central protagonist through an initial acquaintance with lesser figures. Not until this spadework was complete would the central character make a decisive act. Every other major Shakespearean tragedy meets these conditions, although each play naturally stresses some more than others.

The opening scenes of *Hamlet* and *Macbeth* are decidedly atmospheric, catching us up in melodramatic images of the unnatural corruption that will soon rise to the surface. But even as the supernatural enthralls us, we learn a good deal about Denmark and Scotland, and when our attention turns to the heroes, their portraits have already been framed. Hamlet does not appear in scene i and does not speak until well into scene ii, after accounts of past and present events have been given by Marcellus, Horatio, and Claudius. Macbeth first appears in scene iii, after Duncan, the Captain, and Ross have given illuminating descriptions of him. Perhaps more importantly, the initial gestures of both heroes are introductory rather than crucial: neither takes the kind of irreversible step that Lear does in giving up his kingdom and disowning his daughter.

Othello opens in a rather expansive way, the 180-line prologue between Iago, Roderigo, and Brabantio sketching the background and setting the scene for Othello's appearance. Roderigo's stupidity turns the scene into a kind of expository soliloquy (to whom else would Iago dare say 'I· am not what I am'?), and Iago's treatment of him is a revealing dry run. The spider awaits his fly. The opening of *Antony and Cleopatra* is the most formal, an apt harbinger to the play's grand style. Demetrius and Philo enter as chorus, make a brief introductory summary, and point us to an illustrative exhibition: 'Look, where they come!' 'Behold and see.' Antony and Cleopatra enter, give an appropriately physical demonstration of the present state of affairs, and exit as Demetrius and Philo complete the frame with further commentary.

No such exposition awaits the spectator of *King Lear*. The 'choric' scene between Kent, Gloucester, and Edmund, far from preparing us, actually leaves us off guard for both the ritualism and the vehemence of what follows. The main characters act decisively at once, with no clear presentation of background or outline of their motives. Anyone interested in such information must struggle, sometimes in vain, to piece out sequences of causality. Exposition in *King Lear* is an *ex post facto* manoeuvre — and not one the play gives us time to make. Shakespeare does not prepare us for Lear's odd behaviour, or for Cordelia's. It was this aspect of the opening scene that A.C. Bradley found most disturbing. He pronounced the scene dramatically defective 'in so far as it discloses the true position of affairs only to an attention more alert than can be expected in a theatrical audience or has been found in many critics of the play' (p. 251). He even postulated that the scene might have suffered from hasty revision: perhaps the present text was merely a careless abridgment of the original version, pared down because Shakespeare found it too bulky for performance. Perhaps so, but not very likely, Bradley admitted.[13]

In fact, the first scene's *lacunae* seem quite deliberate. Shakespeare has thoroughly removed the carefully placed hints about motivation that abound in his primary source, *The History of King Leir*. There, several reasons are given for Leir's strange conduct: he is sad and distraught because his wife has just died, and he wants to resign the throne to live in devout contemplation; he is ignorant of the affairs and characters of his daughters, 'For fathers best do know to gouerne sonnes';[14] he devises the love-test in order to trick Cordella into marrying the suitor he favours. Likewise, Cordella's silence is linked to her reluctance to wed the chosen suitor; and her two malicious sisters are introduced to us before the crucial scene as jealous of Leir's esteem for her: 'Some desperate medicine must be soone applyed,/ To dimme the glory of her mounting fame,' says Ragan to Gonorill, thereby predisposing us in Cordella's favour. The elder sisters also play a more active role in inciting Leir against Cordella: the stream of vituperation they pour forth against her is so unremitting that Cordella's silence is as much enforced as chosen. None of these intimations appears in Shakespeare's version. Obviously, he is not trying to make the same impression that the anonymous *Leir* playwright made, or that Nahum Tate was to make by embroidering the opening scenes with similar motives.[15] Shakespeare simply presents us with the situation, and makes no attempt to acquaint us with its probable causes. Bradley tries his best to cushion the shock of Shakespeare's omission. Shakespeare does tell us, he observes, that Lear 'loved

Cordelia most and knew that she loved him best,' and therefore Lear's outrage is understandable (p. 250). But Shakespeare tells us this only *after* Lear has disowned her. And Cordelia's muteness, the effective cause of the explosion, vanishes even as the rest of this scene unfolds.

Granville-Barker apologizes for the incredible nature of Edmund's ruse in a different manner: 'Shakespeare asks us to allow him the fact of the deception, even as we have allowed him Lear's partition of the kingdom. It is his starting point, the dramatist's "let's pretend," which is as essential to the beginning of a play as a "let it be granted" to a proposition of Euclid.'[16] Distinguishing between dramatic decorum and real-life motivation is a large step in the right direction; but we are still left with the puzzle of why the offense against common sense is so much greater in *King Lear* than in Shakespeare's other tragedies.

If we assume that there is more method than madness in what Shakespeare is doing here, our investigation becomes a matter of trying to establish the nature of that method, and what he might have hoped to accomplish by using it. Coleridge has provided us with an important hint, in his discussion of the opening scene: 'It is well worthy notice, that *Lear* is the only serious performance of Shakespeare the interest and situations of which are derived from the assumption of a gross improbability; whereas Beaumont and Fletcher's tragedies are, almost all, founded on some out-of-the-way accident or exception to the general experience of mankind.'[17] Associating the opening of *King Lear* with the plays of Beaumont and Fletcher furnishes an illuminating perspective from which to view the scene. For the art of Beaumont and Fletcher is consistently one that sacrifices clarity and plausibility of motive and situation, in order to generate more compelling dramatic moments. This emphasis, like the first scene of *King Lear,* is highly theatrical: it concerns itself more with the immediate forcefulness of the dramatic situation than with tying the causal details of the situation into a realistic pattern.

The opening of *Cupid's Revenge* (1607-8) is typical of the Fletcherian mode, and remarkably similar to *Lear's* first scene. After an initial conversation between three courtiers, the royal family enters in procession, and the duke says he will grant his daughter anything she wishes. She unaccountably requests that all the images of Cupid be cast down; amid great commotion the duke assents, the royal party exits, and further theatrical situations follow. But so close a parallel to *King Lear* need not be invoked; the Beaumont and Fletcher canon is full of situations handled in a similar manner. The lively but implausible artifice of *Cupid's Revenge* also characterizes the wedding masque and its aftermath in *The Maid's Tragedy* (1610) where our astonishment is all the greater because Beaumont and Fletcher spring their 'gross improbability' on us after we have been put off guard by a deliberately casual opening conversation, far longer than the one that opens *King Lear.* A similar emphasis is used for comic effect in the second scene of *The Woman Hater* (1606); there, the authors simply let the bizarre humour of Lazarello activate a whole dynamic scene, an unaccountable and yet self-sufficient display.

The 'assumption of a gross improbability' in *King Lear* is, in fact, character-istic of much Jacobean drama, and not just of the plays of Beaumont and Fletcher. Several other playwrights are also much less concerned with establish-ing a plausible foundation for each situation than with letting each generate an entertaining dramatic exhibition. The opening of Day's *The Isle of Gulls* (1606) illustrates this concern. Duke Basilius takes his family to an island and issues a general challenge: whoever outwits him and succeeds in wooing his daughters may have them in marriage. Day then puts a succession of protagonists into this contrived situation, which provokes entertaining reactions from them. The situation is, of course, reminiscent of Shakespeare's own *Love's Labour's Lost,* a play written under the influence of a man whose art anticipated many fea-tures of early Jacobean drama, John Lyly.[18] But such dramatic construction is extremely rare in the plays of the 1590s, where the improbabilities of Shake-speare and other dramatists are closer to Granville-Barker's 'let's pretend': they are the stock improbabilities which romance and classical comedy have condi-tioned us to accept; and the dramatist's concern to devise a situation that is immediately engrossing and brimming with theatrical vitality does not tend to operate to the exclusion of his development of an expository interest.

A more exclusively situational interest governs the openings of Chapman's *Bussy D'Ambois* (1604) and *The Widow's Tears* (1605), or Field's *Amends for Ladies* (1611), plays written both before and after *King Lear.* Here, the logic behind the situation is never at issue, and to ask for more detailed motivation is to miss the point. The same interest characterizes the deliberately implausible openings of Marston's *Antonio's Revenge* (1600) and *The Malcontent* (1603), and of Jonson's *Cynthia's Revels* (1601). It must be emphasized that by no means all the drama of these playwrights shares this characteristic; in fact, the openings of most of the plays they wrote before 1605 (the date of *King Lear*) manifest a concern for plausibility and/or clear exposition. But since the 'gross improbability' becomes increasingly typical of their drama, and since they seem to point the way to the improbabilities of Beaumont and Fletcher, I feel justified in associating the emphasis with these writers. Their works provide a wealth of antecedents and analogues to the opening of *King Lear.*

Shakespeare's dramaturgy in the first scene of *King Lear* seems to be in keeping with such practice, rather than with the openings of *Hamlet, Othello,* and most other earlier plays.[19] As Bradley concedes, 'this scene acts effectively' (p. 249), and perhaps we have no right to make further demands upon it. In Brecht's phrase, 'if it works, it works.' Typical of much Jacobean drama but not of more naturalistic works, *Lear's* opening satisfies the question 'How?' while ignoring the 'Why?' When Bradley faults the scene because it does not clearly establish 'the true position of affairs,' he displays the literary preconcep-tions of his age. He wants basic motivations and relationships to be apprehensi-ble right from the start, as in a nineteenth-century novel. But *King Lear* does not unfold as a novel transcribed for the stage, and its first scene does not exhibit the narrative coherence that Bradley seeks. Tate, not Shakespeare, endows the opening with such unity and plausibility; and it is perhaps no coincidence that the rise of Tate's version paralleled the rise of the novel and the decline of playwriting. Tate's play answered different expectations. But the affinities of Shakespeare's *King Lear* are more with the world of Chapman, Jonson, and Beaumont and Fletcher.

The advantages that Shakespeare gains from this initial emphasis will be explored at length in later chapters, but their nature may be mentioned briefly. Harley Granville-Barker put his finger on one kind of advantage when he wrote that 'Lear must leave this first scene as he entered it, more a magnificent portent than a man' (II, 25). Many of the characters of this play, and Lear especially, are conceived on a titanic scale. Their struggles have repercussions that are cosmic rather than naturalistic, and that 'Strike flat the thick rotundity o' th' world!' It was probably this aspect of the play that prompted Bradley to write of 'that feeling which haunts us in *King Lear,* as though we were witnessing something universal, – a conflict not so much of particular persons as of the powers of good and evil in the world' (pp. 262-3). For Shakespeare to place these characters' actions in the framework of normal human motivation at the outset would be to diminish their stature irreparably; it would show them too much like us 'particular men and women,' reacting to identifiable stresses rather than reverberating with archetypal meaning.

Given the quality of these characters, another advantage arises from the first scene's bold physiognomy: it prepares us for the play's distinctive method of character presentation. *King Lear* involves us only in those moments when the essential nature of a character manifests itself in action designed to typify it. Instead of planning the dramatic action so that it gradually (and sometimes indirectly) lets us build composite portraits of the characters, as we see them reflecting, planning, and acting, Shakespeare arranges each scene to represent the essence of those involved in it. The process is explosive rather than cumulative, shocking us into a series of full, intense recognitions. Finally, the impossibility of complacent, leisurely reactions to *King Lear* itself suggests a third advantage of the opening scene, an emotive one. By thrusting us into an indecipherable but compelling situation, Shakespeare knocks us off balance. We are unsure of our position. We cannot respond to the scene with confidence in our knowledge of its *données*, yet it involves us immediately and forcefully. And Shakespeare never lets us regain our composure. *King Lear* keeps springing surprises on us. The enigmatic opening scene is an introduction to, and an epitome of, the play's power over us.

III

The first scene of *King Lear* is related to the rest of the play in a number of ways that are characteristic of Jacobean drama. Coleridge suggests one kind of relationship when he observes that later situations *are derived from* the gross improbability, in both *King Lear* and the tragedies of Beaumont and Fletcher (I, 59). In both the first scene contains the seeds of all subsequent action, which seems to follow from the initial situation as a direct result. When Lear makes the wrong choice and banishes Cordelia and Kent, he triggers the physical and symbolic chain reaction that all the later scenes document. The entire concatenation emanates from his decision to break the bond by substituting quantification for a beneficent order. 'Thereafter,' as Maynard Mack notes (p. 95), 'the play seems to illustrate, with an almost diagrammatic relentlessness and thoroughness, the unforeseen potentials that lie waiting to be hatched from a single choice and act.' Lear's auction of Cordelia ('What, in the least,/ Will you require') prefigures Regan and Goneril's reasoning the need for his retainers. France's reference to dismantling 'So many folds of favour,' and Cordelia's pun on 'plighted cunning,' look forward to the play's relentless uncovering and discarding. Kent's 'Thou swear'st thy Gods in vain' anticipates the vast metaphysical impassivity. Edmund's 'Nature' speech takes its impetus from, and rationalizes, Lear's first-scene conduct; in outlook Edmund shows himself Lear's bastard,[20] just as Edgar is Lear's godson. Everything is here *in ovo,* from the elements' treatment of Lear to Edmund's treatment of Gloucester and Oswald's of Kent.

This structural relationship anticipates the shape of a number of Jacobean plays written shortly after *King Lear.* The results of Lear's love-test, for example, are paralleled by the consequences of another folk motif, the rash boon in the first scene of *Cupid's Revenge* (1607-8). The casting down of Cupid's image precipitates an interlocking series of extreme reactions throughout the play; symbolically, the blind god sits above the action in Act V, and comments as the last of these situations runs its course. The opening of Field's *Amends for Ladies* (1611) also provides a blueprint for later dramatic action, in almost allegorical fashion. A wife, a widow, and a maid enter to debate the merits of their relative positions, each claiming that her own status is best – a scene analogous to the patterned interrogation of Lear's three daughters. The play's succeeding action balances each position against the others, testing them all through theatrical situations. Finally, the widow and the maid prove the truth of the wife's assertions by themselves becoming wives, as Cordelia's bond is proved by her sisters' betrayals and her own tragic fidelity.

The opening scenes of John Day's *The Isle of Gulls* (1606) and Robert Armin's *The Two Maids of More-Clacke* (1608) are similarly diagrammatic: like *Lear,* both plays turn on one extreme and capricious action, and then proceed to develop fully all the absurdities inherent in their initial situations. Dramatic action in all such plays consists essentially of permutations and elaborations of what we are given in the first scene.[21] This relationship predicates a departure from the more straightforward narrative progression found in other plays, where later scenes develop the action without relating back so directly and almost diagrammatically to the first scene. (I shall argue in Chapter 2 that *King Lear* departs from many other aspects of narrative progression, and that it shares this structural bias with a large number of Jacobean plays.)[22]

Strictly speaking, *King Lear* does not really begin with the love-test confrontation that has concerned us so far. But the opening conversation of Kent, Gloucester, and Edmund turns a variation on the structural relationship just observed, and is related to Jacobean dramaturgy in several ways. To begin with, the gathering of lesser nobility is an opening that Beaumont and Fletcher were soon to employ in many of their tragedies and tragicomedies. In a standard opening scene, several nobles wait for the entrance of royalty – the main protagonists – to a festival or state occasion. This is how *Philaster* (1609), *Cupid's Revenge* (1607-8), and *The Maid's Tragedy* (1610) open. The nobles' brief exchange provides each play with a point of stability before more extreme kinds of conduct take over, and this glimpse of the mundane heightens the unusualness of what follows. However, Shakespeare's scene is related to the rest of the play in a more far-reaching way. The initial conversation in *King Lear* is an action that has its own independent interests, but it emerges in retrospect as an emblematic abstract of major themes.[23] When we see the panoramic illustration that accompanies this rather cryptic 'motto,' then the allusions to deceptive appearances and to acknowledgment of paternity, the concern with 'proper' conduct and with 'love,' and the use of words like 'weighed' and 'division' carry their full load of meaning. The scene also introduces us to those lapses in charity that will prove so crucial. Love as quantification emerges from references to the shares of Albany and Cornwall (and from the central ambiguity of 'values'), and love as sport from Gloucester's crass account of Edmund's conception.

This use of a preliminary incident resembles the opening actions of several other plays. In *Amends for Ladies* (1611), *The Widow's Tears* (1605), and *Bussy D'Ambois* (1604), the first scenes present basic dramatic issues in a 'dark conceit,' with varying degrees of subtlety. The prime example is *Bussy*, where a tableau in Act I depicts the hero's encounter with Maffé, a steward. Maffé has been sent to give Bussy one thousand crowns, but decides at once to see if the recipient is worth such a generous gift, as he reveals in an aside to the audience. The two trade insults for awhile, until Maffé finally offers Bussy only a hundred crowns, justifying this action in another aside:

> I see the man: a hundred crowns will make him
> Swagger, and drink healths to his Highness' bounty;
> And swear he could not be more bountiful.
> So there's nine hundred crowns, sav'd (I.i.175-8)

But the following lines reveal that he has not seen the man at all. Bussy, always aware of his own worth, recognizes the trick and argues the rest of the money from Maffé, hitting him for his insolence and sending him away. The short scene is emblematic of the play's major themes. Like Maffé, the other characters never 'see the man' in Bussy, and he is doomed to waste his talents – as he struck fear into Maffé – in a milieu that cannot give scope to his virtue, and from which he is hopelessly alienated. His alienation is prefigured in the very mechanics of the scene: it is Maffé who demands our confidence with his asides, while Bussy stands detached from us. Like the opening of *Lear*, this encounter has encapsulated the motifs on which later scenes play variations.

But the abstract of *King Lear* is much more subtle than Chapman's, or the 'prologues' of Beaumont and Fletcher. Shakespeare employs the emblematic opening to create an astonishingly deceptive nonchalance, letting us examine the situation with detachment before we realize how taut it is. The intensely tightened mainspring of dramatic action has been wound up almost to the breaking point before the play begins, and is now presented to the audience in a shadowy perspective: unaware of the scene's potentialities, we respond to it with disinterested fascination. Then, without warning, Shakespeare lets go and it unwinds violently, hitting us with all its force. The enigmas to which Bradley objected serve only to heighten dramatic effect.

Besides functioning as a dramatic overture that contains and sounds out major themes, the first scenes of *King Lear* are prototypes for several structural and thematic patterns. Bradley touched on the basis for this second kind of relationship when, remarking on Shakespeare's careful juxtaposing of unusually extreme characters, he wrote: 'We seem to trace the tendency which, a few years later, produced Ariel and Caliban, the tendency of imagination to analyse and abstract ... This, of course, is a tendency which produces symbols, allegories, personifications of qualities and abstract ideas; and we are accustomed to think it quite foreign to Shakespeare's genius' (p. 264). Abstract concepts achieve dramatic realization and are arranged in symbolic patterns throughout *King Lear.* This is true not only of the play's characterization but of its structural configuration as well. An abstraction will be brought to life in the outlines of one scene, and then later scenes will turn variations on this initial figure.

The first scene is again essential, creating a structural pattern that is echoed and re-echoed in the course of *King Lear.* The scene unfolds as an emblematic test or trial, and its outlines reappear in numerous other places: the 'trial' and condemnation of Edgar by Gloucester and Edmund; Kent's expulsion of Oswald (and its reversal, the censure of Kent by Cornwall); the Fool's satiric re-enactment of the opening scene with Lear; the successive trials of Lear by Goneril and Regan, culminating in his self-exile to the heath; Lear's mad mock trial of his daughters; Cornwall's inquisition and punishment of Gloucester, and Gloucester's self-exile to Dover; Edmund's sentencing of Lear and Cordelia; the trial of Edmund by Albany and Edgar; and the final 'judgment of the heavens,' in the last scene. Similar structural patterning characterizes *Epicoene* (1609), *A Chaste Maid in Cheapside* (1613), *Amends for Ladies* (1611), and *Bussy D'Ambois* (1604). As L.A. Beaurline has written of *Epicoene,* 'Much of the play is like the working out of a series of permutations with a fixed number of constants and two variables.'[24] The variables consist of character and situation, and the playwright places them in a sequence of related combinations. As in a fugue, elements of a given initial statement are recombined to form successive later versions. In *King Lear,* the trial pattern is of primary thematic importance and is responsible for much of the play's emotional impact: the first trial unleashes a harsh, primitive justice that relentlessly reverberates in characters and actions until all of the fatal permutations have been worked out.[25]

Similar to this reiterative pattern is one that presents us with an abstract statement and then proceeds to illuminate it with a series of theatrical illustrations, each one lighting up a component part of the statement. Bradley divined one of them when he noted some 'Biblical ideas ... floating in Shakespeare's mind' and surfacing at times in *King Lear.*[26] So Gloucester's speech about 'these late eclipses of the sun and moon' (I.ii.107-20) points us to several abstract statements, biblical descriptions of the discords auguring the end of the world. The descriptions in Mark 13 (Geneva Bible, 1595 ed.) are especially relevant, because they form almost a synopsis of later scenes:

> Tell us, when shall these things be? and what shall be the signe when all these things shall be fulfilled? And Jesus answered them, and beganne to say, take heed least any man deceiue you ... yee shall heare of warres, and rumours of warres ... For nation shall rise against nation, and kingdome against kingdome ... Yea, and the brother shall deliuer the brother to death, and the father the sonne, and the children shal rise against their parents, and shall cause them to die ... then let them that be in Judea, flee into the mountaines ... And let him that is in the fielde, not turne backe againe to take his garment ... Pray therefore that your flight bee not in the winter ... For false Christes shall rise, and false prophets, and shall shew signes and wonders, to deceiue if it were possible the very elect ... Moreouer in those dayes, after that tribulation, the sunne shall ware darke, and the moone shall not giue her light.

Each of these statements finds its realization in a later scene, and we feel the presence of a powerful apocalyptic theme carried through the dark *Lear* world. The whole teleological chain reaction that Lear has set off culminates in the last scene when trumpets sound (as at the beginning) and characters ask, 'Is this the promis'd end?' 'Or image of that horror?' as the 'judgment of the heavens' fulfils itself. Our sense of a pattern fulfilling itself is heightened by the marked pictorial similarity that the last scene bears to the first. For the first time in the play, most of the main characters of that opening court scene are together again on stage. As Lear tragically experiences the immeasurable love to which he was blind in the beginning, his onetime followers are grouped around him once more, the quick and even the dead.[27]

Edmund has foretold it all, right from the beginning. In the second scene, when Edgar asks him what he is contemplating, he lies and answers: 'I am thinking, brother, of a prediction I read this other day, what should follow these eclipses.' He then enlarges upon the lie, following it up with the words:

> I promise you the effects he writes of succeed unhappily; as of unnaturalness between the child and the parent; death, dearth, dissolutions of ancient amities; divisions in state; menaces and maledictions against King and nobles; needless diffidences, banishment of friends, dissipation of cohorts, nuptial breaches, and I know not what. (I.ii.150-6)

The effects succeed very unhappily, and every disaster that Edmund mentions actually comes about. It is as if the play were designed to illustrate the elements of this general statement, with characters and situations manipulated to meet its preimposed conditions. R.B. Heilman observed that a similar technique is employed, on a smaller scale, following Edmund's 'Nature' speech at the start of this scene: 'Now, the announcement of his plan follows immediately upon his exposition of Nature, and it is connected with the statement of his nature theory by the word *then* – precisely as if his scheme followed as a logical projection of the theory into action.'[28] As Edmund effects a realization of his theory, so Shakespeare projects his own abstracts into dramatic realities in the course of *King Lear.*

It is a technique originated by neither Edmund nor Shakespeare, and found in many contemporary plays. Chapman's *Bussy D'Ambois,* written about a year before *King Lear,* bases its structure on just such a juxtaposition of abstract statement with theatrical action. The very first line delineates the limits within which Bussy will play out his tragedy: 'Fortune, not Reason, rules the state of things.' Bussy at once opposes this maxim by associating himself with virtue rather than reward ('We must to Virtue for her guide resort,' I.i.32), but then wilfully follows the course of Fortune. He initiates a process in which his virtue is warped by the fortunes of successive illustrative situations; these situations realize aspects of the play's opening paragraph, and leave Bussy with only the gestures of nobility. Even the hollow tableau of his death ('I am up/ Here like a Roman statue,' V.iii.143-4) is prefigured in the opening lines, when he compares great men to 'Unskilful statuaries' forging a Colossus.

Taking a different approach, Tharsalio rejects Fortune as a 'blind imperfect goddess' in the first line of *The Widow's Tears* (1605). He instead accepts Confidence as his guide, and the rest of the play documents the victories of Confidence over Fortune in both plot and subplot. In less theoretical terms, Fletcher's *The Faithful Shepherdess* (1608) sets up in its opening lines the extreme philosophical position around which succeeding action gravitates. Clorin affirms an otherworldly chastity that, after other characters have displayed positive and negative permutations of it, provides the comic solution to the play's near-tragic dilemma; and like Shakespeare's Edmund, Clorin functions as both a character and an embodiment of the concept identified with her at the beginning. Similarly, Middleton's *Your Five Gallants* (1605) opens with a Presenter pointing us to an emblematic procession of the play's heroes, each of whom is identified with one of the five types of roguery that thread in and out of the play.

In *King Lear* it is Shakespeare's desire to realize abstract concepts dramatically, a practice that strongly influences the nature of characters, themes, and actions. All of these combine to illustrate thoroughly the reciprocal obligations attendant upon man's social existence. This idea is the basis of the final kind of relationship that we will explore between I.i and the rest of the play; it nearly comprehends the others, and shows them glowing with the luminescence of a common theme. Abstract, cryptic, and biblical statements, illustrative and reiterative patterns, meet here. As Maynard Mack observes, 'Shakespeare's imagination appears to have been ... fully oriented toward presenting human reality as a web of ties commutual.'[29] Seen in this light, Lear's love-test is a symbolic violation of a commutual bond, and its enormity is driven home to us by a succession of perspectives on the 'web of ties.' Some of these have been traced above, from different angles. Another one is the servant-master relationship, a perspective first displayed by Kent and Lear in the opening scene. Kent speaks out against his master's conduct at the risk of his own welfare, demonstrating the selfless dedication that the relationship can involve. Later incidents reveal that it can also involve a whole spectrum of very different reactions: after the initial statement, Shakespeare provides illuminating variations on it in the relationships of Oswald and Goneril, the Fool and Lear, the First Servant and Cornwall, the Old Man and Gloucester, and the Captain and Edmund. A series of juxtaposed opposites also dramatizes the commutual bond: the first scene pits France's generosity against Burgundy's materialism; later scenes hold up Kent's selfless loyalty against Oswald's selfish sycophancy; and towards the end of the play the guileless husband, Albany, is opposed to Edmund, the scheming adulterer. With the complete consort before us, we recognize virtue as a matter of necessity, not choice; without it, unaccommodated man is little more than an animal.

But the most deeply probed of commutual bonds in *King Lear* is that of paternity. It is another note sounded right at the beginning:

> KENT Is this not your son, my Lord?
> GLOU. His breeding, Sir, hath been at my charge.

Gloucester's reply may be frank, but it refrains from describing Edmund as his 'son.' When he says 'I have a son, Sir,' he is referring to Edgar. Although Gloucester claims that he treats his children as equals, he grants Edmund no higher title than 'the whoreson.' This conversation sets the pace for later practice: not once in almost three acts will Gloucester refer to Edmund as his son, though he will so describe Edgar many times. Here, Gloucester's reluctance reverberates almost immediately in Lear's furious words to Cordelia: 'Here I disclaim all my paternal care' (I.i.113). This, in turn, is re-echoed in Gloucester's reaction to his son's alleged treachery: 'I never got him' (II.i.78). In short order, each parent has blindly disowned the only child of whom he has reason to be proud. But later events will force Lear and Gloucester to acknowledge not only Cordelia and Edgar, but also Edmund, Goneril, and Regan. Both will come to the painful realization that they have fathered their monstrous offspring, and that this paternity cannot be renounced. They bear witness that man must own up to the evil he has brought into the world as well as the good.

When it finally comes, Gloucester's verbal acknowledgment of Edmund seems to trigger his immediate disillusionment. Immediately after Cornwall has blinded him, Gloucester cries out, 'Where's my son Edmund?' In reply, Regan tells how Edmund has betrayed him, and at once the blind old man sees all: 'O my follies! Then Edgar was abus'd./ Kind Gods, forgive me that, and prosper him!' (III.vii.91-2). The moment of acknowledgment coincides with the moment of remorse, just as it has for Lear on the heath:

> Is it the fashion that discarded fathers
> Should have thus little mercy on their flesh?
> Judicious punishment! 'twas this flesh begot
> Those pelican daughters. (III.iv.72-5)

Both Gloucester and Lear come to acknowledge their children with their sins.

Shakespeare affirms these bonds long before his characters do, though in more indirect ways. In the second scene of the play, for instance, an unmistakable link is established between Gloucester and Edmund. No sooner has Edmund finished his defiant soliloquy on Nature ('Why bastard? Wherefore base?') than Gloucester enters and immediately picks up the questioning cadences: 'Kent banished thus? and France in choler parted?/ And the King gone tonight?'[30] Similarly, Lear and his wicked daughters share the same mercantile imagery and zeal for quantifying, in the first scene; and the controversy over retainers in Act II simply shows Regan and Goneril treating Lear to a rehearsal of his own quantitative values. Even a fool can see the relationship, and does: 'I marvel what kin thou and thy daughters are' (I.iv.189).

Shakespeare's extensive use of the paternity motif in *King Lear* had no precedents in his source material; in fact, the hero of *King Leir* emerges almost guiltless, and displays no resemblance to his evil daughters. The dramatization of this concept originates in Shakespeare's version. Nor is it paralleled in any other contemporary play. Only Shakespeare, in Bradley's words, 'had been musing over heredity, and wondering how it comes about that the composition of two strains of blood or two parent souls can produce such astonishingly different products' (p. 266). The emphasis on blood ties looms large from the first scene, where our attention is caught by Lear as father rather than as king of Britain, and where family divisions strike us as so much more vital than political ones. This focus on the generational conflict becomes a fixed perspective in *King Lear*: no other Shakespearean tragedy subjects us to such a barrage of various actions that rend apart the web of family relations. Of course, the theme does not receive its final statement in this play. It carries over into the warmer atmosphere of the late romances, and there generation becomes a means of regeneration.[31] But *King Lear* is the first full dramatic realization of this concept.

Similar concepts, however, were receiving the same kind of treatment from other playwrights. As the paternal and social bonds are dramatized in this play, so the tenets of Stoicism receive dramatic exploration in several of Marston's comedies and Chapman's tragedies, and so less noble ideas are brought to life in the comedies of Middleton. Every character and situation in *A Chaste Maid in Cheapside* (1613), for instance, yields but another variation on the theme of warped marital relations; delighting in sheer artifice, Middleton gives the sense that he is realizing every possible combination. Characters in Jonson's *Epicoene* (1609), too, variously embody the concept of lost or distorted sexuality.[32] Such self-conscious patterning was vital to Jacobean drama, where so many playwrights cultivated and rewarded an interest in sheer virtuosity of technique. In joy and in sorrow, the characters of these playwrights dance in patterned allegiance to artificial rhythms.

Such rhythms also run through *King Lear.* But there, they blend unobtrusively into a finer music. Although *King Lear* displays more pronounced patterning than any other Shakespearean tragedy, the pattern does not intrude. From the beginning, it serves to reinforce rather than infringe upon a profound and archetypally resonant emotional experience. In fact, the compelling emphasis on family relations works on us in a manner more suggestive of Greek than of Jacobean tragedy; and like the Greek dramatists, Shakespeare makes us feel how every violation of this bond, every turn of the pattern, is a betrayal of one's own blood. The discussion of characterization in Chapter 4 will cause us to consider some of the specific means by which Shakespeare evokes and controls this response.

What fascinated Bradley about the stress on paternity in *King Lear* was, as noted above, that 'two parent souls can produce such astonishingly different products.' The difference is most astonishing between Lear's children. Edgar and Edmund may be morally antithetical, but Cordelia and her sisters stand as spiritual antipodes, the angelic versus the demonic. Perhaps this is Shakespeare's most emblematic touch, and the aspect of *King Lear* for which the opening scene, incorporating so much of the artifice of Jacobean drama, is a most necessary preparation. The scene is extremely stylized in its character presentation: Lear's questions and rewards unfold in a recitative-and-aria pattern of parallel speeches as he progresses from eldest daughter to youngest. The basic moral antipathy is conveyed in equally formal terms, as Cordelia follows up each of her false sisters' performances with a similar aside. After Goneril's parade of empty mouthings, Cordelia turns to us in genuine panic: 'What shall Cordelia speak? Love, and be silent.' The contrast between her and her sister could not be more striking, and Cordelia's aside gains our immediate sympathy. All Elizabethan playwrights frequently used the aside in this manner, to forge a link between an admirable character and the audience. Here, Shakespeare strengthens both link and artifice by giving Cordelia a second aside following Regan's speech: 'Then poor Cordelia!/ And yet not so; since I am sure my love's/ More ponderous than my tongue.' The parallel asides undercut the tableaux in which they appear (each one comes between and reflects on a sister's hollow oath and her father's blind reward), and demonstrate this polarity in an altogether fitting way.

Cordelia, in particular, exists here as a dramatized emblem. There is never any question of this Cordelia's being romantically repelled (as in *King Leir*) or attracted (as in Tate's play) by anybody. Unlike Desdemona or even Ophelia, Cordelia has none of the dimensions of the romantic heroine. It is her nature to be more singular. She behaves less as a realistic character than as Shelley described his Prometheus, 'the type of the highest perfection ... impelled by the purest and truest motives to the best and noblest ends.' To point us towards this figurative kind of characterization – one that the formal nature of the scene makes us readier to accept – Shakespeare even gives her words that paraphrase the marriage response: '[I] Obey you, love you, and most honour you,' says Cordelia, indicating by such terms the sanctity of her bond to Lear. Because she is so emblematically conceived, her motives and her ends will not brook questioning; the critic must not imitate Lear and ask Cordelia to justify herself.

In an essay appearing in *Some Facets of 'King Lear,'* Sheldon P. Zitner defends Cordelia's silence as representative of another kind of patterning. He writes:

> We are perhaps so influenced by our sense of what is owed by subjects and daughters that we are ready to accuse Cordelia of a virginal coldness in not humouring the old man. But this is to substitute modern 'realistic' deductions about personality for inductions from the design of language. Cordelia's silence, like her plainness, is the response that 'honour's bound [to] / When majesty falls to folly.' It is part of a verbal pattern, not to be judged according to the implications of such responses in 'real' life. (p. 7)

Zitner argues persuasively that her silence epitomizes the play's insistence that words can become valid only when they follow deeds that define them. Advocating a similar response to Cordelia, John F. Danby also finds real-life motivation inadequate to account for her behaviour, and turns to a non-Shakespearean precedent for confirmation: 'Almost everyone has strained to detect in her the traces of her father's pride. We might equally well, I suggest, discuss Griselda's long-sufferance as disguised self-interest or peasant stupidity. Cordelia, when she says nothing is the sheep before the shearers that must be dumb. She is quite simply the truly patient woman and daughter.'[33]

While sympathizing with the drift of Danby's remarks, I doubt whether the example of Griselda is entirely applicable here. When Dekker portrays Griselda on the Elizabethan stage (*Patient Grissil*, 1600), he takes care to motivate her actions and make them more plausible – much more so than Chaucer did. Dekker seems to have felt a need that Shakespeare, in *King Lear*, did not. Useful as such interpretations (Zitner's, Danby's, and my own) may perhaps be in delineating the general shape of Cordelia's characterization, they do not in themselves explain our response to her as spectators. To recognize a pattern is not to say that we immediately and without hesitation find ourselves giving unqualified approval to Cordelia's conduct.[34]

As spectators, we can accept the emblematic portrait of Cordelia only on faith, and wait for this faith to be confirmed later in the play when an anonymous Gentleman reaffirms her symbolic nature ('There she shook/ The holy water from her heavenly eyes,' IV.iii.30-1), or when he or another cries to Lear:

>   Thou hast one daughter,
>   Who redeems nature from the general curse
>   Which twain have brought her to. (IV.vi.206-8)

Or when Shakespeare gives these words to Cordelia herself: 'O dear father!/ It is thy business that I go about' (IV.iv.23-4). Alone among the characters in *King Lear,* Cordelia carries much of the play's Christian symbolism; she brings an otherworldly light to the sunless *Lear* world. And her conduct in the opening scene – however we respond to it – is a perfect introduction to her. As Russell Fraser has written, her muteness there 'is not so much a reflection of character as it is the embodiment of an idea.'[35] The emblematic and 'unmotived' conduct associated with Cordelia in the opening scene gives an accurate impression of her nature throughout the play. France recognizes her worth, but (as Shakespeare emphasizes by giving him a language of rhymed paradoxy) he is from another world. The darkness of this world does not comprehend her.

2

Structure: 'The Dramatic Effect of the Great Scenes'

The first scene of Act V is typical of a peculiar structural emphasis in *King Lear*; and as we set out to map the labyrinthine *Lear* world by investigating its structure, we might begin by treating this emphasis as an Ariadne's thread, to see where it leads us. Edmund, Regan, and their retinue open V .i by entering with drum and colours. We do not know where they have come from or where they are going, and no attempt is made to enlighten us. Instead, Edmund and Regan discuss whether or not he has made love to Goneril. Two scenes have elapsed since Regan's last appearance, and five since Edmund's, with no indications that they were together so long and intimately as their present conduct implies. The primary concern of this scene is completely different from those of the two previous ones, which centred on Gloucester's suicide attempt. Edgar, offstage since the scene before last, is the only character from either previous scene to appear here, and he disappears again in the space of ten lines.

Each scene in *King Lear* absorbs us as completely as does this one, making such unique demands on our attention that we tend to forget our sense of before and after. The play conveys the impression that each scene projects its own drama, depicting only that instant when the essential nature of a character or situation manifests itself. Cordelia's 'No cause, no cause' may be applied to an effect that the play's structure has upon us: we feel no gradual accumulation of causes, no careful supplying of connectives, and not even a thorough elaboration of consequences. If one opens the play at random to any scene after Act II, when the storm takes over, one finds it nearly impossible to say just what actions come immediately before or after.

Bradley noticed this quality and claimed that 'It is far more difficult to retrace in memory the steps of the action in this tragedy than in *Hamlet, Othello,* or *Macbeth*. The outline is of course quite clear; anyone could write an "argument" of the play. But when an attempt is made to fill in the detail, it issues sooner or later in confusion even with readers whose dramatic memory is unusually strong' (p. 260). Yet anyone who has ever presented *King Lear* on the stage knows how well-nigh impossible it is to tamper with – how essential each action is in its place, how fitting are the parallels and contrasts that unfold. Even while accepting the justice of Bradley's statement, we find our-selves paradoxically in agreement with Kenneth Muir: 'The play, far from exhibiting any signs of loose, episodic structure, is more closely knit than any of the tragedies, except *Othello*.'[1]

Chapters 2 and 3 will *not* attempt a Hegelian synthesis of these antithetical views. Rather, they will try to affirm how apposite both impressions are, when seen from the perspective of the early Jacobean theatre; for each critic seems to have fixed his sights on one countenance of a Janus. Muir praises the art that, after culling material for two plots from a variety of heterogeneous sources, manages to create a unified structure. It is a tight concatenation of events that both issue from the central character and serve to illuminate him for us, and as such it is the flower of a traditional structure found in Elizabethan plays dating back to the early Marlowe. Bradley seems unaware of this unified progression, so dismayed is he by another aspect of *King Lear*. Taking a more affective approach to its structure, he recoils from a play filled with scenes that are so powerful in themselves that they minimize our sense of cumulative progression. In finding Shakespeare too exclusively 'set upon the dramatic effect of the great scenes' (p. 258), Bradley points us to a different structural heritage. The strong, self-sufficient scene characterizes drama from Marston through Massin-ger and beyond.[2]

The structure of *King Lear* masterfully fuses basic attributes of several dra-matic traditions, and we can enlarge upon Bradley's observations by ex-amining some affinities to the structural emphases of Jacobean drama. Shakespeare buttresses his 'great scenes' with a number of effects that also convey a somewhat disjunctive impression, each one tending to inhibit our sense of the structure as a smooth developmental sequence, and thereby afford-ing Shakespeare the means for creating some of the most memorable contours of the *Lear* world. The Jacobean usage of momentary effects and poses, dramatic emblems, and suppression of story elements will occupy centre stage in the three main sections of this chapter, to be followed in Chapter 3 by an examination of two structural features shaped by both early and late Elizabethan practice: the stage-managed situation, and the plot-subplot configuration.

Before concentrating on those aspects of *King Lear* that tend to reinforce Bradley's impression, we consider briefly why his objections are not more widely shared by later critics. What is it that makes Kenneth Muir see a 'closely knit' structure, or Maynard Mack 'an almost diagrammatic'[3] unfolding, where Bradley finds 'confusion?' The answer lies partly in the play and partly in the nature of Bradley's approach. The play's verbal and thematic texture has yielded innumerable patterns and symmetries to the probing of modern criti-cism, and many different interpreters have either discovered or assumed an 'organic unity.'[4] Such approaches, if sometimes too subtle, have nevertheless made us sensitive to harmonies that escaped Bradley's ear. But there is also another kind of unity, one that reaches far back into the history of popular drama and that, perhaps, more aptly merits the description 'organic.' It is that unity provided by the gargantuan presence of the play's hero. As mentioned above, there is a sense in which the play's structure both issues from the central character and serves to illuminate him for us. Lear's first-scene blunders initiate a series of perspectives on his situation. The chaotic incidents that follow all relate directly to him – betrayals, folly, madness, the storm; even Gloucester (was ever subplot more like the main action?) is an alter ego. This concatenation is a more sophisticated version of the episodic progression that David Bevington finds in *Tamburlaine*, and is a heritage of the moral plays and hybrid chronicles of popular drama:

> Marlowe chooses an enormously varied number of incidents and unifies them by thematic treatment ... the incidents in the life of Tamburlaine, both admirable and deplorable, are chosen with care to represent from many points of view, and through successive iteration, the greatness of Tamburlaine's character. The episodes reveal his capacity in love for generosity, loyalty, and a sense of justice, his capacity in war for impassive cruelty, treachery, endurance of hardship and pain, invincible resolution, and ruthless lust for dominion.[5]

Variations on this structure can be traced through such later works as *Sir John Oldcastle* (1599) or *Thomas Lord Cromwell* (1600), where the entire series of characters and events exists to do little more than illuminate aspects of the hero's character. Or more artful approaches towards it can be found in *Hamlet*, where – aside from parallels in a partially developed secondary plot – the hero's problems echo through the speeches and actions of other characters (Gertrude, the First Player), or through the play-within-a-play and the graveyard scene. Viewed in this context, the incidents, characters, and settings of *King Lear* form a vast hall of mirrors reflecting Lear, though of course each also leads a more complex and independent existence than the two-dimensional reflectors of earlier drama; so complex and independent that the resulting configuration probably bears a closer resemblance to Wölfflin's concept of 'multiple unity' than to his 'unified unity.'[6] Yet throughout this complex structure we never lose our consciousness of Lear himself, at the centre.

Bradley cannot respond to such unity, and tries in vain to reconcile the copiousness of *King Lear* with more familiar, nineteenth-century interpretations of dramatic unity. He looks at the work's immense scope and despairs: 'all this interferes with dramatic clearness' (p. 247). As he finds more and more pieces that refuse to fit, one can picture him shaking his head and criticizing Shakespeare's art in terms of Pistol's estimate of Falstaff: 'He loves the gallimaufry.' Yet Bradley's failure to see the unity of *King Lear* betrays a general critical penchant of his that can be of great value in our study of the play's structure. Bradley's essay on *King Lear* exhibits a constant predilection towards affective criticism. His concern is always with what we *feel* at a given moment in the play, how we react to what takes place, and this concern is evident in a kind of Augustinian reiteration: page after page, we meet phrases like 'has made us feel,' 'we may feel,' 'we feel now,' 'what we feel,' 'such feelings ... possess us,' 'give way to another feeling,' 'we are inclined to feel.' This attitude contributes much to both the weaknesses and the strengths of Bradley's work. Students of Shakespearean drama must always lament the fact, for instance, that a critical mind of such power was denied acquaintance with a vital tradition of theatrical production; given this lack, Bradley's affective response produces grotesqueries on Othello's courtship or Lady Macbeth's children. But at its best, the response serves to anchor our judgment. It keeps us rooted in the play as felt experience, rather than floating in clouds of abstract speculations that could have no possible bearing on an audience's reaction to the play. Bradley's response to drama entails a close following of the play as a score that is played on our emotions, and he therefore most often devotes his attention to specific dramatic experiences. The approach sometimes leads him to miss the forest for the trees; but since we read him in an age when many critics are so concerned with charting the boundaries of forests that they forget the unique beauty of each tree, we are in little danger of sharing his blind spots and have much to gain from his insights.

The most significant gain, for our purposes, follows from Bradley's affective response to structure. 'Is the general reader and play-goer ... altogether in the wrong? I venture to doubt it' (p. 244), he proclaims, and allies himself with audience reaction instead of with critical apologetic. As a result, he feels what I think is a very real Jacobean trait in *King Lear*, the somewhat detached quality of scenes like V.i. The trait might be missed by a critic more concerned with the play as a whole than with the effect of its parts on us. But from a closer vantage point, structure seems frequently to consist of somewhat disjunctive moments. Perhaps this impression is the primary reason one should avoid using the term 'chronicle' in describing the structure of *King Lear*, despite the nature of Shakespeare's sources. 'Chronicle' implies a suppression of the total effect in favour of following the outline of a story, and the chronicle history was the most extreme example of that kind of structure that Elizabethan drama produced.[7] The structure of *King Lear* differs greatly from that emphasis; and the nature of the difference may be apprehended by approaching it through a brief outline of another kind of structure.

Most Jacobean playwrights departed from the chronicle history's predominantly narrative structure, in which each situation tended to channel its energies into a cumulative movement, and where the articulation of 'great scenes' was subordinated to a steady progress. The Jacobeans placed themselves at the opposite extreme, emphasizing the strong individual scene and paying less attention to narrative movement than was common in even the comedies and tragedies of the 1590s. Such plays as Chapman's *May-Day* (1602) and Middleton's *The Phoenix* (1604) display radical versions of this structure as they loosely string discrete scenes on a slight situational framework.

The Phoenix may be viewed as a paradigm. The play is characterized by brief and often unconnected tableaux, such as the one in which Tangle, an unscrupulous lawyer, makes his first appearance. The prince and his companion have just arrived at an inn, where the groom tells them that the man who just alighted is a crafty knave. Tangle then takes over the scene, as he displays his craftiness at length by negotiating a complicated case with two opposing suitors. This action is only tangentially connected with what comes before and after it: in the previous scene, a Captain has mentioned in passing that he knows a crafty lawyer; and in the following one, the Captain hires Tangle for a short intrigue. Significantly, the two suitors who have aided in Tangle's exhibition here are never seen again.

Even more isolated is a later scene in the play, which abruptly depicts a situation in an affair between a jeweller's wife and a knight, neither of whom has been mentioned before. The play's action then shifts to another strange situation, and a connection between the two is made only when the second scene is well in progress. Along with many other characters, the two adulterers are unmasked by the prince during a long scene towards the end of the play, in which all the separate situations are briefly revisited in order to create a semblance of structural unity. Like his Jacobean colleagues, Middleton became more adept in later plays at relating his strong scenes to each other, but the scenes themselves remain central, and narrative matters remain well in the background as we shall see.[8]

One source for this structural emphasis may perhaps be found in the theatrical conditions under which many early Jacobean plays were performed: in 1599-1600 private theatre productions resumed at St Paul's and at Blackfriars after a lapse of almost a decade. These productions were mounted by companies composed entirely of children, and their writers attempted perhaps to compensate for the actors' limitations and relative inexperience. In early works like *Histriomastix* (1599) and *The Maid's Metamorphosis* (1600), or Jonson's *Cynthia's Revels* and Marston's *Jack Drum's Entertainment* (both 1600), a highly wrought metre and frequent songs accent individual moments rather than uniform movement; action gives way to ornament, and each play tends to become a series of set pieces. Because the all-boy casts were probably unable to involve the audience in a sustained mimesis of adult action – such as had been developed at the public theatres while the private houses were dormant in the 1590s – the structure of these plays stresses the individual scene rather than the continuous progression. It is a structural emphasis that strongly resembles the work of an earlier dramatist who wrote for child companies, John Lyly.[9]

Many Jacobean playwrights did write for the child actors during the early 1600s: Jonson, Marston, Chapman, Middleton. But lest we attach too much importance to the child companies as a source for the new emphasis on the individual scene, we should recall that this emphasis is also noticeable in the immensely popular and influential humours plays of Jonson and Chapman, performed by adult companies before the private theatres reopened. These plays consist of Chapman's *An Humourous Day's Mirth* (1597) and Jonson's two *Every Man* works (1598 and 1599). All three plays take the audience through a series of humourous tableaux, lively situations on which attention focuses temporarily. The situations are not subsumed into a narrative development, and manifest a pronounced structural autonomy.

This structural emphasis continued even after adults had replaced the boy actors at Blackfriars. In Beaumont and Fletcher's tragicomedies, 'We [still] have a series of disjunctive scenes rather than a steady progress.'[10] The strong scene is at the heart of the Jacobeans' work, and perhaps we can finally attain the clearest perspective on its origins by viewing both the child players and the humours vogue as forces tending to accelerate a development that was already underway: the gradual evolution of English drama away from the rambling narrative plays of the 1570s and 1580s towards a later tradition that has been helpfully summarized by Joseph W. Donohue, Jr:

> A homogeneous dramatic tradition extends from the plays of Beaumont and Fletcher to those of Romantic writers like Joanna Baillie, 'Monk' Lewis, Charles Maturin, Richard Sheil, and many others. This tradition may be aptly termed 'the affective drama of situation.' Plays of this sort have a structure based on a series of circumstances and events unconnected by a strict logic of causality (or Aristotelian 'action'); their situations are deliberately brought out of the blue for the purpose of displaying human reactions to extreme and unexpected occurrences. In these plays the intelligible unit is not the thematic part, placed within a coherent series of other parts, but, as in Fletcherian drama, the scene, which exists in effect for its own sake.[11]

As Bradley half guessed, the strong scene is at the heart of *King Lear* too. The opening may again be referred to since it is typical of the play's concentrated scenes. Without warning, it thrusts us into a situation of brutal, exaggerated conflict between people we know nothing about. Only later do we find out that the absurd love-test that provokes this reaction is bogus: 'I lov'd her most, and thought to set my rest/ On her kind nursery' (123-4), Lear discloses *after* he has disinherited Cordelia. Lear's outburst is partially explained only after it occurs, when we learn that his anger was triggered by the collapse of a carefully planned scheme. Cordelia's reticence, the direct cause of her father's explosion, fades away unexplained. Shakespeare has presented us with a strong, self-sufficient scene rather than with the first chapter of a chronicle history.

It may be observed that the disjunctive quality of many scenes in *King Lear* is perhaps emphasized by the unusually large number of end-of-scene soliloquies which, instead of looking forward in a transitional way to future action (like Edmund's soliloquies at III.iii and V.i), reflect on what has occurred and so round off their scenes as more discrete units. These include Edmund's soliloquy closing I.ii, the Fool's at I.v, Kent's at II.ii, the Fool's at III.ii, and Edgar's at III.vi.

However, Shakespeare reinforces the disjunctive impression of his strong scenes with several devices and emphases that also have a wider Jacobean currency: momentary effects and poses, certain types of dramatic emblems, and suppression of story elements. In considering them, one is highly conscious of dealing with an area that troubled A.C. Bradley, for some of the examples from *King Lear* appear on his list of the play's 'defects,' so labelled because his preconception of the 'well-made play' kept him from regarding them as the product of design rather than of accident. But even where such effects are perhaps the result of carelessness – a term that experience has taught us to apply to Shakespeare with great caution – one finds that their drift is strong and unmistakable. They all throw the individual dramatic moment, the single frame rather than the moving picture, into the spotlight.

I

Such is certainly the effect when Shakespeare suddenly brings to our attention issues or attitudes that then seem to disappear as precipitately as they appeared. For example, a character named Curan enters at the start of Act II and asks Edmund, 'Have you heard of no likely wars toward, 'twixt the Dukes of Cornwall and Albany?' The wars never materialize and the rumour is briefly mentioned at two other times (III.i.19-21 and III.iii.8-9) so widely spaced that it becomes completely lost in more major issues; and Curan himself vanishes after this encounter. Curan's rumour colours the atmosphere of the tumultuous family division, into which we are thrust at once, by raising the even more fearful spectre of political chaos. But once the reference has served its purpose, it disappears.

The same process takes place towards the end of II.ii, when Kent eases his punishment in the stocks by reading a letter from Cordelia. Just as another letter he carries, from Lear to Gloucester, seems here to have faded into the blue, so this letter comes from nowhere: we have no reason to think that Kent would now welcome a communication from Cordelia, much less value it a 'miracle,' since he has not mentioned her since the first scene; and the diligence with which he carried out Lear's hasty command would hardly have made him readily available to messengers from Cordelia. But the letter, of which we never hear more than a dozen garbled words because Kent falls asleep before he finishes reading it, serves its dramatic purpose. It raises hopes by putting Cordelia in the light of a marvelous redeemer ('miracles' 'seeking to give/ Losses their remedies'), and it ends the scene by conveying to us a sense of polarization among the characters as it throws Kent and Cordelia together against their malicious opposites and a hostile Fortune.

These abrupt and disconnected happenings are unusual in Shakespearean drama, but many similar incidents can be found in other plays of the same era. Curan's walk-on is equalled in its suddenness by that of the Painter who appears in Act V of *Antonio and Mellida* (1599) just so that Marston can parody *The Spanish Tragedy*, and is surpassed by the entrance of an enchanter and attendant fairies in Act II of *The Wisdom of Doctor Dodypoll* (1599). That group bursts in on what has hitherto been an absolutely mundane if mad world, augments the comic confusion, and then fades out again.[12] Or one can turn to more serious drama and compare Kent's letter to that which Marston's Sophonisba receives in Act II of the play named for her. Sophonisba is being held captive by the tyrant Syphax, who has opened the scene by dragging her in by the hair and telling her that her husband is dead, when their conversation is interrupted by the entrance of a page with a letter for her. She reads the letter silently, and learns that her husband is in fact alive – as she announces to us after Syphax exits. The letter is as abrupt and implausible as Kent's, but it makes as striking an impact on the scene, bringing light to a previously hopeless situation. By appreciating the importance of the strong scene to Jacobean playwrights, we can better understand the logic behind such effects as prompted Herford and Simpson to write of *Cynthia's Revels*: 'In place of action as a coherent whole, we find a number of embryonic or fragmentary actions, very loosely and inorganically connected.'[13] Other such actions from *King Lear* include: the Fool's disappearance; the morality-like apparition of an Old Man in IV.i; the fortuitous entrance of Oswald at II.iv.186; and the music invoked at IV.vii.24.[14]

Complementing the play's disconnected characters and incidents are those actions in which major characters assume unexplained postures for momentary effect. The scene depicting Kent's fight with Oswald (II.ii) displays this quality. Kent provokes and beats Oswald, behaves insolently to Edmund and Cornwall (neither of whom he has any reason to dislike), and delivers a bombastic speech (73-85) that makes Oswald laugh and Cornwall suspect him of madness. He has nearly jumped out of character to force events to a crisis, and he settles safely back into the old mould after triggering the confrontation; a partial explanation of his conduct only comes some time after this exhibition (II.iv.27-41). But Kent's strange behaviour has energized a conflict that is both theatrically ebullient and revealing of those drawn into it. As well, the conflict has epitomized the 'court versus country' dichotomy that is so important to the ethical vision of *King Lear*, and that receives fuller expression in another strange pose later in the play.

The later incident, strongly objected to by Bradley (p. 257), occurs after Edgar's 'miraculous' rescue of his father. When Oswald enters in pursuit of Gloucester, Edgar assumes a country dialect as he opposes the courtly intruder. After killing Oswald, he resumes his normal speech, without giving either us or Gloucester a reason for the disguise. Those readers who are so inclined can invent a plausible explanation: that Edgar launches into peasant dialect because he is *dressed* like a peasant; it is unlikely that a man of upper-class speech would be helping a 'publish'd traitor' while disguised as a peasant, and he does not want to spark any suspicions in Oswald who knows Edgar well, as Edgar (IV.vi.254). Such suspicions might tip off Gloucester to Edgar's real identity. But a decent performance of the scene helps to show why Shakespeare found any explanation superfluous. The confrontation catches us up in its excitement and strikes us as profoundly appropriate: Edgar represents and champions the peasants with whom Lear and Gloucester have been brought to sympathize, and his pose here helps us to feel more deeply the significance of his victory. It is the first victory since the play began of the victims over their tormentors, and the first indication that those who are not well spoken have a fighting chance against the 'glib and oily' opportunists. Audiences *feel* the rightness of this opposition and exult in its outcome – the fight often draws applause and even cheers – even if they are not consciously aware of its symbolism. The scene satisfies the needs of an audience rather than the more leisurely curiosity of a novel-reader.

Such curiosity made Bradley protest against the logic of Edgar's writing a letter to Edmund, who lives in the same house with him, the delayed unmaskings of Kent and Edgar, and Edmund's delay in revealing his sentencing of Lear and Cordelia. Kenneth Muir (pp. l-li), largely with tongue in cheek, finds naturalistic explanations for each of Bradley's objections: Edmund's delay could have been caused by his loyalty to Goneril or by the gradual workings of repentance, for instance, and Edgar's by a wish to impose a penance on his father or to rehabilitate himself in the world's eyes before revealing himself; Lear's figure of fifty followers to be dismissed, quoted although Goneril has not set a figure, could have been arrived at by telepathy, etc. I feel that it is less important to 'explain' the improbabilities, however whimsically, than to realize that every one of them may be justified as contributing in large measure to the impact of Shakespeare's strong scenes. Edmund's delay, for instance, functions magnificently in working our anxiety up to fever pitch during the suspenseful last scene.

Bradley noticed many other 'improbabilities' and 'inconsistencies' in *King Lear*, observing that Shakespeare introduced 'what was convenient or striking for a momentary purpose without troubling himself about anything more than the moment' (p. 258). Lear does seem to employ more than the usual share of attendant lords and anonymous gentlemen who materialize briefly to swell a progress or start a scene or two. But Shakespeare's method becomes more understandable as such when one realizes that it had ample precedence in the work of his contemporaries. Kent's strange behaviour is mirrored by that of Iacomo in Act I of Marston's *What You Will* (1601), or that of Justiniano in *Westward Ho* (1604), who shifts between prodigal, jealous husband, and genial intriguer according to the mood of each scene; and the Fool's disappearance is paralleled by those of Echo in *Cynthia's Revels* (1601), and Maffé after the epitomic scene at the beginning of *Bussy D'Ambois* (1604). Like Curan's rumour and Cordelia's silence, these incidents exist to illuminate individual moments, and are quietly snuffed out after they have served their purpose. It is in the study rather than in the theatre that they call attention to themselves as improbabilities.

II

Like these momentary effects and poses, Shakespeare's dramatic emblems call attention to the single frame rather than the moving picture. When characters arrange themselves into fleeting but memorable tableaux, pictorial realizations of abstract themes, they create an instantaneous detachment from the flow of events. They make us relate the picture to previous words or pictures, and reflect on the total significance of each configuration. This is true whether the emblematic effect derives from a single physical configuration or from the juxtaposition of similar actions in different scenes – the two kinds of dramatic emblems that the following discussion will explore. All of the tableaux that

Shakespeare creates in *King Lear* have this in common: like bas-relief details on a plane composition, they do not quite yield up their individuation to the whole of which they are parts. Each tableau fosters an awareness of the singularity of the light it sheds on the main situation instead of completely subsuming that light to a single cumulative impression. Furthermore, they all either ignore or resist the forward-moving impetus of a developing sequence of events: the solitary tableau stands apart from such an impetus, briefly motionless, while the juxtaposed or patterned emblem encourages a retrospective view of the action. Instead of keeping our attention fixed constantly on an unbroken line of development, Shakespeare also calls for an awareness of dramatic structure as an object of static or retrospective contemplation. The emblematic technique of *King Lear* thus accords with, and reinforces, a structure characterized by strong scenes.

Before we turn our attention to particular emblems in *King Lear*, further differentiation needs to be made. In his illuminating article on 'Emblems in English Renaissance Drama,'[15] Dieter Mehl distinguishes three types of dramatic emblems: direct borrowings or quotations from emblem books; full allegorical scenes that comment on a play's action (e.g., dumb shows); and significant combinations of verbal and pictorial expression in the course of a scene. It will be evident that the dramatic emblems which this discussion distinguishes in *King Lear* bear closest resemblance to Mehl's third type, in that we will not be concerned with direct borrowings or full allegorical scenes. But an important distinction must still be made between his third type of emblems and those to be discussed in relation to *King Lear* and Jacobean drama. In every example adduced by Mehl, it is the characters in a scene who give full emblematic interpretations to objects or relationships around them. They give the impression of having themselves read emblem books. I am interested primarily in those scenes where it is only the audience who perceives such meaning. These scenes are so constructed as to encourage *us* to trace emblematic figures, while the characters are unaware of them and are engaged in other activities. There is thus a fundamental difference in the relationship of audience to play: Mehl's emblems have been worked into the surface of the play, so we experience them through the characters even as we continue to be involved in the unwinding dramatic action; the emblems I shall cite in *King Lear* exist as emblems apart from any characters' consciousness, and require us to stand momentarily back from the action in order to perceive their outlines and their significance.[16] They briefly interrupt our involvement in the flow of events in order to foster a more profound involvement in the world of the play.

The type of emblem which engages my attention in *King Lear* occurs in earlier Shakespearean drama, though less frequently. In all his plays, Shakespeare is concerned with verbal and thematic echoes of popular emblems (Mehl's first type). Writing on the history plays, James Hoyle feels that when Shakespeare goes beyond such echoes to create emblematic stage configurations in the early plays, at least in the Henriad, the characters involved in them usually display an awareness of the pictures' meanings: 'His characters have become self-conscious about the relationship to metaphor and convention of their own complex and immediate intuition of themselves.'[17] Two scenes from the tragedies would also seem to conform to this description. When Othello holds the candle over Desdemona, and when Hamlet holds up Yorick's skull, each is quite conscious of his emblem's meaning, and proceeds to interpret it. But one of the most famous emblems in Shakespeare constitutes a notable exception: Hal expresses no awareness of the emblem we see as he stands between the recumbent figures of Hotspur and Falstaff, after the battle at Shrewsbury; and the elm and vine *topos* is used in a similar emblematic way in *A Midsummer Night's Dream* (IV.i.39-42) and *The Comedy of Errors* (II.ii.172-9), as Mehl points out (pp. 54-5). It should be evident that I am not trying to assert the uniqueness of such emblems to *King Lear*. My concern is with their unusual abundance there, and with the ways in which they support some aspects of the play's structure.

The first scene of Act IV ends with one of these groupings. Paradox leaps to life when Edgar, supposedly mad but really the sanest man in the play, leads out a blind Gloucester who has finally gained a clearer vision of himself. No iconographer could portray it more concisely. Lear calls our attention to an equally symbolic tableau in Act II. Fleeing from Goneril's ingratitude, he has arrived for a visit with Regan; but even as he complains of the treatment that brought him, Goneril enters. Regan immediately shows where her allegiance lies, as Lear's shocked exclamation indicates: 'O Regan! will you take her by the hand?' (II.iv.196). By holding hands, the two sisters provide us with an unmistakable emblem of their affinity, and of Lear's folly in thinking they would be different. The gesture is focused on for its symbolic implications, and exists primarily in terms of them.

We may say the same of a series of emblematic entrances in *King Lear* which also resonate with dramatic irony because the characters involved in them do not perceive the emblems. The first occurs when Lear unconsciously foretells the course of Albany's career. Wrapped up in self-pity, Lear follows the stage direction *'Enter* ALBANY' with a proverb uttered in response to his own condition but providing the picture of Albany with a bitterly prophetic motto: 'Woe, that too late repents' (I.iv.266). Lear then unconsciously drives the point home as he realizes Albany's presence and continues: 'O! Sir, are you come?' In contrast, the next emblematic entrance takes place with lightning speed and shocking effect, as motto precedes illustration. Getting much the worst of his scuffle with Kent, Oswald cries for assistance: 'Help, ho! murther! murther!' (II.ii.43). Immediately in response there enters a true type of the allegorical figure he has invoked, as the stage direction indicates: *'Enter* EDMUND, *with his rapier drawn.'* The end of this scene brings yet another emblematic combination of word and picture. Kent settles in for his night in the stocks by calling for benevolence from another allegorical presence: 'Fortune, good night; smile once more; turn thy wheel!' he says, drifting off to sleep. The wheel turns, but again in a downward direction appropriate to the play's increasingly tragic world, as Edgar enters breathless, hunted, and desperate, resembling one of those illuminated manuscript figures at the bottom of Fortune's wheel. In this world, characters must tolerate 'false Fortune's frown' (V.iii.6) rather than bask in her smile. The most critical of the play's emblematic entrances literally lights up the storm scenes. The Fool, chilled to the bone, is appalled by Lear's nakedness and resorts to a simile to express his feelings: 'Now a little fire in a wild field were like an old lecher's heart; a small spark, all the rest on's body cold' (III.iv.114-16). As if on cue ('Look! here comes a walking fire') in comes the old lecher whose moral blindness will soon be translated into agonizing physical terms: '*Enter* GLOUCESTER, *with a torch.*' The emblematic prop of Gloucester here, like that of Edmund in his entrance, helps to fix our attention on the picture's symbolic nature, even as it fulfils its more usual dramatic function.

Similar emblematic tableaux abound in Jacobean drama, where one might expect the emphasis on strong scenes to foster this kind of display. Of course, all types of emblematic imagery appear in English drama long before the Jacobean period,[18] but emblems of Mehl's third type do seem especially prevalent in Jacobean drama: of the nine examples he gives, six are from Jacobean plays. After describing several emblematic groupings and gestures, Mehl remarks on 'the close relationship between Elizabethan dramatic imagery and the method of the emblem writers,' and observes that 'In plays of the early seventeenth century, this relationship becomes even more marked' (p. 55).

Chapman, for instance, uses the technique to image his hero's isolation in Act IV of *Byron's Tragedy* (1608). As the outcast Byron stands at centre stage with a single confidant, other nobles enter and walk around him in couples, whispering together but refraining from communication with him. The result is an emblem of alienation, as effective as the emblem of affinity observed between Regan and Goneril in *King Lear*. Similarly, the moving tableau at the end of Shakespeare's play – where Lear and Cordelia form a kind of *Pietà* – has its analogues. The body of Marston's heroine is borne in to her presence chamber and is richly adorned in the gruesome last scene of *Sophonisba* (1605), showing us the price that this 'wonder of women' has paid for freedom; and the famous ending of *Bussy D'Ambois* (1604) presents us with another 'Roman statue,' this one in a more martial pose than Shakespeare's. The tableau is an image of Bussy's deterioration: he is left with only the pose of nobility, his noble deeds having been dissipated in the play's corrupt world. The final scenes of all three plays gain in impact by being both dramatically and graphically striking.

Shakespeare also uses costuming for emblematic effect. As Heilman has observed, clothes symbolism is an important leitmotif in *King Lear*;[19] and we can see it achieving stage realization through the gestures of many characters. For instance, when Kent accuses Oswald of being made by a tailor, he opens our eyes to the visual proof of Oswald's concern with outer rather than inner worth. The opposite concern is visible in the nakedness of Edgar and Lear on the heath, where Shakespeare follows the practice of Renaissance iconographers in depicting Truth without clothes.[20] Lear's madness comes to life in the same way: Cordelia first sketches him as 'Crown'd with rank fumiter and furrow-weeds,/ With hardocks, hemlock, nettles, cuckoo-flowers' (IV.iv.3-4) – noxious weeds, some associated with death and insanity. Shortly afterwards Lear completes the picture by appearing on stage in this very costume (IV.vi.81).[21]

Chapman had anticipated this effect in the first act of *Bussy D'Ambois*. Bussy enters dressed in tatters, and proclaims that 'Fortune, not Reason, rules the state of things.' Then, later in Act I, Henry states that his French court is a mirror of confusion, while the foppery of the English court masks an inner worth that the French do not possess. At that moment, Bussy enters dressed in fantastic court attire (I.ii.56),[22] and the emblem's meaning is plain: besides showing that he has accepted Fortune rather than Reason, the clothes associate him with the outer affectation and inner worth of the English court.

Even when scenes do not contain pictorial tableaux of abstract themes, Shakespeare often manages to create the pictorial vividness and the momentary detachment of his theatrical emblems by juxtaposing the same kind of action in two different scenes. In the play's first scene, Lear's mercenary conduct and imagery demonstrate a zeal for quantifying that recoils back on him in the retainers incident of Act II when Regan and Goneril treat him to a bold rehearsal of his own values. A more immediate juxtaposition emerges in Act III. When Cornwall gives orders to apprehend Gloucester, Edmund's reaction comes in an aside: 'If I find him comforting the King, it will stuff his suspicion more fully' (III.v.20-1). In the next scene Edgar, busy comforting the King, also voices his reaction in an aside: 'My tears begin to take his part so much,/ They mar my counterfeiting' (III.vi.60-1). The contrast between the two brothers could not be sharper: they appear like back to back pictures of Vice and Virtue in an emblem book. Conversely, an unmistakable link is forged between Gloucester and Edmund in II.i, when Gloucester's repeated questions form a variation on those his son has just asked in the Nature soliloquy.

Such pointed juxtaposition of similar or contrasting actions also occurs in other Jacobean drama, as may be seen in Jonson's *Epicoene* (1609). Tom Otter and his wife open Act III with a terrific argument, during which he is reduced to timid monosyllables under his wife's continuous barrage of expletives; neither is aware that the argument is being observed by Truewit, Clerimont, and Dauphine. The scene finds its counterpart in Act IV, when the three gallants feed Tom's courage with alcohol, and watch as he explodes into an equally fierce denunciation of Mistress Otter; unfortunately for Tom, the hidden observer this time is Mistress Otter herself. The two scenes are mirror images, and the second one picks up immense theatrical vitality from this kind of paralleling. The same is true of Edward Sharpham's *The Fleer* (1606), where the opening scenes of Act III present the parallel actions of several characters in even closer juxtaposition as we watch the fortunes of two absurd lovers fall into perfect alignment. The technique goes far beyond a basic plot-subplot echoing in that it encourages us to engage in a detail-by-detail paralleling of the two scenes.

It is a technique that also proved useful in Jacobean tragedy, as when Marston employed it to emphasize a turning point in our response to the characters of *Antonio's Revenge* (1600). When Antonio enters in scene V of Act III, he forms a tableau that reveals his absolute commitment to violence: his arms are bloodied, and he stands with a torch in one hand and a dagger in the other. This emblem is the more telling because it duplicates exactly the entrance of the villainous Piero at the start of Act I. The emblem is the same, only the faces are changed. Chapman employs a similar emblematic contrast in *Bussy D'Ambois*, when Bussy's entrance with two pages at V.ii ironically duplicates the entrance Monsieur had made in I.i. Bussy has taken on the trappings of the man who was previously his antithesis.[23]

Two implications of the tableaux and juxtaposed actions of *King Lear* remain to be considered, the first being more of a caveat. It must be emphasized that these effects do not act on the involved spectator in a mechanical way, simply directing him in and out of an intense awareness of those 'bas-relief' moments in the play's texture. Rather, they should be viewed as working to reinforce or oppose the *tendency* in him towards greater or lesser awareness of such moments, ripples in the complex stream of an audience's response. Conversely, if we apply Maynard Mack's two poles of 'engagement' and 'detachment'[24] to an audience's vision of the whole rather than of its parts, of sequence rather than of moment, we may say that Shakespeare's dramatic emblems (like his momentary effects and poses) exert pressure towards 'detachment' from the sequential whole; but we must realize that this pressure is subtle and intermittent.

Secondly, the presence of so many dramatic emblems in *King Lear* calls our attention to a conception of dramatic action that Shakespeare employs here to an extent unique among the tragedies (although it is found more often in his romances). We can state this conception most simply by saying that the action in *King Lear* concerns itself primarily with defining the essences of characters and moral issues rather than with following a gradually realized course of developments. The major exception to this statement is of course Lear himself whose actions trace an arc resembling that of the Marlovian hero mentioned at the start of this chapter, or that of his morality play prototypes. But the actions surrounding and contributing to this central progress subscribe mainly to the characteristics discussed above. Each strong scene points us directly to the essence of those characters and issues involved in it. The process is itself an emblematic one, but Shakespeare's dramatic emblems are only its most formalized results. Alongside them stand such actions as the storm on the heath, Gloucester's blindness (as Mack writes in *'King Lear' in Our Time*, 'blindness is not what will follow from adultery, but what is implied in it' [p. 70]), Lear's madness, or the fall from Dover Cliffs. Each of these actions unfolds so as to point us directly towards meaning on an essential rather than a literal level; each is, as Rosemond Tuve wrote of Milton's personifications, 'a way of talking about the absolutely not the contingently real.'[25]

Many of the incidents that troubled Bradley because they lacked contingent reality yield meaning to an interpretation that seeks instead 'a perfect picture' of 'the general reason of things' (the phrases are Sidney's). So, for example, the fight between Edgar and Oswald in IV.vi, an unlikely coincidence, reverberates with this kind of meaning. Aside from the court-country opposition that the fight crystallizes, it conforms to our growing awareness of Edgar's place in the *Lear* world: he shows himself ready to become an active opponent of Edmund by here destroying Oswald, who represents the lesser evils of his betters. Similarly, the trial by combat between Edgar and Edmund, to Bradley an act of supererogation (p. 256) and to D.G. James 'a piece of hollow stage trumpery,' is *essential*, as Carol L. Marks has observed: 'In this first ceremonial occasion since the opening scene, a good child defeats an evil.'[26] The combat further demonstrates the role of ceremony-initiator passing to Edgar, who has already assumed the lesser role of stage manager – a role to be explored in detail later in Chapter 3. Such examples reveal, then, that the nature of action in *King Lear* is shaped to an unusual extent by the hand of ultimate significance rather than by that of contingent reality. Two conclusions relevant to the main concerns of this chapter follow from this realization. Bradley's naturalistic expectations must again fail him, whereas a critical approach that views action and gesture as a window to essential meaning (like the approach of R.B. Heilman, for instance) can mine great riches in *King Lear*. And Shakespeare's choice of this form of action shows the deep eclecticism of his art, for even while it sustains emblems like those of Jacobean drama it hearkens back to the metaphorically determined structure of the morality plays, ancestors of all Elizabethan drama.

III

In turn, this morality heritage points to yet another Jacobean trait, a third corollary of Shakespeare's strong scenes. When we investigate the effects on our response to the play of those actions where ultimate significance determines form, we find that the actions contribute to a sense of narrative discontinuity. By focusing our attention exclusively on a series of events where meaning explodes into action, and neglecting both the preparation and the after-effects of these explosions, Shakespeare diminishes story interest in *King Lear*. Suppression of story elements is another emphasis that *King Lear* shares with other dramas of its age. Jacobean playwrights seem to have radically departed from the predilection for sustained narrative that characterized so much earlier drama. At this point in my own narrative, an account of these centrally important narrative and anti-narrative traditions should place some of the seeming anomalies of Shakespeare's structure in a more meaningful light. But first, because of a common critical tendency to use the terms 'narrative' and 'plot' interchangeably, I want to make it clear that I am distinguishing between them here.

Thus, in arguing that Jacobean tragedies display an anti-narrative bias, I am not claiming that these tragedies are not well plotted. Indeed, such tragedies and tragicomedies as Beaumont and Fletcher's are among the most elaborately plotted in the history of drama, even though they ignore narrative continuity and narrative fulness. I believe that a great deal of confusion in the criticism of Jacobean drama has arisen from an unfortunately ambiguous use of the word 'plot.' The OED defines 'plot' as meaning, in literary contexts, the 'plan or scheme of any literary creation,' but looser usage of the term has often made it synonymous with 'story' and therefore with 'narrative': so Webster's Third International dictionary defines 'plot' as 'the plan or pattern of events *or the main story* of a literary work' (italics mine). The confusion seems to have crept into the work of even so precise a writer as T.S. Eliot, when Eliot writes that 'Jonson employs immense dramatic skill: it is not so much skill in plot as skill in doing without a plot' (*Essays on Elizabethan Drama*, New York, 1956, p. 75). There is a need for someone to trace the application of the term to Jacobean drama, with the aim of putting future criticism on firmer ground. I would assert here that Jacobean drama displays immense 'skill in plot' while doing largely without sustained or full narratives.

On the other hand, the Presenter who comes forward in Act I of Heywood's *The Four Prentices* (c. 1600) voices a concern that was basic to sixteenth-century popular dramaturgy:

> Now to auoide all dilatory newes,
> Which might with-hold you from the Stories pith,
> And substance of the matter wee entend:
> I must entreate your patience to forbeare,
> Whilst we do feast your eye, and starue your eare.[27]

In preparing the audience for the dumb show that will follow, he indicates how narrative elements predominate in these plays: the 'Stories pith' and 'substance' are most important, and the fundamental interest is in narrative incident. The very fact that he must apologize for deleting some action, so that more crucial events may be represented, shows the extent to which episodic narrative incidents are featured in place of integral dramatic *situations*.

This concern largely determined the structural composition of numerous adventure plays, comedies, and tragedies, not to mention that of the primitive and widely collaborative chronicle histories. *The Four Prentices*, for instance, is simply a series of exciting narrative episodes that trace the stories of four brothers, their sister, and their father. In various combinations, the six protagonists shuffle into one adventure after another; and like Sidney's old men held from the chimney corner by the 'well-enchanting' tale, we follow each episode through its inception, development, and conclusion. Not for Heywood is the bold *King Lear* practice of jumping from one high point to another; he carefully guides us over every slope of his narrative. A father and his two sons demand similar attention in Dekker's *Old Fortunatus* (1599), which prepares the spectator for such structural movement from the beginning, when the Prologue announces that he will serve as Chorus 'Not when the lawes of Poesy doe call,/ But as the storie needes.'[28] The laws of Poesy are sacrificed to the maintenance of narrative continuity. The fabric of both plays is a magic carpet that transports an audience through a succession of wonderful adventures, and the structure of both works is determined by demands of the narrative.

In writing these plays at the turn of the century, Dekker and Heywood were creating dramatic anachronisms, throwbacks to such overwhelmingly narrative works as *Clyomon and Clamydes* (c. 1570) and *Common Conditions* (1576). But more major dramatists had been developing a different kind of structure during the 1580s and 1590s. If we observe the course of Marlowe's dramatic career, for instance, we find a pronounced movement away from predominantly narrative concerns. *Tamburlaine*, written at the beginning of his career (i.e., 1587), follows its hero's fortunes through a long series of incidents – 'his rare and woonderfull Conquests,' as the 1590 title page puts it. The Prologue to Part One promises to 'lead you to the stately tent of war,/ Where you shall hear the Scythian Tamburlaine/ Threat'ning the world with high astounding terms/ And scourging kingdoms with his conquering sword';[29] and in Part Two the Prologue announces that 'what became of fair Zenocrate,' 'Herself in presence shall unfold at large.' The emphasis is on 'what' rather than on 'how,' and the dramatist seems to be viewing his work as something to be imparted rather than experienced. On the other hand *Doctor Faustus*, written some five years later, gives the story away before the action starts. Its Prologue completely disposes of a string of narrative details, so that the play itself may centre on more dramatically crucial events. To be sure, *Doctor Faustus* proceeds to move us through a conspicuous, if more circumscribed, series of often spectacular incidents; but these are arranged to relate vitally to the hero's spiritual crisis, always in the foreground, and their circumstantial developments are curtailed accordingly.

A similar movement characterizes Shakespeare's work in the early 1590s. Somewhat on the order of *Tamburlaine*, the Henry VI plays attempt through long chains of power struggles and battles to 'present the chronicled event with convincing documentary detail,'[30] while the Henry IV plays depart brilliantly from this narrative focus, and anticipate the structural achievement of later tragedies. But even the profoundly selective use of narrative in a play like *Hamlet* does not quite prepare us for the anti-narrative bias of *King Lear* and many other Jacobean dramas. *Hamlet* still familiarizes us with background events, through speeches of the Ghost, Claudius, Gertrude, and others, so that we may follow the inception, development, and consequences of actions. We are shown the foundations of characters' later behaviour, through such scenes as I.iii (the interview of Polonius and Ophelia), II.i (Polonius and Reynaldo), the start of II.ii (Claudius with Rosencrantz and Guildenstern, then with Voltimand and Cornelius), and IV.vii (Claudius and Laertes). Interstices are carefully filled in: we find out in detail what happened to Hamlet at sea, how Laertes was probably behaving in Paris, how Ophelia met her end, even why the players have left the city. After the fates of all the characters (even Rosencrantz and Guildenstern) have been worked out – mostly on stage – the future of Denmark is also clearly determined. In the end, when Hamlet bids Horatio to absent himself 'from felicity a while/ ... To tell my story,' his desire to get the story right seems to voice a concern evident in the play as a whole.

The concern for narrative continuity and fulness is largely absent from Jacobean drama. Examples of this shift in emphasis are numerous, covering the entire spectrum between scenes that suppress their story content, and scenes that run absolutely counter to the advancement of a story line. To illustrate the former, one might begin by noting how differently the romantic intrigue is handled in Dekker's *The Shoemakers' Holiday* (1599) and in Middleton's *A Chaste Maid in Cheapside* (1613). Dekker tells a tale of triumphant love, letting us follow closely the fortunes of a main character who tries, against parental opposition, to win the girl he loves. Conversely, the romantic story of Middleton's play has been dismissed by critics as a neutral 'frame' on which he can 'hang the more interesting comedy of fleshly passions and follies.'[31]

One reason Jacobean playwrights can evolve strong and fully realized scenes is that they do not permit story material to infringe upon the dramatic moment. Indeed, several plays give potentially broad story elements very short shrift: the central disguise intrigue of Marston's *What You Will* (1601) is almost obliterated by extensive lively departures from the play's story line; the love of Ovid and Julia comes to nothing, in Jonson's *Poetaster* (1601), and nobody much cares; and the obvious love affair between Hercules and Philocalia never materializes in Marston's *The Fawn* (1605). In fact, like the Fool in *King Lear*, Philocalia disappears altogether. These instances may all be dismissed as due to authorial carelessness, but even so, it is a carelessness that strongly suggests where the writers' interests lay, and it is an emphasis supported by other examples. In Act III of *The Gentleman Usher* (1602), Chapman deliberately moves away from the advancement of a narrative interest, in order to create a strong comic scene. The ridiculous Bassiolo tries to persuade Margaret to reciprocate Vincentio's affections, and volunteers to write a love letter for her in hopes of bringing the affair to consummation. But the resulting letter, hilariously composed on stage, is an exercise in futility: Chapman has already shown us that Margaret loves Vincentio even before the scene began. Her coyness here is patently artificial, and furthers Chapman's desire to create another strong scene rather than to follow the course of an evolving romantic interest. Such dramatic predilections have even caused one of Chapman's critics to object to the scenes of *Sir Giles Goosecap* (1602) because they 'tell no story.'[32]

Typical of the disregard for narrative interests in Jacobean tragedy is the first act of *Bussy D'Ambois*. The hero opens this play with a soliloquy that gives us no information about the time or place of the action, or about his own circumstances. Instead, his speech sets up a philosophical framework to be tested by the situations into which Chapman will place him. Bussy's background will in fact remain a blank for the rest of the play. After his soliloquy, Monsieur enters and invites Bussy to come to the court of his brother, Henry III. Monsieur explains in soliloquy that he needs all the strong followers he can get, because he secretly aspires to the throne. Yet as soon as these ambitions are voiced, and provide a means for Chapman to get Bussy into the court, they disappear until the end of Act III, emerging again only in conversation. The play goes no further in exploring the relationship between Monsieur and Henry, nor do we ever find out what Henry thinks of his brother. After Monsieur's exit in Act I, a

retainer of his named Maffé enters to test Bussy's mettle. We are given absolutely no information about Maffé or his background, and he disappears from
the play after this scene. His abrupt materialization is duplicated later in Act I
by that of Brisac and Melynell. They appear while Bussy is quarrelling (also
abruptly) with three other courtiers; they immediately take sides with him, and
are killed along with their three opponents in the duel that follows. We learn
nothing else about them. Instead of moving smoothly in and out of well-estab-
lished narrative backgrounds, as is the rule for instance in *Hamlet* or *Macbeth*,
characters come and go, and collide with each other in dramatically intense
situations. Here and elsewhere in Jacobean tragedy, story interests are neglect-
ed in favour of bare confrontations that emerge through speeches and counter-
speeches, poses and juxtapositions.[33]

King Lear shows a similar disregard for story interests. Maynard Mack alerts
us to this characteristic when he notices an absence of 'scenes recording the
genesis or gestation of an action – scenes of introspection or persuasion or
temptation like those which occupy the heart of the drama in *Hamlet, Othello*,
and *Macbeth*' (p. 91). 'Genesis' and 'gestation' are provinces in the realm of
narrative, and this realm does not lie within the boundaries of the *Lear* world.
We might even extend Mack's list of examples beyond those scenes that build
up to momentous decisions, to include a whole range of scenes that prepare or
complicate or follow through almost any kind of action. Shakespeare shows no
concern with our pinning down exact cause-and-effect relationships or tracing
probable sequences. When Bradley tries to do this with Act II (See Note U:
'Movements of the Dramatis Personae in Act II'), he turns *King Lear* into a
badly constructed jigsaw puzzle with half the pieces missing. He remarks that
'it needs the closest attention to follow these movements. And, apart from this,
difficulties remain' (p. 449). Act II does not ask us to 'follow the movements.'
We experience Edmund's staged fight, Gloucester's rage, Kent's fight with
Oswald, Cornwall's retribution, Edgar's persecution, etc. Along with the rest of
the play, Act II presents us with moments of acute revelation and crisis. To
wonder what the characters are doing in between these moments is to examine
the wrong side of a tapestry. Like the other Jacobean plays mentioned above,
King Lear sometimes demonstrates an anti-narrative emphasis by snuffing out
potentially interesting story material, and sometimes frustrates the advancement of a story line with scenes that provide nothing in the way of narrative
development. The treatment of Cordelia's marriage gives the audience its first
experience of the former kind of practice. France enters with fine dramatic
flourish in scene i, metaphorically and perhaps dramatically a knight in shining
armour. His chivalrous rescue of Cordelia manifests a strong alternative to
Lear's quantifying value system, and when his most climactic speech adds to
the scene's gravity by shading into stately couplets ('Gods, gods! 'tis strange
that from their cold'st neglect/ My love should kindle to inflam'd respect'), he
cuts a figure of great narrative potential, worthy to stand beside Lear and Kent.
But Shakespeare has expended all this dramatic energy just for the purpose of a
strong scene. As far as our narrative interest in it is concerned, France's mar-

riage to Cordelia might as well not have taken place, for we never see them together after this first scene. France exits soon after his speech and never comes back. Cordelia herself fares little better. Her story has an end as well as a beginning, but the middle is missing. Obviously the play's heroine, she leaves the stage in I.i and returns only at IV.iv. Shakespeare gives her a scant 85 or 90 lines in the whole play – about as many as the First Gravedigger in *Hamlet*. More than any other heroine in the canon of Shakespearean drama, Cordelia moves in shadows, neither exciting nor satisfying even the kind of curiosity that surrounds the actions of her prototype in *The History of King Leir*.

We see the actions of many characters in *King Lear* through a similarly dark glass. Like the affair of the heart between France and Cordelia, Edmund's affairs with Regan and Goneril take place literally behind the scenes. Instead of following the contours of a developing relationship after Edmund and Goneril exit together from III.vii, Shakespeare simply reveals a powerful attraction when we next see them in IV.ii, as if their attachment were electromagnetic. As Oswald says of Albany, 'never man so chang'd,' nor woman either. Their relationship is the *donnée* for an absorbing dramatic situation; how it was initiated and developed does not matter. Edmund's other obscure affair, with Regan, would make equally poor romantic fiction. Like the unexpected emergence of Edgar into the forefront during the last two acts, indeed like the precipitate first scene of the play, the situation impresses spectators by its dramatic effectiveness and thematic appropriateness rather than by the way in which its causal details are not neatly tied into a complete narrative pattern.

Greater actions are likewise muffled. The conflict of Britain and France, normally an Elizabethan theatrical event of some magnitude, here stays in the background (like the apparent feud between Albany and Cornwall); and can we say that, for the author of *Richard II*, political caution would have been the only reason for this disregard? Even in a more patriotic era, such concerns did not inhibit the *King Leir* playwright from a full staging of the invasion. Shakespeare's Kent mentions an invasion at the beginning of Act III, but then everybody seems to forget about it until much later in the play. Even the crucial battle in Act V is, as mentioned in Chapter 1, a distant background to the reactions of Edmund, Gloucester, and Edgar. As Bradley wrote, 'There is something almost ludicrous in the insignificance of this battle, when it is compared with the corresponding battles in *Julius Caesar* and *Macbeth*' (p. 255). The battle takes place entirely offstage. But then so do the deaths of Cornwall, Regan, Goneril, Gloucester, and Cordelia – an astonishing departure from Shakespeare's usual practices, when one thinks of the final acts of the other major tragedies.

In addition, there are actions in *King Lear* that ignore, or run absolutely counter to, the advancement of a story line. These are frequently numbered among the play's most memorable scenes. The long, brilliant conversation between Lear and the Fool in I.iv, for example, simply gives us another perspective on the events of the opening scene. And as Granville-Barker observed, 'The three ... scenes of Lear's madness show us Shakespeare's art at its boldest.

They pass beyond the needs of the plot' (II, 33). We become too caught up in the drama of Lear's mind to bother with tracing the course of more circumstantial and yet less real events. The retainers incident also shows us that events themselves are sometimes less important than the extremes of conduct to which they can give rise. The length and consequences of the argument are out of all proportion to the nature of the issue – whether one has fifty or twenty-five retainers is not in itself a tragic problem – and to the absurdly petty way in which quantitative estimates are hurled back and forth. The basic issue exists as a platform for an abrasive confrontation between Lear and his daughters; it provides the underpinning for a significant and dramatically satisfying scene. Typically, the hundred knights whose existence has sparked the confrontation remain in the shadows.

Shakespeare derives extraordinary advantages from this anti-narrative emphasis. He can choose material for his 'great scenes' from a much wider range of action than strict adherence to narrative unity would permit. Each scene can involve us directly in another extreme upheaval, its force undiminished by the need to tailor the individual effect to fit a story sequence. The pace that results is breathless, as we plunge into one crisis after another. This result of Shakespeare's anti-narrative emphasis is, I suspect, primarily responsible for the admirable intensity of Grigori Kozintsev's film version of the play, in contrast with his profound but slow-moving version of *Hamlet*. He could let the latter unfold like a nineteenth-century Russian novel, but *King Lear* did not give him that option.

This radical departure from narrative concerns marks a turning point in the evolution of Shakespeare's style, and (among other features) distinguishes *King Lear* from the other great tragedies. It points ahead to the late romances, rather than back to *Hamlet* or *Othello*. David Grene has perceptively described the role of narrative in the late romances, and his words deserve repetition in this context because of their applicability to *King Lear*. Shakespeare sets the disposition of his action, Grene writes, 'against the importance of cause and effect, as they would be understood in the ordinary world – even, in a way, against the importance of sequence. Events happen and are significant; the hinges, on which the blocks of action turn, are not ... Shakespeare no longer thought that it mattered to write a plausible story that connected these events ... [The] reader does not have to enter into the reality of the process of the story.'[34] To be sure, plausibility has not been left altogether behind: the *Lear* world yields neither magician nor miraculous music. Would that it could. But we are a long way from either the tight narrative unity of *Othello* or the sequential discursiveness of *Hamlet*.

It was his failure to recognize this crucial difference between *King Lear* and the other tragedies that prompted Bradley to wonder if Shakespeare had carelessly shortened *King Lear*:

> There are, it has sometimes struck me, slight indications that the details of the plot were originally more full and more clearly imagined than one would suppose from the play as

we have it; and some of the defects to which I have drawn attention might have arisen if Shakespeare, finding his matter too bulky, had (*a*) omitted to write some things originally intended, and (*b*) after finishing his play, had reduced it by excision, and had not, in these omissions and excisions, taken sufficient pains to remove the obscurities and inconsistencies occasioned by them. (p. 446)

Bradley goes on to state that 'the play would obviously gain something if it appeared that, at a time shortly before that of the action, Gloster had encouraged the King in his idea of dividing the kingdom, while Kent had tried to dissuade him' (p. 447). What the play would gain would be the narrative fulness of a nineteenth-century novel, but that is what *King Lear* deliberately does not provide. Again and again, an absorbing situation materializes and then disappears, with little attempt made to tie up its 'loose ends.' This kind of technique would not work in a novel or short narrative, where the reader is encouraged to pause and to probe; but as a dramatic device it succeeds. As this chapter has shown, it is one of many such effects that manifest themselves and are replaced by others, before we have time to question the inner logic of any one of them.

In fact, much of Bradley's 'confusion' seems to arise because he brings narrative expectations to the play. He complains that 'The number of essential characters is so large, their actions and movements are so complicated ... that the reader's attention, rapidly transferred from one centre of interest to another, is overstrained' (p. 255). But the sheer number of characters and incidents is not at fault here; *Hamlet* has more characters than *King Lear*, and any Shakespearean history play features an even greater variety of characters and incidents. It is the lack of narrative continuity (indicated by his protest at being 'rapidly transferred from one centre of interest to another') that sits at the centre of his troubles. With his attention fixed on what Grene calls the 'hinges' of action, he is looking at the play through an inappropriate lens.

But recognition of the anti-narrative emphasis of *King Lear* has important implications for more recent criticism than Bradley's. There seems to be a general presupposition among critics of Shakespeare that the form of Elizabethan drama is invariably characterized by a solid narrative core. Seldom expressed because taken for granted, this presupposition influences conclusions about structure, characterization (especially the search for absolute consistency of expression), and formal conventions. It is voiced most cogently by Dame Helen Gardner when she writes that 'There is an irreducible narrative element in all Elizabethan tragedies, and pre-eminently in Shakespearian, as if the serious representation of reality involved the presentation of man living in and through time and its meaning was to be understood through the developing experience of an individual.'[35] The statement needs qualification. It holds true for earlier Elizabethan drama – it is, in fact, a paradigm of the Marlovian structure – but not for those plays influenced by a later tradition, as this chapter has tried to show. Gardner quite rightly maintains that the 'pattern of a single life,' underlying all Christian thought in the Middle Ages and early Renaissance, exerted great pressure on tragic form; but when she concludes that Elizabethan tragedy is a 'presentation of process' in contrast to the 'presentation of crisis' that classical tragedy consisted of, we must recognize that the distinction does not apply to all Elizabethan drama. Even while its hero follows a version of the Marlovian course charted at the start of this chapter, *King Lear* brings us back to a tragedy of crisis. Its structure impresses us as a succession of strong and sometimes disconnected crises, rather than as a process; and as we shall see in Chapter 3, the existence of a subplot serves to strengthen this conception of tragic action, because the spotlight is not thrown on a single man's story.

Yet even as we conclude discussion of the anti-narrative elements in *King Lear*, another earlier dramatic tradition offers a precedent for this Jacobean structural emphasis. When Jacobean playwrights departed from the narrative bias of previous Elizabethan drama, they were unknowingly returning to the structure of an earlier form of popular drama. As Glynne Wickham demonstrates, 'The Morality Play is ... structured on contention or debate and not on progressive, typological narrative; and it is no coincidence that such secular institutions as the Tournament and the legal or academic Disputation are accommodated within Morality Plays while finding no place within the Cycles. For the same reason the Morality Play could as easily be stretched to accommodate discussion of social and political conduct as personal conduct.'[36] Here, then, is the antecedent of that brilliant conflation of personal, social, and political crises that, in Richard Wilbur's phrase, 'rocket the mind' in *King Lear*. As the morality play evolved, however, it absorbed an ever greater share of story material,[37] until it came to resemble the predominantly narrative form that later dramatists departed from. Shakespeare, in observing this departure while still maintaining the archetypal spiritual journey of his central protagonist in all its wholeness, touches and reconciles some of the most diverse aspects of his dramatic heritage.

3

Structure: Figures and Configurations

Many of the structural characteristics of Jacobean drama tend to keep us from becoming deeply involved with the characters and actions of numerous seventeenth-century plays. Frequent momentary effects and emblematic tableaux, coupled with a suppression of detailed exposition and narrative, create a discontinuous flow of events. Our attention is subjected to persistent interruptions and abrupt changes, and these impede the concentration needed for continuous involvement.[1] The Jacobean concept of an extreme, self-enclosed play-world can also discourage involvement, setting up a wall of conspicuous artifice between our life and that of the play: when playwrights like Marston or Beaumont and Fletcher depart from real-world standards of behaviour and probability, they inevitably distance us from their creations.

Such distancing can contribute to the effects of comedy, or to the deft emotional balancing act that is Fletcherian tragicomedy; but it is an impediment to tragedy. The Jacobean tragedies of Chapman, Marston, or Fletcher may win admiration for the ideals that their heroes display, but we are too conscious of the author's hand, and too remote from the heroes to be fully engrossed in their struggles.[2] To be sure, tragedy does not depend for its effect on a response like that of Fielding's Mr Partridge; real spectators never lose their awareness of the stage, the actor as actor, the play as a *shaped* experience. The wonder of mimesis is that we can be made to tuck this awareness in a bottom drawer of our consciousness, and to feel for the actors as the characters they portray. But where a dramatist's technique intrudes on the shaping that makes us enter even so tentatively into his world, the necessary tragic empathy will be diminished.

Spectators have sometimes protested against the shocks that Samuel Johnson found unendurable, but nobody has ever accused *King Lear* of failing to involve an audience. One reason for its emotive power is that Shakespeare follows a precedent set by the morality plays and confirmed by Marlowe: he keeps his hero at the centre of the play's complex structure, and so avoids the dissipation of response that occurs in such works as *The Revenger's Tragedy* or *The White Devil*. Indeed, the statement that John Russell Brown makes about *The White*

Devil in the introduction to his edition of the work (London, 1966) applies as well to many other Jacobean plays: 'In this play, intimate feeling for a single character is intermittent only: none of its characters draws attention wholly to himself for more than a few consecutive lines; as we tend to identify ourselves with one character, we are forced back ... It is a restless technique' (pp. xlv-xlvi).

Also, by pointing his strong scenes towards ultimate significance (as the morality plays did), Shakespeare lets them foster a more profound involvement with characters and actions than the structure of many contemporary plays allowed. And even as he responds to more contemporary dramatic practices, he turns as well to early dramatic traditions for figures and configurations that encourage our deep involvement in the world of *King Lear.* One such figure, a strong presence in much Elizabethan drama, is the character I have chosen to refer to as the 'stage manager.' I have preferred this term to the more traditional 'intriguer' because I am concerned with a limited and particularly theatrical aspect of the intriguer's role – the devising and arrangement of scenes, and the manipulation of other characters through them. The term 'stage manager' emphasizes such activities, along with the scene-painting and handling of props that frequently accompany his own role-playing.

In *King Lear,* Shakespeare masterfully draws on early and later traditions of stage-managing to help shape characters and situations that evoke our profound involvement; and some of the most striking attributes of the *Lear* world result when he adopts an authorial approximation of the stage manager's highly manipulative art in creating the structure of the play as a whole. He shows a similar boldness in adapting what was probably the most significant structural contribution of Elizabethan drama, the multiple plot. Although the plot-subplot configuration was used by every generation of Elizabethan dramatists, *King Lear* is the only Shakespearean tragedy with a fully articulated subplot. The second part of this chapter will explore some of the advantages that Shakespeare derives from it, and will relate it to the emotive effects of his other structural designs.

I

Many of the 'great scenes' in *King Lear* seem to evolve along lines suggested by Edmund's words about Edgar: 'and pat he comes, like the catastrophe of the old comedy' (I.ii.141-2). The scenes appear to be stage-managed. Characters are manipulated into prearranged situations that are designed to elicit the most extreme, and the most revealing, reactions from them. These situations are intricate constructs, fabricated by other characters, in which the deluded object of the ruse unconsciously plays a part in someone else's 'comedy.' The stage manager plans the course of the action, sometimes revealing his plans to the audience in detail before the other characters enter; during the scene, he patently assumes a role designed to further his ends – but unlike the other characters, the audience sees through the stage manager's role-playing to the motives behind it; and he may even employ some of the trappings of the theatre in his production: props, background noises, costumes, and the like. Such scenes serve a dual purpose, both advancing the fortunes of their 'authors' and providing us with an illuminating exhibition of the characters involved.

A paradigm of the stage-managed situation in *King Lear* is provided by the first scene of Act II, where Edmund functions zestfully as scriptwriter, actor, and director. He has even set the stage in the previous act, by showing the forged letter to Gloucester and advising Edgar to bear arms: now, as a result, 'My father hath set guard to take my brother;/ And I have one thing, of a queasy question,/ Which I must act' (II.17-19). The acting begins at once. He cues in Edgar ('Brother, a word; descend: brother, I say!'), throws him off guard with a warning of immediate danger, stages a quick sword fight, and ushers his confused and speechless brother out. Then, having roused the household by his shouts during the fight, Edmund devises a stage prop for the next encounter by wounding himself: 'Some blood drawn on me would beget opinion' (34). Though the wound does not beget Gloucester's opinion of Edgar, it nurses it; given a speaking part larger than Edgar's, Gloucester disinherits him and vows to make Edmund his heir. It has all gone according to plan. Edmund's interlude furthers his own interests, and calls forth the essential natures of its three characters – Edgar's trustful innocence, Gloucester's quick-tempered lack of trust, and Edmund's duplicity.

Edmund is the main stage manager of *King Lear*, and he sets up a number of revealing performances: Gloucester's outburst at reading the forged letter (I.ii), Cornwall's desire to revenge himself on Gloucester and reward the more accommodating son (III.v) – this leads directly to Gloucester's blinding – and the pairing-off of Regan and Goneril against each other (V.i.55-65). In devising such explosive situations, Edmund reflects both an earlier figure from popular drama, the Vice, and a contemporary, the wily comic intriguer. It is worthwhile to reconstruct here the trappings of both figures, for they can reveal the threads that Shakespeare chose to pick up when he wove the creation of Edmund out of the old and the new. Fortunately, Bernard Spivack has already charted the history and the identifying characteristics of the Vice in *Shakespeare and the Allegory of Evil* (New York, 1958), and the short general description that follows owes much to his fine work.

Arising out of the morality tradition as a personification of the process by which temptation gradually breaks down the soul's defences, the Vice became the most familiar theatrical personage on the early popular stage. As his role expanded, the outlines of his character took on a fixed and recognizable shape. Like the clowns of later drama, the Vice stood as intermediary between audience and play. Through soliloquy, he would make the audience his confidants as he announced his evil nature and briskly devised a scheme to lead some innocent dupe to moral catastrophe; and with great relish he would keep them posted through later soliloquies and asides. He skilfully managed the scenes effecting the dupe's downfall, and his goal was the overthrow of those religious (and, in later plays, social and political) values to which playwright and audience subscribed.

From the moment Edmund boldly announces his credo in I.ii, Shakespeare's depiction of him satisfies many particulars of this archetypal description. His bastardy, both an identity and a calling, aims a devastating blow at the commutual bond that is vital to the *Lear* world's moral foundations, undermining all the necessary hierarchies. Like the Vice, too, Edmund stage-manages scenes for us with great gusto, plays on the naiveté of his dupes, and ingratiates himself with those he plans to use. 'Your seruaunt wyll I be,' says Folye to Manhood.[3] 'I shall serve you, Sir,' says Edmund to Cornwall (II.i.116).

But the main difference between Edmund and the Vice is as noteworthy as these similarities, for it reveals the creative vision that moves Shakespeare's conception far beyond the sterotype, and beyond his earlier version of the Vice, Iago. What Edmund is not may be perceived from Spivack's description of the Vice's personality: 'Free from human limitation, he is equally free from human passion and responsibility, and his residual emotion is a limitless, amoral merriment ... Professional and impersonal, he is immune to the gravity of his aggression – a gravity that exists everywhere in the play except in him' (p. 195). Edmund becomes humanized in the course of *King Lear*. Like Lear, he discovers the limitations and passions that being human bestows on him. His speech at the end of V.i ('To both these sisters have I sworn my love') shows a genuine perplexity qualifying his sureness, as his own success threatens to overwhelm him. Later, his drive for status makes him accept the aristocratic trial by combat with Edgar, and Edmund's newly acquired class pride does him in:

> But since thy outside looks so fair and war-like,
> And that thy tongue some say of breeding breathes,
> What safe and nicely I might well delay
> By rule of knighthood, I disdain and spurn. (V.iii.142-5)

Poor parvenu! The very last turn of the wheel, Edmund's attempt to save Lear and Cordelia and his pathetic 'Yet Edmund was belov'd,' pierces through the archetype to disclose a miniature of the same tormented humanity revealed in the full-length portrait of Lear suffering on the heath.

Except for Shakespeare's grand variations on the type, the Vice largely disappeared from the stage after the advent of established professional theatres in London during the 1570s and 1580s. Vestiges emerge in Marlowe's Barabas (*The Jew of Malta*, c. 1589) and Chettle's Lorrique (*The Tragedy of Hoffman*, 1602),[4] but the Vice never achieved anything like his earlier prominence, and except for the occasional reminiscence his name vanished altogether. A main thesis of Spivack's book is that the Vice was outdated by a more intricately characterized drama, and by the disappearance from popular dramaturgy of the specific religious framework that gave life to his fundamentally allegorical being. This interpretation is no doubt true, but it needs to be supplemented to account for the near-extinction on the public stage not only of the Vice, but of characters fulfilling his role as stage manager (Shakespeare's plays are, as usual, full of exceptions). Two further explanations can be suggested here. First, a figure without the Vice's moral associations took over his close relationship with the audience. The clown, a resident favourite in every public-theatre company, had no devilish heritage and could be worked into all kinds of plays; but his antics often lost structural importance by being thrust into a comic subplot, where he would usually just ape the actions of main plot characters. He went from manager to obstreperous underling. The second explanation grows out of our discussion in Chapter 2 of the relationship between drama and narrative. As Glynne Wickham observes, 'The precedence given to historical narrative in the Cycles [was] reserved for theme or argument in the Morality Play.'[5] With the coming of chronicles and romances to the stage, this situational bent of plays in the morality tradition gave way to a new emphasis on narrative presentation. Playwrights now invited audiences to follow characters through various adventures instead of letting them watch the characters be manipulated in and out of a series of demonstrations. To invoke Helen Gardner's distinction again, in relative terms drama passed from 'the presentation of crisis' (or of debate or essence) to 'the presentation of process.'[6] When a playwright tries to make his audience enter into a developing story, the stage manager becomes superfluous, his presence an intrusion on the play's narrative unity. One reason for the disappearance of the Vice, then, is that during the 1590s plays were no longer structured in such a way as to make use of his prodigious stage-managing talents.

If Shakespeare could not look to many 1590s public-theatre plays for models of the stage manager, he could find them in abundance at the private houses during the early 1600s. The wily intriguer who often stage-managed was a stock character during the first decade of private-theatre dramaturgy, from the time Paul's and Blackfriars started up again at the turn of the century. Before one can argue for the importance to *King Lear* of this tradition of stage-managing, it is necessary to outline its origin and nature, since the terrain has not already been mapped out.

Humours comedy seems to be the primary source for the comic structure in which the private-theatre intriguer flourished. As described in Chapter 2, the public-theatre humours comedies of Jonson and Chapman constituted a complete departure from narrative drama. Structurally, each play consisted of a series of strong scenes in which characters displayed their quirks or 'humours.' These situations were not linked by a developing narrative, and had no intrinsic coherence except that they offered variations on the humours concept.[7] However, this kind of structure had its disadvantages. A play with so many singular strengths can have trouble bringing them together to form an artistic whole and holding our interest over a five-act span.

Jonson overcame the difficulty by performing a virtuoso balancing act. He substituted an aggregative unity for the usual linear unity by letting each scene illuminate a facet of his humours theory, and the unrelenting comic force of his 'family portraits' gave the plays their theatrical velocity. The prodigious power of his comic invention held the play together and sustained interest. Chapman, on the other hand, solved the problem by nominally linking the humourous displays as steps in one main character's recipe for comic diversion. This relatively passive predecessor of the intriguer reveals the play's structural principle at the start when he tells a friend that he will 'sit, as it were, and point out all my humourous companions.'[8] While Jonson's solution was inimitable, being so much a part of his individual talent, Chapman's was available to later playwrights. Consequently, when humours comedy became extremely popular in the early years of the private theatres, playwrights turned to the intriguer. His presence helped retain coherence when less versatile writers than Jonson tried to sustain so many autonomous scenes. Structural integrity in these plays was thus achieved by allowing the intriguer to contrive and manage the scenes in which other characters would display their humours; each situation was the result of his scheming.[9]

With the decline of humours comedy, the intriguer and his wiles assumed even greater importance, as 'intrigue comedy' became a formidable mode in itself. The mode developed gradually during the first years of private-theatre performance, as dramatists seem to have realized the limitations of structuring a play around extreme characters: humours comedy soon ran out of humours to exploit, and playwrights turned to a means of comic expression rooted in the dramatic structure that humours comedy had used as a simple platform. While the strong scene maintained its pre-eminence, it now focused on extremity of situation rather than of character. The intrigue became an organic element, determining the situations of an art whose essence was situational. The comic intriguer created in each scene the extreme conditions that elicited entertaining reactions, and such intrigues often involved him in stage-managing.

Although this type of play reached its peak in comedies written by Middleton at about the same time that *King Lear* was performed, intimations of it are found in earlier works. In the last act of Dekker's *Satiromastix* (1601), for instance, Quintilian creates an extreme situation by apparently poisoning his daughter, with her permission. Masquers enter with the 'dead' Celestine in a chair, and so provoke radical reactions from the other characters. When this exhibition has served its purpose and has abated the lascivious king's desires, Celestine awakes, and Quintilian reveals that he tricked them all by giving her a sleeping potion. Quintilian has stage-managed the entire scene by contriving the ruse, arranging for the masquers' entrance with their centrally important stage prop, and playing the role of bereaved father in front of the other characters. Marston's Freevill stage-manages a more extensive situation in *The Dutch Courtesan* (1604). He and Malheureux agree to make it look as if Malheureux has killed him, as the courtesan wishes, so that Malheureux can win her favour. But instead of being available to exonerate Malheureux at a prearranged hiding place, Freevill disguises himself as a pander, playacts through a scene with the courtesan to observe her reaction to his reported death, and even assists in apprehending the 'murderer.' Still in disguise, Freevill then plays out the deception through encounters with several other characters, and finally reveals the ruse by removing his disguise only moments before Malheureux is to be executed.[10]

Middleton's best-known comedies abound in stage-managed scenes. The intriguer is the central character in these plays, and the scenes issue from his schemes. *A Trick to Catch the Old One* (1605) is Middleton's greatest early achievement in this mode; there, Witgood places every other character but the courtesan in a succession of stage-managed scenes, all emanating from his primary intrigue. The second scene of Act IV is typical of Witgood's art. He enters his uncle Lucre's house sighing, and his penitent gestures and words prompt Lucre to comment on how greatly the former prodigal has changed. Lucre promises him £300 a year – ostensibly out of generosity but really out of greed, for Lucre hopes to mend his own fortunes after the regenerate Witgood's imminent marriage to a rich widow. Lucre does not realize that his nephew is also playing a part, for the widow is in fact Witgood's former mistress, and has already been secretly married off to yet another avaricious dupe. After Lucre's exit, Witgood soliloquizes on the success of his performance. It should be noted that in this play, as in his other intrigue comedies, Middleton draws the audience's attention to the virtuosity of the stage-managing rather than to the intriguer's character: he minimizes our involvement with Witgood, and does not use the intrigue as a means of character portrayal. Shakespeare makes significant departures from this usage, which should be borne in mind when considering the activities of Edmund and the other stage managers in *King Lear.*

Edmund's intrigues are matched by those of several other characters; and returning to *King Lear*, one finds that the private-theatre tradition just outlined provides (as the history of the Vice alone does not) illuminating precedents for their stage-managing.[11] It is no vestige of the Vice that clings to Edgar, for instance, when he mercifully stages Gloucester's 'miracle' in Act IV. This most selfless intriguer enters in deceptive costume, *'dressed like a peasant,'* and – playing on his father's physical blindness to save him as Edmund had played on his spiritual blindness to destroy him – he makes Gloucester believe they are climbing Dover Cliffs. He then concocts the most convincing piece of scene-painting in all Shakespearean drama, a flood of mundane, sensuous details that are all the more startling for their appearance in the abstracted desert of the *Lear* world. Like the private-theatre intriguer, Edgar tricks his dupe by making a desired goal seem concrete and within reach, and creates an extreme theatrical situation in the process. Gloucester performs according to plan: 'He fals,' as the Quarto notes. Then, changing roles, Edgar paints a new setting (where 'the shrill-gorg'd lark so far/ Cannot be seen or heard') and a fabulous fiend for the blind old man, and achieves the desired result of his intrigue. Edgar's stage-managing has turned a potentially tragic incident into tragicomedy, with the very existence of an intrigue and its attendant ironies qualifying the pathos of Gloucester's physical condition.

In most stage-managed situations, in fact, dramatic irony adds a considerable edge to our experience of the scene. Such is the case earlier in the play, during the retainers incident. Unknown to Lear, Goneril has set the stage by telling

Oswald to 'breed from hence occasions' (I.iii.25). These occasions give rise to the retainers conflict, during which Lear unconsciously acts out the role that Regan and Goneril have prepared for him. It is perhaps a mark of the sisters' aristocratic hauteur (Regan's clothing is 'gorgeous' and Goneril can command fifty of her servants to tend Lear) that, unlike Edmund, they let their deputies set the scene, and enter only later themselves like prima donnas. But as in the opening love-test, they have rehearsed well. In the first confrontation with Lear, Goneril's intricate opening speech betrays much preparation:

> Not only, Sir, this your all-licens'd Fool,
> But other of your insolent retinue
> Do hourly carp and quarrel, breaking forth
> In rank and not-to-be-endured riots. Sir,
> I had thought, by making this well known unto you,
> To have found a safe redress; but now grow fearful,
> By what yourself too late have spoke and done,
> That you protect this course, and put it on
> By your allowance; which if you should, the fault
> Would not 'scape censure, nor the redresses sleep,
> Which, in the tender of a wholesome weal,
> Might in their working do you that offence,
> Which else were shame, that then necessity
> Will call discreet proceeding. (I.iv.209-22)

Only two sentences thread their laboured way through these fourteen lines. The first sentence makes us wait until the third line for its cargo of verbs, and the awkwardness of 'not-to-be-endured riots' exposes its lack of spontaneity. The labyrinthine syntax of the second sentence (including three 'bys,' two 'ands,' one 'but,' one 'nor,' three 'thats,' and three 'whiches') unfolds in highly wrought periodicity, with a series of abstractions that artfully gloss over the ugly threats within. The Fool's four-line speech goes by before Lear, reeling, can reply, and his shocked and solid rejoinder presents an absolute contrast: 'Are you our daughter?' Its incredulous brevity shows that Lear has been taken completely unawares by Goneril's performance. And Lear is doubly fooled, as his later words indicate: 'I have another daughter,/ Who, I am sure, is kind and comfortable' (314-15), he shouts at Goneril. But as we already know, both daughters are in league against him, and he reacts just as Goneril wanted: he is acting on cue.

Two other stage-managed scenes even include sound effects. The first and shorter scene marks the reunion of Lear and Cordelia, and is managed by the Doctor after Cordelia delegates the task to him. Ever self-effacing, she lets him 'proceed/ I' th' sway of [his] own will' (IV.vii.19-20); and so he has Lear brought in wearing 'fresh garments,' urges Cordelia to draw near, and orders 'Louder the music there!' He then delicately orchestrates the two voices of reunion, prompting Cordelia three times when to speak and when to be silent, and finally brings the scene to a close: 'Desire him to go in; trouble him no more/ Till further settling.' The scene seems a deliberate departure from the form of other stage-managed scenes in the play: like them, it is a situation prearranged by one of the characters, who takes an active role in shaping and determining its course of action; and it employs the theatrical trappings of costume and music. But the striking difference is that here, the aim of the scene is solely to heal the object of the stage-managing rather than to delude him, and so no role-playing is involved. Cordelia speaks what she feels, not what she 'ought to say,' and the difference between her and the other characters in the *Lear* world is as marked as it was in the play's first scene. This stage-managed act of recovery follows and echoes that of Gloucester by Edgar, another healing intriguer ('Why I do trifle thus with his despair/ Is done to cure it'). The relationship between the two scenes is clearly also one of contrast between Edgar's methods, which involve deception, and Cordelia's, which do not. The contrast will be examined later in this chapter, in the context of larger differences between Cordelia and Edgar.

Edgar himself acts the role of stage manager for the second scene with sound effects, towards the end of the play. He enters (v.i) in disguise to set the scene, handing a letter – both stage prop and catalyst – to Albany and ordering him:

> Before you fight the battle, ope this letter.
> If you have victory, let the trumpet sound
> For him that brought it: wretched though I seem,
> I can produce a champion that will prove
> What is avouched there. (40-4)

After the battle Albany acts on cue, interrupting a call for sound effects by Regan ('[*To Edmund*.] Let the drum strike, and prove my title thine'), and substituting for her play what Goneril proclaims as 'An interlude!' (v.iii.90). The trumpets sound, and Edgar enters in yet another disguise, feigning not to recognize his brother: 'What's he that speaks for Edmund Earl of Gloucester?' Then, in a reversal of roles from their earlier stage-managed fight in II.i, Edgar acts as director ('Draw thy sword') and tricks Edmund: by playing on his brother's pride, just as Edmund had taken advantage of Edgar's trusting nobility, he makes him agree to a duel that he really need not enter. 'This is practice, Gloucester,' Goneril observes accurately but too late. Albany then marks the interlude's climax by holding up the letter, precipitating Goneril's hurried exit, and Edgar ends the ruse by revealing himself. The careers of Edmund and Goneril, inaugurated by their own successful stage managing, have been brought to an end by Edgar's.

All of the stage-managed scenes in *King Lear* resemble those of private-theatre drama in that an intriguer creates each time the extreme situations that elicit theatrically potent reactions from other characters. But as I intimated at the outset of this discussion, Shakespeare departs in several ways from the treatment given such scenes on the private-theatre stage; three of these variations merit consideration here. His most significant departure involves the relationship between these scenes and the process of characterization. I have emphasized that private-theatre drama rivets our attention to the clever execution of an ingenious situation instead of using each situation primarily as a means of character portrayal. The figures manipulated through such scenes are usually type characters – rakes, misers, jealous husbands – and in fact the intriguers of a playwright like Middleton are interchangeable from one play to another. But Shakespeare's stage-managed scenes, like his dramatic emblems, are designed to be pointed revelations of those characters involved in them, or of important stages in the characters' development.

The love-test that opens the play is a clear example. Lear stage-manages a formal pageant, 'The Loving Daughters and the Generous King,' knowing full well beforehand what course he intends the plot to follow. The grand entrance, the stage prop (his map), and the formulaic questions elevate form above content – just as the speeches of Regan and Goneril do. Cordelia's refusal to act her role, however, sets off his terrible outrage, and the Generous King hardens into a fierce tyrant. The unfolding of this scene conveys Lear's paradoxical nature with great economy, both the domineering strength and the pathetic need for public reassurance. The stage-managed form turns out to be a pellucid image of Lear's character.

Similarly, the fact that Edgar chooses to *become* an intriguer in the Dover Cliffs scene is intensely significant: it shows that he has renounced his passivity and is now, for the first time in the play, working out his own destiny by helping someone else, acting rather than reacting. Of course, he has still to cast off his protective disguises and stop 'acting.' Yet it is revealing that for the rest of the play Edgar replaces Edmund as main intriguer and as main chorus (through his soliloquies and asides). Through Edgar's wily reversal of roles we witness the making of the future king, and come to accept him as such. No private-theatre dramatist hangs so much meaning on the mere assumption of an intrigue – or on the avoidance of one: Cordelia's refusal to play stage manager during the reunion scene reveals a basic difference between her character and Edgar's (and between the main plot and subplot, as the latter part of this chapter will demonstrate). Bradley put his finger on the difference when he wrote that Edgar 'learns by experience' (p. 305), while 'what happens to [Cordelia] does not matter' (p. 325). By 'what happens' he meant her death, but the words apply to any action. Edgar's nobility manifests itself through acting and suffering, while Cordelia's simply *is*. We cannot speak of her as learning or developing in any way, for her character is an immutable essence rather than something subject to change. By having her delegate the stage-managing to the Doctor – one of her first gestures after a three-act absence – Shakespeare underlines that remoteness from the tides of action and influence first intimated by her unyielding presence in I.i.

Stage-managed scenes characterize those who unwittingly act in them as well as those who design them. Stage-managing in *King Lear* is adapted to a world that is truly, to cite R.W. Chambers' apt quotation from Keats, a vale of soul-making;[12] for the situations into which characters are manipulated are those in which they can play a crucial and revealing role in saving or condemning themselves. Thus, Edmund's play in II.i provides a platform for calling forth Edgar's trusting innocence and Gloucester's choleric lack of trust; and so the Dover Cliffs scene brings Gloucester to a new recognition of his role in a larger play, and enables him to tap the previously hidden resources in his being that are necessary to 'bear/ Affliction till it do cry out itself/ "Enough, enough," and die.' As Mack has written, 'almost every character in the play, including such humble figures as Cornwall's servant and the old tenant who befriends Gloucester, is impelled soon or late to take some sort of stand – to show, in Oswald's words, "what party I do follow." One cannot but be struck by how much positioning and repositioning of this kind the play contains' (p. 90). Shakespeare achieves much of this positioning through the manipulations of his stage managers. Thus, Edgar's production in Act V puts Edmund on trial in more than one sense: though his fate is literally decided by the combat, we judge his performance by the attitudes that the duel and its aftermath induce from him. Lear, too, is given an opportunity to redeem himself during the Doctor's presentation, and responds with softened accents that show a complete transformation from the proud despot of Act I.

In a second departure from private-theatre practice, Shakespeare shades the concept of intrigue with positive or negative overtones at various points in *King Lear*, so that we are sometimes far from approving of it. This technique serves the purpose of answering an important query that Alfred Harbage has posed about the place of intrigue in a tragedy: 'The most obvious objection to intrigue in tragedy, apart from the fact that it can overtax the constructive skill of the playwright, is that it amuses us, makes us wish momentarily for its success, and creates in us a certain admiration for the intriguer and tolerance for his aims.'[13] None of the private-theatre playwrights mentioned earlier had to cope with this problem: their intrigue plays were all comedies, and our admiration and amusement at the stage manager's skill could only contribute to the prevalent comic mood. But Shakespeare had to reckon with Edmund, an uncommendable character whose skilful stage-managing takes place within the context of a tragedy. Shakespeare solves the problem by looking to an older dramatic tradition and, as we have seen, invoking as Edmund's shadow the sly but condemnable figure of the Vice. Edmund's intrigues succeed, but they follow hard upon the Vice's calling card in I.ii, that traditionally heinous self-announcement that can hardly win friends for him. In addition, Shakespeare endows Edmund's victims with the sympathetic and identifiable vulnerability of the traditional morality play dupe, as he is described by Spivack: 'The action presents an unsuspecting dupe, an *innocent* – guileless and gullible because he is the epitome of frail humanity ... turned inside out and made a plaything by a consummate artist in the craft of deceit' (p. 176). We feel too close to Edgar and frail Gloucester to find ourselves in Edmund's camp or wish even momentarily for his success. We become more compassionate towards

Edmund only after he has left his Vice trappings behind him and given up stage-managing.

Shakespeare also maintains the tragic tone of *King Lear* by departing from private-theatre practice in a third way, to tinker with the intrigues of his other main stage manager, Edgar. Edgar's schemes rarely come off without a considerable hitch; they leave him looking almost as victimized as the objects of his intrigues. His disguise as poor Tom may save his own neck, for instance, but it frightens the Fool out of the hovel just when Lear is on the threshold of much-needed sleep. Lear is unintentionally pushed over the brink to madness by 'the last man who would willingly have injured [him],' as Bradley notes (p. 287, n.1). Edgar's delayed unmasking to his father fares even worse: it turns out to be a 'fault' that makes 'his flaw'd heart,/ Alack, too weak the conflict to support!/ 'Twixt two extremes of passion, joy and grief,/ Burst smilingly' (V.iii.196-9). Even the trial by combat has its tragic side effects, taking Albany's mind off the fate of Lear and Cordelia ('Great thing of us forgot!') and giving the Captain time to do his 'man's work.'

Similarly the Dover Cliffs scene, by giving one critic (and probably some uneasy spectators) the feeling that it is 'a remarkable piece of virtuoso stage-craft that does not quite come off,'[14] increases our feeling that Edgar's actions are invariably marked by a well-intentioned awkwardness. No sooner has Gloucester thrown himself to the floor than Edgar, with mounting alarm, looks at the motionless form and fears that his 'conceit' has brought the same mortal result as a real jump. We all know otherwise, but the play's first audiences didn't; they would have shared Edgar's fears in those few moments, and shared his relief when Gloucester shows signs of life. At such times Shakespeare's deliberately flawed intriguer wins our sympathy through his fallibility, and the bond that he establishes with us outlasts even the priggish *sententiae* on which he relies before experience teaches him better. As stage manager, Edgar presents a moving contrast to his brother, whose victims even enter on cue and for whom every accident 'weaves itself perforce into [his] business' (II.i.16).

Apart from the similarities and differences between the intrigues of *King Lear* and those of private-theatre drama, the concept of stage-managing can prove useful in approaching one of the most deeply felt and frequently observed attributes of the *Lear* world – the complete disharmony between the nobler characters and their circumstances. The structural emphasis that I believe contributes to this impression appears in other Jacobean drama, and an examination of it there can be of value in helping us to recognize its place in *King Lear.*

A number of Jacobean tragedies may be thought of as resembling *The Alchemist* (1610) in structure. There, Jonson makes one stage-managed situation generate all the extreme reactions that constitute the play's dramatic action: Face and Subtle manipulate other characters in and out of Lovewit's house in contrasting arrangements, playing numerous roles to facilitate their deception; the play is a series of stage-managed scenes that are really variations on a single basic circumstance. It is this structural configuration that the tragedies resemble. Of course, in those Jacobean tragedies that display similar structures, no Lovewit materializes at the end to set everything right; nor are intriguers at the heart of the stage-managing. Instead, playwrights themselves play the intriguer by engineering a complete and tragic disparity between the hero and the world of the play.

In applying the term 'stage-managing' to such dramatic structures, I am engaging in a metaphorical usage rather than a literal one: I do not want to suggest that these playwrights had the concept of stage-managing in mind when they created their tragic worlds. But the metaphor of stage-managing seems an apt way to apprehend and describe the sense of prearranged, manipulated, and arbitrary disharmony between hero and play-world generated by many Jacobean tragedies. Like the stage-managed scenes discussed above, the world of these plays strikes us as a patent construct, every aspect of which is designed to put the hero on trial; this is a specialized refinement of the self-enclosed play-world described in Chapter 1. It is certainly true that opposition between a hero and his environment is an essential characteristic of all tragedy, but Jacobean tragedy seems to be unique in conveying this strong sense of a manipulated disparity. Instead of having action issue from character, the dramatist places an extreme character in an equally extreme (and usually warped) situation designed to oppose and frustrate every aspect of his being. He is manoeuvred through a series of ingeniously abrasive trials, and usually chooses to perish rather than compromise or capitulate.

Critics have sometimes remarked on this kind of 'stage-managing' in Jacobean tragedy, but have missed the mark in identifying it as the peculiar style of one or another playwright. T.M. Parrott, for instance, wrote that 'the peculiar tragic theme of Chapman is the conflict of the individual with his environment and the inevitable issue of that conflict in the individual's defeat.'[15] The perception definitely applies to a work such as *Bussy D'Ambois* (1604), where Chapman sets up an arbitrary theoretical framework to govern the play's world ('Fortune, not Reason, rules the state of things'), places in that world a hero whose beliefs are diametrically opposed to the framework, and devises a succession of incidents that bring the two into conflict. In the end, Bussy is crushed by the hostile environment, which leaves no room for his virtues to take root and flourish. Chapman's Byron (*The Conspiracy and Tragedy of Charles Duke of Byron*, 1608) and his Clermont D'Ambois (*The Revenge of Bussy D'Ambois*, 1610) travel the same path; Clermont even finds ultimately that his only prerogative is suicide, an absolute rejection of his world.

But this stage-managed course is also followed by other tragic heroes in Jacobean drama. Marston's eponymous heroine in *Sophonisba* (1605) is manoeuvred through a world that is designed to be in every respect the opposite of her nature. As in *Bussy D'Ambois*, too, the play's opening carefully sets up and underlines the contrast between the protagonist's admirable virtues and an unredeemably depraved world. As with Chapman, critics have felt such theatrical territory to be the exclusive preserve of Marston. One of the most perceptive Marston scholars writes of 'the total lack of relation between nature and man' in the Antonio plays, and views *Antonio's Revenge* (1600) as an attempt to answer 'a new and fruitful question ... what happens to an Antonio when he is forced to act in [a] depraved and villainous world? This was to become one of Marston's most serious and persistent themes.'[16] This critic also feels the power of Marston's visions of a dark battle 'between a corrupt world and the integrity of the individual.' The vision (and the stage-managing that gives it a local habitation) is shared by Marston's Jacobean colleagues. A similar relationship between hero and world prevails in Tourneur's *The Atheist's Tragedy* (1611) and Webster's *The Duchess of Malfi* (1613-14). One may find it also in the tragedies of Beaumont and Fletcher, where characters are dashed to pieces against similarly inexorable situations: such is the fate of Amintor and Aspatia in *The Maid's Tragedy* (1610), where the authors resort to an extreme version of the 'divine right of kings' theory for the play-world's inflexible framework; and of the lovers in *Cupid's Revenge* (1607-8), a tragedy in which Cupid himself stage-manages the structure. The tragicomedies of Beaumont and Fletcher may be viewed as variations on this kind of stage-managing: Fletcherian tragicomedy manoeuvres its characters through situations designed to *seem* inexorably tragic, and calls attention to the ingenuity of an art that rescues them at the last minute.

Discussion of the 'stage-managed' world in Jacobean tragedy brings a fruitful context to the study of *King Lear*, because its structure displays many resemblances to this configuration. Of course, these resemblances do not negate the central affinity to earlier popular drama noted at the start of Chapter 2. What connects Lear with a hero like Tamburlaine is that the structures of the plays in which they appear seem to issue from their characters. But within this area of general similitude, a fundamental distinction must be made. The structure of *Tamburlaine* consists of scenes designed to bring us into closer acquaintance with the hero by showing us facets of his character; but Shakespeare designs *King Lear* less to illuminate Lear than to put him and his court on trial. Like the heroes of Jacobean tragedy, Lear confronts an abrasive world shaped to make him suffer the consequences of what he is and what he has done. The play's scenes demonstrate how its hero suffers and changes through these deep-laid confrontations rather than how his multifaceted nature unfolds before us.[17]

To a much greater extent than Shakespeare's other tragedies, *King Lear* bases its structure on the stage-managed situation. The literal stage-managing of Edmund and Edgar evolves situations for the subplot. The main plot's incidents all stem from Lear's stage-managed pageant in the opening scene, and work out the consequences and implications of that scene in a series of probative situations. Lear sets out as intriguer, but his scheme backfires and he finds himself victimized by the *Lear* world. The contrived love-test is followed by more insidiously contrived 'trials' that issue from the *Lear* world rather than from any character's intrigues, and that rack both the hero and the whole range of main protagonists. In the first scene, for example, Cordelia and Kent are victims of an incompatibility with their environment. In another time and place their words would never produce the effects they do in Lear's carefully staged exhibition. Similarly, Kent and Edgar are manipulated into tragic incongruity in Act V: their delayed unmaskings, meant to occasion joyous reunions, are met with Gloucester's death and Lear's desolate incomprehension. Lear alone makes his clear and unpressured choice in I.i, and an ineluctable chain reaction follows. It is as if the *Lear* world has gone berserk, overwhelming the characters' well-intentioned and very human gestures. Schlegel discerned this feature which distinguishes *King Lear* from the other tragedies when he wrote: 'The principal characters here are not those who act, but those who suffer.'[18] If we run down the list of *dramatis personae*, it is hard to find a character who does not confront a chain of incidents that are 'instruments to plague [him].' Undeniably, Hamlet finds himself in a hostile environment; Macbeth dances to some extent to the witches' music, and Othello to that of Iago; but only *King Lear* closes off so thoroughly, to such a host of characters, the possibility of self-willed action or its success.

This technique is, I believe, largely responsible for the extraordinary emotional identification that *King Lear* awakens in us, even though some of its characters deserve Bradley's reference to them as 'somewhat faint and thin' (p. 263). Comparing the play with *Othello*, William Blissett describes the heroes' emotional effect on us: 'Lear for all his age and royalty and folly, which might be expected to distance him, is much more a piece with our inner experience, perhaps because there is not a blessed thing that he can do ... whereas Othello ... could reverse the plot at any moment.'[19] Nor is there a blessed thing that any of the characters can do, try as they will. They are all subject to an irreversible situation that unfolds remorselessly to upset their expectations. Two aspects of Shakespeare's art emerge through this last statement: first, that Shakespeare is working through a contemporary practice to realize in it the seeds of a universal tragic effect − for this ineluctable combination of character and circumstance winds itself around the core of all great tragedy, classical and modern; secondly, that the direction of Shakespeare's dramaturgy in *King Lear* is situational. That is, the situation rather than the characters' intentions seems to be the primary determinant of the action: emphasis is not so much on their actions as on their reactions to a set of extreme circumstances that are forced on them. Structure is less a progression of willed events than a series of imposed situations. As an interpreter of later situational dramas writes of their structure: 'Plays of this sort have a structure based on a series of circumstances and events unconnected by a strict logic of causality ... their situations are deliberately brought out ... for the purpose of displaying human reactions to extreme and unexpected occurrences.'[20] More than the other tragedies, *King Lear* resembles this type of situational drama.

It is a structural emphasis that might be expected, in light of both the anti-narrative thrust of *King Lear* and the creation of a self-sustained play-world that provides more diverse and extreme conditions than naturalistic presentation would allow, because both these aspects of the play spotlight the intense dramatic moment. They are time-saving conventions that allow Shakespeare to dispense with dissipative connections and colourless logic – Henry James's 'clumsy Life again at her stupid work' – and to deal exclusively with the crises of situations. To coincide with this emphasis, Shakespeare even trims the verbal flora of the *Lear* world. In a discerning essay on 'Some Aspects of the Style of *King Lear*,' Winifred Nowottny has remarked on 'the absence from *Lear* of resplendent imagery ... indeed of poetry that survives quotation out of context.'[21] There are notable patterns of imagery – as the work of Heilman and others plenteously affirms – but the images are so tightly woven into their situational contexts that it becomes extremely difficult to find any passages (such as Hamlet on the dram of evil, or Macbeth on the poor player) that seem satisfying and complete in themselves when excerpted. Mrs Nowottny maintains that this circumstance arises because 'imagery that projects the conflict or quality of the hero ... is unnecessary where the hero is physically the image of his own tragedy' (p. 50). But the need for 'resplendent' verbal imagery is also lessened because of the large number and variety of theatrical images and emblems. Verbal images are frequently supplemented by stage images, in line with the play's emphasis on the dramatic situation. Without sacrificing a richness of verbal texture, Shakespeare is moving in the direction of Fletcherian tragicomedy's blank verse – more closely bound up with the immediate responses of characters to specific situations, because of the authors' overwhelming concern with situational drama.

In fact, the entire situational bent of *King Lear* seems to anticipate the central achievement of Fletcherian dramaturgy, itself the fullest flower of the private-theatre tradition. This achievement has been summarized by Andrew Gurr: 'Beyond any dramatist of their time the collaborators were adept at the theatre of situation; the extraordinary ingenuity of plotting ... gave them the accomplishment of metaphysical conceits of situation on stage.'[22] Yet just as Donne's metaphysical lyrics make us suspect him of a greater passion for devising poems than for baring his soul, so the situations of Beaumont and Fletcher involve us more with a virtuoso art than with the characters who experience them. They are instruments of detachment, so ingeniously contrived that our attention is bound to be centred at least as much on the stage manager's dexterity as on the object of his art. How wonderful, then, that *King Lear* manages to be so emotionally compelling even while its structure fosters the drama of situation. One reason for our strong involvement has already been discussed, the central situational focus on character. We shall now look briefly at several other reasons, means of involvement rather than detachment.

Unlike the tragic heroes of Chapman or Marston, Lear himself determines the nature of the situations that will put him and his kingdom on trial. It is his inverted value system, prizing word over action and form over essence, and his shattering of reason and tradition by force, that set up the ground rules of the *Lear* world. Not just a fly to wanton gods, Lear makes his initial choice from a position of free will and great authority. In occupying this central position of responsibility, Lear resembles less a Bussy or a Sophonisba than an earlier dramatic hero like Faustus or Tamburlaine, each (initially at least) master of his own house. The emotional effect of this arrangement on us is also similar: Lear and his sufferings become as terribly real because he is in some measure responsible for them. We are made to feel that the tragedy's inevitability grows out of his character, not out of the playwright's construction of an airtight design.

When the series of catastrophes begins after Lear's tragic choice, Shakespeare also maintains our involvement through an intricate adaptation of other dramatic traditions and emphases. We might note first how he parallels the experiences of his characters with our experience of those disjunctive effects studied in Chapter 2. The feelings of Gloucester ('all ruinous disorders follow us'), Kent ('man's nature cannot carry/ Th' affliction nor the fear'), Lear ('this dreadful pudder o'er our heads'), Edgar ('O world!/ ... thy strange mutations make us hate thee'), [23] and all the other characters who pluck allegiance from our hearts, are echoed by Bradley's 'confusion' and our impression as spectators of being adrift in the *Lear* world. The vagueness of locale is partially responsible for our unease, for there are no distinct places where we can get a foothold, but its main causes are the frequency of purely momentary effects and the absence of narrative continuities. These result in our being constantly assaulted with changing situations, and so they deny us the reassurance that would come from an overview of a settled or predictable set of circumstances. Not that we would be able to pin our feelings down to these causes while in the theatre; they seem to work on us like dramatic imagery, without drawing attention to themselves.

What I would argue here, therefore, is that Shakespeare realizes and sustains a great emotional potential from techniques that other Jacobean playwrights employ more self-consciously to reinforce their structural emphasis on the strong scene. He makes the experience of the spectator approximate in a minor way that of his characters, and their disorientation becomes more compelling as we experience a lesser version of it. Gloucester's words, 'the night comes on, and the bleak winds/ Do sorely ruffle; for many miles about/ There's scarce a bush' (II.iv.302-4), come when we are already feeling something like the inversions in nature and mind that Shakespeare chooses to express to us through the dominant metaphors of storm and madness. Throughout *King Lear*, then, Shakespeare has used the somewhat disjunctive impressions created by a structure of strong scenes to maintain our deep involvement with his characters' experiences.

To further this end, Shakespeare also turns to a popular dramatic tradition. Elizabethan drama had always reached out to its public through frequent allusions to homely details and local places, and such plays as Dekker's *The Shoemaker's Holiday* (1599) or the anonymous *The Merry Devil of Edmonton* (1602) achieved great success with the practice.[24] It promoted audience involvement by turning the dramatic background into a comfortable duplicate of the audience's own environment, creating warm feelings of identification that would broaden to include a play's characters as well. It held spectators by giving them something familiar to cling to. In *King Lear*, we too need something to cling to, so that the placeless world and the absence of story interest do not leave us thinking of the play's characters as floating in a situational test tube, the abstracted environment of Heath or Castle. Shakespeare responds to the challenge by coming up with a extraordinary array of familiar sights. *King Lear* catches us up in a constant stream of references to people (lawyers, barbers, tailors, Bedlam beggars, cockneys), places (taverns, brothels, sheep-cotes, jakes), and things (eggs, oysters, worsted stockings, holy water, toasted cheese) – not to forget Tray, Blanche, and Sweetheart – that fill out its abstract world and endow it with a fine concreteness. We feel that the spectacle we are watching is, to alter Eliot's phrase from *Little Gidding*, remote and yet identifiable. Granville-Barker marvelled at Lear's 'call for a looking-glass, his catching at the feather to put on Cordelia's lips, the undoing of the button,' and recognized that 'These things are the necessary balance to the magniloquence of the play's beginning and to the tragic splendor of the storm.'[25] They are also the necessary ballast to such a changeable universe. Solid objects from the everyday world provide us with fixed points of reference throughout the kaleidoscopic situations of *King Lear*, and help them to 'Speak what we feel.'

II

Among the many structural features that set *King Lear* off from the other tragedies, the most conspicuous is probably its fully developed subplot. No other Shakespearean tragedy features a two-plot structure, which has been described as making demands on the playwright 'in direct conflict with the demands of tragedy.'[26] Shakespeare evidently thought it worthwhile to risk the unusual and the hazardous in *King Lear*, and we shall now explore some of the special advantages gained by his daring move. As a preliminary step, however, I want again to place Shakespeare's choice in the context where he made it, by relating his plot-subplot configuration to the form's traditional use on the Elizabethan stage.

The two-plot structure grew up along with the Elizabethan theatre. As David M. Bevington has shown, it arose in direct response to a demand for variety in themes and characters: when employed with the practice of doubling, it enabled the popular companies to multiply the value of their limited resources, compounding the number of people and actions that could be dramatized.[27] But as Lear learns, the art of our necessities is strange. Long after theatres grew so large and affluent that the structure was no longer necessary, it remained popular. It satisfied the clamour for an abundance of narrative material, and its subplot gave the indispensable clowns a permanent home – regardless of genre, *pace* Sidney. Playwrights adapted it to every dramatic form – chronicle histories, domestic dramas, comedies, and (with least success) tragedies.[28]

In its most basic form, the plot-subplot relationship entails a simple patterning in the stories of two plots that unfold in isolation from each other. A typical example is Heywood's *If You Know Not Me You Know Nobody: Part II*, a work that Polonius would probably call a 'historical morality comedy' written in the same year as *King Lear*. The play's main plot glorifies Charity through the person of the legendary Thomas Gresham, who enriches the needy in a succession of episodes. Later in the main action, Thomas and Lady Ramsey show that they have profited from his example and become similarly charitable. In the subplot, the merchant Hobson readily gives money to help the Queen (as Gresham had done on a larger scale) and relieves the impoverished peddler Rowland, who (like the Ramseys) himself aids the poor. The play brings similarities to our attention by letting us make connections between the larger outlines of each sequence, instead of encouraging us to compare specific scenes or actions. The two plots are linked by Gresham's prodigal nephew, who swindles both his uncle and Hobson; otherwise, neither plot makes its discoveries available to the other. Furthermore, the characters in each move about in ignorance of their structural counterparts' affairs, and only the audience profits from the recognition of similarities.

More ambitious playwrights, however, used the configuration to do much more than add or reinforce thematic developments. For them, the double plot became a means of juxtaposing situations and, as with dramatically juxtaposed emblems, inviting comparison between them. A telltale sign of this emphasis is the pronounced counterpointing of scenes and speeches from the two plots, a practice that frequently obtains in the works of such playwrights as Marston, Chapman, or Middleton.[29] Indeed, given the strong situational bent of Middleton's intrigue comedies, one might expect his use of the multiple plot to involve such situational counterpointing. His plays often hold up the gestures of characters from different plots and match them against each other in order to call our attention to the parallelism of specific scenes, actions, and speeches. Furthermore, in contrast to the rather isolated communities of plot and subplot characters in *If You Know Not Me*, characters from the multiple plots of Middleton's works are often highly aware of each other's activities. Dryfat's speech in Act V of *The Family of Love* (1602), for instance, deliberately points up parallels for the characters:

> Master doctor Glister hath a cradleful and a bellyful, you see, thrust upon him; and master Purge a headful. – Your wife is an angry honeyless wasp, whose sting, I hope, you need not fear – and yours carries honey in her mouth, but her sting makes your forehead swell; – your wife makes you deaf with the shrill treble of her tongue, – and yours makes you horn-mad with the tenor of her tale.[30]

Shakespeare's handling of basic plot-subplot parallels, apart from the more distinctive uses to which he puts the multiple plot, relates *King Lear* to this tradition of elaborate counterpointing. Throughout the play, he underlines connections for us with juxtaposed actions and speeches. In Act II, for example, a symbolic tableau memorably establishes several important parallels. As scene iii opens, Kent is in the stocks, asleep. He is wearing the disguise he assumed after

Lear banished him, and has just read a letter from Cordelia, the other outcast. Now Edgar enters to another part of the stage and tells us:

> I heard myself proclaim'd;
> And by the happy hollow of a tree
> Escap'd the hunt ...
>
> ... .
>   and am bethought
> To take the basest and most poorest shape
>
> ... .
>   Poor Turlygod! poor Tom!
> That's something yet: Edgar I nothing am. (1-21)

Like Kent and Cordelia, Edgar is now an outcast; and even as Kent sits near him in disguise, he too resolves to disguise himself. As if these plot-subplot parallels were not enough to underline the affinity, Shakespeare reinforces them with a verbal echo: Edgar's 'nothing' repeats Cordelia's unfortunate answer to Lear.

Actually, Cordelia's reply has echoed in the subplot long before this. When Gloucester asks Edmund what letter he is hiding, Edmund repeats the same original phrase: 'Nothing, my Lord' (I.ii.31). The second scene of *King Lear* is in some respects a mirror image of the first, with the roles of Regan and Goneril played by Edmund, Lear by Gloucester, and Cordelia by Edgar: the foolish old man is again taken in by a 'play' of deception, and the worthy child again falls into disfavour. Edmund's reply here confirms him as Cordelia's antithesis, a villain who masquerades in innocuous words; and it paves the way for our association of Edgar with Cordelia, in their respective plots. Like the symbolic tableau in Act II, juxtaposing this second scene against the first emphasizes those elements that the subplot has in common with the main action. Shakespeare also underlines the connection in several related speeches, given by plot and subplot characters who have been manoeuvred into similar situations. The blind Gloucester's speech on how 'distribution should undo excess' (IV.i.66-70) repeats, in essence, the short speech that follows mad Lear's 'O! I have ta'en/ Too little care of this' (III.iv.32-6); and Edmund's defence of bastardy (I.ii.6-15) is echoed in Lear's defence of adultery (IV.vi.112-20), where an allusion by Lear calls attention to the parallel: 'Glou-cester's bastard son/ Was kinder to his father than my daughters/ Got 'tween the lawful sheets.'

Lear is mistaken, of course: Edgar has saved his father from Dover Cliffs just minutes before, while in the previous scene Edmund was reported as 'gone,/ In pity of his misery, to dispatch/ His [Gloucester's] nighted life' (IV.v.11-13). This is one of several discrepancies between what characters in one plot say about those in the other, and what the real state of affairs is there. Edgar makes a similar mistake when he says that Lear 'childed as I father'd' (III.vi.113), and Gloucester errs in his earlier analogy: 'This villain of mine comes under the prediction; there's son against father: the King falls from bias of nature; there's father against child' (I.ii.114-17). Shakespeare has turned a profound variation on traditional practice by making each character's statement about the other plot reflect ignorance and misinformation rather than true knowledge, for such statements image a tragic atmosphere of isolation. They convey the feeling that truth and communication are hopelessly remote ideals, never to be realized in the *Lear* world. Even when characters do touch on a truth, they are unaware of it – as when Gloucester commiserates with the disguised Kent about Lear:

> His daughters seek his death. Ah! that good Kent;
> He said it would be thus, poor banish'd man!
> Thou say'st the king grows mad; I'll tell thee, friend,
> I am almost mad myself. I had a son,
> Now outlaw'd from my blood; he sought my life,
> But lately, very late. (III.iv.167-72)

The relationship between 'seek his death' and 'sought my life' is one of contrast, not similitude, but Gloucester does not realize this; and later when he does, the realization is his death.

Artful as such variations on the multiple plot structure may be, Shakespeare did not turn to the configuration in *King Lear* just for their sake. If we examine how that structure functions in shaping our response to the play, more essential reasons for his choice emerge. The rest of this chapter will investigate some of its primary dramatic effects, looking mainly at benefits derived from the subplot, and then at impressions made by the two plots as they unfold together.

When Bradley wrote that we regard Lear 'almost wholly as a sufferer, hardly at all as an agent' (p. 280), he touched on a central characteristic not just of Lear's journey but of the entire main action in *King Lear*. Schlegel's remark testifies to the same characteristic: 'The principal characters here are not those who act, but those who suffer' (New Variorum, p. 449). Although characters and audience are led through psychological and elemental turmoil, the main plot has very little action. Hardly anything takes place, in comparison with *Macbeth* or *Othello* or even *Hamlet* (which turns thematically and theatrically on the delaying of its principal action, but has so much more going on as well). Story interest is minimal, as Chapter 2 observed, and after I.i characters are carried along, manipulated into one test after another, instead of achieving a series of objectives or creating the outlines of the world around them. What *happens* outside of the subplot can be summarized in a trice: Lear rejects Cordelia, goes to each of her sisters and is rejected in turn, suffers the outrage of the heath, is reunited with Cordelia, and breaks under the final iniquity of her death. We are presented with a number of emotionally compelling variations on the trial situation. We react strongly to them, but our attention is fixed on the inner life of the characters rather than on their achievements in the realm of action. This intense focus is of course one of Shakespeare's greatest accomplishments, but alone it would have its drawbacks in a work written for the Renaissance stage. Shakespeare had learned from practical experience that drama is the imitation of characters in *action*, and he was not about to anticipate Byron's 'dramatic poem,' Shelley's 'lyrical drama,' or even one of Chapman's relentless spiritual peregrinations. Also, the 1603 failure of Jonson's eloquent but inanimate *Sejanus* (a play in which Shakespeare acted) provided a lesson close at hand. He circumvented the problem by supplementing the Lear story with a subject that, despite its many topical similarities to the main plot, stimulates a profoundly different response.

It is a commonplace that Gloucester's struggles are largely physical, in contrast to Lear's spiritual trials. In addition, the subplot both adds specific incidents to the play and makes us feel through its prolific intrigues that purposeful action is itself possible in the *Lear* world. For the two intriguers, first Edmund and then Edgar, initiate and carry out a long chain of purposeful and exciting actions – duels, power plays, love affairs, and a 'miracle.' Their activities would satisfy the keenest appetite for incidents, and are the source of Bradley's complaint about 'the pressure of persons and events' (p. 256) in *King Lear*. Edmund, in fact, climbs by these actions all the way up the ladder from a 'whoreson' who 'hath been out nine years' to within an arm's reach of the throne. Repeatedly, the subplot sows the seeds of action in *King Lear*, thus performing the task for which it was first devised during the 1560s and 1570s. It also gives the course of action a more even shape. For just as the main plot begins more precipitately than the other tragedies, doing in one scene what they take two acts to accomplish, so it ends in a more concentrated way: all the developments that are usually spread out over the later acts are here condensed into the play's breathless last scene, anticipating the exciting situational complexity of *Cymbeline's* final scene. The subplot in *King Lear* fills in the interstices. Gloucester's story unfolds at a more normal pace over the first three acts; and in Act IV, after Lear's storm and before his recovery, the subplot 'prevent[s] the play from dying when the storm blows itself out' by providing a strong, rising plot interest to hold our attention.[31]

Gloucester's story not only unfolds more normally, but introduces us to a more normal, approachable world than the main action. This is a second advantage that Shakespeare derives from his subplot. Lear and his family are titans. When the play opens, Lear wields an authority far greater than any other king in Shakespeare, and his later sufferings are far more profound. Two of his daughters display unfathomable malice ('Hang him instantly,' 'Pluck out his eyes,' they cry like harpies) and lust, and the other 'redeems nature from the general curse' (IV.vi.207). We might view the actions of such gigantic creatures with a detached fascination – like Gulliver in Brobdingnag – if the subplot characters and actions did not bridge the gap for us. This is one reason why Shakespeare evidently thought it vital to develop such close parallels between the two plots. The subplot is the dull mirror through which our eyes can bear to see an eclipse of the sun. It provides a more accessible verbal medium, as Clifford Leech has perceived,[32] and its whole scale of characterization is more apprehensible. Error takes root there as mere weakness or corruption: unlike

Lear, Gloucester always seeks the easy way out, and Edmund's villainy stems from ambition rather than from motiveless malice. Virtue also 'treads on the ground,' as Edgar's perilous experiences indicate. A short aside in III.vi points up the difference between him and Cordelia. Lear's mock trial evokes Edgar's pity, making him turn to us and say: 'My tears begin to take his part so much,/ They mar my counterfeiting' (60-1). Counterfeiting is something Cordelia would never do; her virtue does not make compromises, as we know from I.i. Nor are Edgar's palpable tears like the 'guests' in Cordelia's eyes, 'which parted thence,/ As pearls from diamonds dropp'd' (IV.iii.22-3).

Another reason that the subplot is so approachable arises out of its nature as primarily an intrigue action. The intriguers create a more intimate relationship through asides and soliloquies, sharing their secrets with us. They invite us into the very making of the play. Their victims, too, strike us as less awesome than figures like Lear or Cordelia, because we have watched from a position of superior awareness as their every reaction was predicted and manipulated by our very human confidants, rather than by 'the great Gods' who oppose Lear. Placed in this less exalted position, the subplot figures can even – like the dupes of intrigue comedy – become funny. In fact, most of the mordant humour of *King Lear* (apart from the Fool's wit) occurs in the subplot, from Edmund's snickering to the black comedy of Gloucester's 'suicide.' Earlier, Gloucester has even played the traditional comic *senex* who finds himself royally outwitted, and so perhaps Edmund speaks truer than he knows when he calls Edgar 'the catastrophe of the old comedy,' whether it be Roman comedy or the comic subplot of so many Elizabethan plays.

This satellite world that can tolerate humour is absolutely necessary if we are to endure and assimilate the shocking concentration of the main plot. It literalizes the happenings of the main action and so makes them more bearable, much in the way that comedy makes our fears bearable through exaggeration. The subplot, then, resembles those 'passages of less intensity' that Eliot found necessary in a long poem, 'to give a rhythm of fluctuating emotion essential to the musical structure of the whole.'[33] And the whole of *King Lear* does have a musical structure, in which the distinct parts blend and harmonize. Although discussion has up to now centred exclusively on one of the parts, the subplot, the rest of this section will try to respond to some of the harmonies that emerge from this symphonic balance of the two plots.

In a structure consisting of so many strong scenes, the plot-subplot configuration works as a unifying force. It brings situations together by setting up patterns of echoes in place of the tight sequence of more narrative drama. One such pattern in *King Lear* seems to be derived from the humble but popular Elizabethan genre of domestic drama. Domestic dramas may be seen as falling into three main structural types; all of them are woven into *King Lear*, turning plot and subplot into variations on common themes. One of these structural types delineates the inception and commission of a domestic crime, as well as the apprehension, trial, and punishment of the guilty characters. The anonymous *A Yorkshire Tragedy* (1606) and *A Warning for Fair Women* (1599) both exhibit this structure, as does the main plot of Heywood's *A Woman Killed with Kindness* (1603), where the trial and punishment are conducted by John Frankford rather than by any civil authorities. Lear himself follows this pattern. He breaks the commutual bond by disinheriting Cordelia and banishing Kent. For this crime, he is tried by the Fool and by himself, and is punished by Regan and Goneril, the elements, and – at the death of Cordelia – the 'judgment of the heavens.' Another structural type traces a rake's progress: the focus here is on the course of a domestic vice (such as adultery or prodigality), its repercussions, and the final reclamation of a character from its clutches.[34] In each play, a main protagonist follows vice until it leads him to the brink of catastrophe, at which point his reformation is effected, usually through the effort of a loving wife. The story of Gloucester unfolds around this pattern (and Lear's story provides a distant echo, just as Gloucester's experience conforms more vaguely to the first structural type). He embraces, and is nearly destroyed by, adultery and its issue; but his true son reclaims him from the brink of Dover Cliffs and brings him to a state of penitence.

Patience is the basis of the third structural type, displayed in three public-theatre plays.[35] In each case, a main character's patience undergoes a series of trials, until he or she is finally restored to a suspicious relative's good graces. Lear directs us to the exemplars of this structure in *King Lear*, when he tells us 'No, I will be the pattern of all patience;/ I will say nothing' (III.ii.37-8). Both Cordelia and Edgar (and thus both plots) follow this course, each saying 'nothing,' suffering exclusion, and finally achieving vindication. Yet even in echoing these popular dramatic forms, Shakespeare's art was opening itself to other genres and audiences: the redemption of parents and children is a theme that worked its way into the plot-subplot configurations of all of those late romances performed in the private theatre at Blackfriars as well as at the Globe.

Like the subplot itself, this pattern of domestic crises helps to involve us in the cosmic upheavals of the *Lear* world by translating them into the medium of personal relationships. It particularizes the universal without diminishing it. This same end is achieved by other aspects of the two-plot structure. The dual emphasis on Gloucester's physical being and Lear's spiritual being dramatizes the perpetual duality of body and soul.[36] Similarly, in the contrasting spiritual journeys of Lear and Edmund, we can see the two moral options open to Renaissance man – 'the alternating and progressive rise of the hero from fallen innocence to spiritual victory' or 'the progressive decline of the corrupted man to ultimate damnation.'[37] The quotations are from David Bevington's description of two kinds of morality plays; and their applicability to the two plots of *King Lear* shows the structure of that play once again hearkening back to (and incorporating) the earliest themes of popular drama.

Yet even while the two-plot structure makes universal issues palpable, it also exerts a broadening effect: the experiences of Lear and Gloucester, paralleling and elaborating on each other,[38] turn the play from the ordeal of an individual to the image of a world. Shakespeare's two-plot structure thus contributes greatly to both the creation of the *Lear* world and our acceptance of it – a world that is superficially different from our own, but at its core is so undeniably the same. The words of Polixenes, as he explains a different art to Perdita in *The Winter's Tale*, describe the kind of structure that his creator evolved for *King Lear*:

> You see, sweet maid, we marry
> A gentler scion to the wildest stock,
> And make conceive a bark of baser kind
> By bud of nobler race. This is an art
> Which does mend nature – change it rather – but
> The art itself is nature. (IV.iv.92-7)

In *King Lear*, Shakespeare unites the 'gentler' or more genteel structural figures and configurations of Jacobean tragedy with the more common 'stock' of comedies, morality plays, and other popular traditional forms. He creates a work of art that transcends the achievements of its parent strains, yet it is one that ultimately involves us not in the intricacies of its art but in its truth to our own nature.

4

Characterization: Fools and Madmen

Although seventy years of critical scholarship have come and gone since Bradley wrote about characterization in *King Lear*, his description still provides the clearest appraisal of what distinguishes the *Lear* world's characters from their counterparts in other Shakespearean tragedies. Bradley's description may serve here as an introduction to the approach that this chapter will take:

> Fine and subtle touches could not be absent from a work of Shakespeare's maturity; but, with the possible exception of Lear himself, no one of the characters strikes us as psychologically a *wonderful* creation, like Hamlet or Iago or even Macbeth; one or two seem even to be somewhat faint and thin. And, what is more significant, it is not quite natural to us to regard them from this point of view at all. Rather we observe a most unusual circumstance. If Lear, Gloster and Albany are set apart, the rest fall into two distinct groups, which are strongly, even violently, contrasted: Cordelia, Kent, Edgar, the Fool on one side, Goneril, Regan, Edmund, Cornwall, Oswald on the other ... the radical differences of the two species are emphasized in broad hard strokes; and the two are set in conflict, almost as if Shakespeare, like Empedocles, were regarding Love and Hate as the two ultimate forces of the universe. (p. 263)

With an eye for the problematical, Bradley recognizes that the characters of *King Lear* are less complex than those of the other tragedies, and he senses some connection between this 'thinness' and the sharp moral dichotomy along which Shakespeare aligns them. His instinct is right. The difference between Gertrude's adultery and Goneril's, between Claudius' ambition and Edmund's, or between Hamlet's shifts for survival and Edgar's, consists primarily of a lack of moral ambiguity in the *Lear* characters. The good characters never wilfully commit evil acts, and the bad characters never feel pangs of remorse in the midst of their villainy.[1]

Nor does Shakespeare let us even imagine them in such positions, for the entire thrust of characterization seems aimed at creating and maintaining this moral dichotomy. With the exception of Cornwall, characters in the groups Bradley mentions are polarized in the first act; and even Lear, Gloucester, and

Albany have been compelled to take sides by the end of the play. We take sides with them. Shakespeare constantly asks us to assess the moral natures of his characters, and' to pronounce on their good or evil conduct. The good characters win our allegiance as they struggle against their persecutors, familiarity with whom awakens nothing more positive than contempt. Shades of gray never appear. Indeed, character presentation in *King Lear* is what we might expect from a play compounded of so many trials, since trials recognize only the guilty and the innocent.

Character presentation in *King Lear* becomes less strange than it was to Bradley when it is viewed in light of a tradition of dramatic characterization that defined its characters principally in terms of such moral polarities. Shakespeare adopts many features of this traditional mode, sometimes modifying or deliberately exaggerating them for special effect. His use of the Fool draws on a broader dramatic and literary heritage, and will be considered in the second half of this chapter; yet Shakespeare's art here complements the play's bold method of characterization, and works with it to sustain a relationship between characters and audience that is (like so much else in *King Lear*) unique among the tragedies.

I

We begin with a brief abstract of a convention of character presentation in its most basic form, a pattern recognizable in the composition a large number of Elizabethan plays. Conventional presentation of characters in such drama involves, at the outset of each play, a definite establishment of the characters' moral positions; and it dictates that later appearances simply reinforce, rather than modify, our initial moral impressions. Thus, as each play unfolds, characters act precisely as we would expect on the basis of these *données*, and our sympathies are set accordingly. The result is that the dramatist steadily evokes either positive or negative feelings through moral approval or disapproval. This technique was based on an understanding that, in M.C. Bradbrook's words, 'characters did not develop,'[2] and on the assumption that the most important (and sometimes the only) information that a dramatist should present about a character was whether that character was good or evil. In such plays, good characters exhibit their election by being noble, which means that they are chaste, charitable, and/or courageous. Evil characters have wider scope, for they display their wickedness by subverting good in a variety of ingenious ways. Whichever colours they show, their conduct does not call for our examination or analysis; it is typical.

Such is the outline of a tradition of character presentation to which many lesser playwrights adhered slavishly, but which some of their more accomplished colleagues used as a foundation for more intricate designs.[3] Tourneur's *The Revenger's Tragedy* (1606) clearly belongs to the latter class, yet we can easily see the conventional lines in its characterization. They appear most conspicuously in the tag names with which Tourneur indicates the moral bent of each major protagonist: the chaste heroine is Castiza, the Duke's lascivious son is Lussorioso, etc. But these conventional lines emerge through the action as well. For instance, Castiza opens Act II with a soliloquy in praise of chastity, saying that she has no estate but her honour. This honour is immediately tried by Vindice, who enters and attempts to win her for Lussurioso. All he wins from her is a box on the ear, however, and she exits with an angry challenge:

> Bear to him
> That figure of my hate upon thy cheek
> Whilst 'tis yet hot, and I'll reward thee for 't;
> Tell him my honour shall have a rich name
> When several harlots shall share his with shame.[4]

Castiza never yields to Lussurioso's advances, and remains exemplary throughout the play. Her conduct contrasts with that of her mother, Gratiana, whom Vindice solicits immediately after his unsuccessful interview with Castiza. Gratiana shows her weakness from the beginning of the encounter by listening patiently to Vindice's arguments instead of confronting and repulsing him at once, as her daughter did. Castiza's rejection heightens the immorality of Gratiana's conduct. Similar polarization occurs in Heywood's *The Rape of Lucrece* (1607), which pits the virtuous trio of Lucrece, her husband Collatine, and a noble friend named Brutus against the tyrannous family of Tarquin. As in Jonson's *Sejanus* (1603), the main characters' moral worth is established through a conversation of senators in Act I, and receives immediate reinforcement: Tarquin enters and captures the crown by stabbing his father-in-law to death. Not to be outdone, his wife Tullia shows she is of the same breed by walking over her father's body as she exits.

The example is extreme, but it provides a telling contrast to a kind of characterization that Shakespeare obviously rejected in *King Lear*. In the tragedies and tragicomedies of Beaumont and Fletcher, there are numerous extreme events like those in Heywood's play, meant to evoke pathos or indignation; but the unswerving moral emphasis is gone. Also, it is often the case that the first appearances of characters do not establish the conduct that we can expect from those characters in subsequent scenes. The consequences of both traits is that later actions do not reinforce initial moral impressions. Frequent turnabouts in character are to be expected, and are numerous: Philaster, for instance, experiences many sudden changes in nature and outlook to suit the contexts of differing situations in the 1609 play named after him; Evadne displays a similarly erratic character in *The Maid's Tragedy* (1610). Our involvement has little to do with the characters' moral natures, and is sporadic rather than constant. As Arthur C. Kirsch observes, Beaumont and Fletcher manifest 'a conception of characterization which is discontinuous and deliberately indecorous.'[5]

In *Cymbeline*, as Kirsch demonstrates (pp. 294-6), Shakespeare chose to employ this conception of characterization. But in *King Lear*, a play that shares many structural, generic, and thematic motifs with *Cymbeline*, he instead developed his characters along lines that resemble the very different conventional presentation outlined earlier. For reasons that will become clear, he found its less theatrically sophisticated techniques more readily adaptable to the needs of his tragedy. Before we turn to *King Lear*, a more extensive scrutiny of character presentation in Jonson's *Volpone* might be instructive, providing a paradigm against which Shakespeare's achievement may be considered. Both playwrights managed to build major works along the lines of a tradition largely associated with minor dramatic efforts. In *Volpone* (1606), it is revealing to see how extensively Jonson adapts his character presentation to coincide with the methods described above. I should emphasize here that I am not comparing specific characters or even types of characters, but methods of characterization – similarities in the means that a playwright uses to shape our response to his characters rather than similarities between the characters themselves. I have chosen *Volpone* for this purpose because it is the most familiar and the most dramatically successful of the plays in which Jonson applies this convention, but the same methods may also be seen as central to characterization in his tragedies, *Sejanus* (1603) and *Catiline* (1611). They apply especially to Jonson's depiction of his villainous central characters (Sejanus, Macro, Catiline) and their virtuous opponents (Drusus, Cicero) in these plays. Characterization in most other Elizabethan plays (including Shakespeare's) may clearly be seen to fall somewhere in between the two extremes distinguished above: indecorous and discontinuous, or rigidly moral and consistent.

Volpone opens Act I by worshipping his gold. For all its vitality and theatrical effectiveness, the gesture nevertheless gives us a first look at Volpone through a lens strongly coloured with moral judgment. Later scenes reinforce this impression: his delight in the 'very pretty' entertainment of dwarf, eunuch, and hermaphrodite, for instance, and the symbolic relationship that we sense exists between them ('He's the true father of his family,' Mosca tells Corvino later in the scene); the animalism that he shares with the creatures he coaxes into his den; and the repulsive symptoms that become associated with him – counterfeit as far as his physical being is concerned, but creating an atmosphere of disease that we feel is appropriate on another level. By such means Jonson distances us from Volpone even as we are fascinated by his ingenuity. Thus, after his attempted rape and his slander of Celia alienate him even further, it is our sense of moral repugnance that brings us to feel the inevitability and the aptness of Volpone's final humiliation.

Jonson defines his minor characters in *Volpone* even more emphatically along these lines. The first act reveals, in succession, Voltore, Corbaccio, and Corvino in terms of unfavourable moral impressions. Opposing this nefarious array are Celia and Bonario, both morally impeccable. From the moment Corvino drags her in by the hair in Act II, Celia is the picture of the wronged wife, all chastity and submission.[6] Her humiliation by Volpone strengthens both the audience's negative feelings about him and their positive response towards her. Similarly, Bonario's first appearance shows that he too is virtuous, as he is ready to forgive Mosca when the latter appears penitent (III.i); and his very

credulousness in such a scheming world wins our sympathy. Magnificent reinforcement of this positive moral impression comes later in the act when he
dashes in to rescue Celia from the clutches of Volpone:

> BON. Forbeare, foule rauisher, libidinous swine,
> Free the forc'd lady, or thou dy'st, impostor.
> But that I am loth to snatch thy punishment
> Out of the hand of iustice, thou shouldst, yet,
> Be made the timely sacrifice of vengeance,
> Before this altar, and this drosse, thy idoll.
> Lady, let's quit the place, it is the den
> Of villany; feare nought, you haue a guard:
> And he, ere long, shall meet his iust reward.[7]

Bonario's later humiliation serves the same purpose as Celia's, in terms of
audience response; and their final vindication, demanded by the sympathies
that have been established, is a triumph of right over wrong. Through the subtle
threads of Jonson's art, one can see the conventional dramatic victory of virtue
over vice. To make this victory even more impressive, and to depict his good
characters solely in terms of their moral worth, Jonson has even denied his
virtuous couple any romantic connection.

Shakespeare denies Cordelia and Edgar any romantic connection in *King
Lear*, although Tate changed that in his version. But many other aspects of
character presentation in *King Lear* also conform to Jonson's practices in
Volpone. To begin with, the opening scene elicits the same strong sympathies
and antipathies. After Goneril's hollow oratory in the love-test, Cordelia's
words ring with a genuine urgency: 'What shall Cordelia speak? Love, and be
silent.' As observed in Chapter 1, Shakespeare presents the sisters in absolute
contrast, and gains our immediate sympathy with Cordelia's aside. Asides were
a common means of characterization in all Elizabethan drama; and since they
put characters in direct contact with the audience, they could function in
making good characters more sympathetic or evil characters more repellent.
Following Regan's speech, Cordelia's second aside reinforces our impression of
the sisters: 'Then poor Cordelia!/ And yet not so; since I am sure my love's/
More ponderous than my tongue.'

There is no precedent for such personally moving asides in Shakespeare's
source, *The History of King Leir*: there, Cordella's words bespeak a position of
moral superiority, and deliberately undercut those of her father. When Leir
exclaims 'O, how thy words reuiue my dying soule!' after Gonorill's speech,
Cordella responds with 'O, how I doe abhorre this flattery!' Similarly, his 'Did
neuer *Philomel* sing so sweet a note,' after Ragan's speech, is met with the
equally alliterative 'Did neuer flatterer tell so false a tale.'[8] For all their moral
rectitude, these asides fail to involve us in a poignant personal dilemma. They
call for assent rather than compassion. Thus, we may assume that Shakespeare

has deliberately modified them not only to highlight the moral antithesis, but to make Cordelia more sympathetic.

Characterization in the opening scene continues along these lines. Kent's plea for clemency, coming after Lear's explosion, further advances the polarization. His self-sacrificing speech simultaneously gains sympathy for himself and confirms our opinion of Cordelia:

> LEAR The bow is bent and drawn; make from the shaft.
> KENT Let it fall rather, though the fork invade
> The region of my heart ...
> ...
> Thy youngest daughter does not love thee least;
> Nor are those empty-hearted whose low sounds
> Reverb no hollowness. (144-54)

Kent's words are as revealing of his character as Cordelia's asides were of hers, and they associate him with the conventional dramatic role of the wise counsellor, the selfless nobleman who remains loyal even when his king rashly ostracizes him.[9] The way Kent evokes sympathy for Cordelia here also prefigures the function of his conversation with the Gentlemen in III.iii, which surrounds the figure of Cordelia with reverent affection before her long-awaited appearance in the next scene.

France is even more positive in his attitude towards Cordelia, praising her virtues and prizing them above any dowry (241-61). The treatment that Kent and Cordelia receive at the hands of Lear, and their parting words, also seed our responses. Kent's farewell speech commends Cordelia's action ('The Gods to their dear shelter take thee, maid,/ That justly think'st and hast most rightly said!') and dares Regan and Goneril to act on their high-sounding words; and Cordelia's speech gives the fullest indictment yet of her sisters:

>   I know you what you are;
>   And like a sister am most loth to call
>   Your faults as they are named. Love well our father:
>   To your professed bosoms I commit him:
>   But yet, alas! stood I within his grace,
>   I would prefer him to a better place. (269-74)

Up to this point, the natures of Regan and Goneril have been sketched in dark but somewhat softer shades; they have made hypocritical speeches to Lear – Kent and Cordelia called our attention to the hypocrisy – and have not raised a finger to help their unfortunate sister. Now there are hints of deeper faults, and these are reinforced by the selfish, disrespectful plans they make in plain prose, alone on stage as the scene closes.

Their descent into prose necessitates a momentary departure from this survey of initial impressions in *King Lear*, because it directs attention to some characterizing effects of dramatic speech. It is well known that Shakespeare had no rival among Elizabethan playwrights in his ability to endow characters with distinctive speech patterns; this is one opportunity for character presentation that the average public-theatre writer lacked. Although many scholars have explored the relationship between character and speech in *King Lear*,[10] a few minor observations remain to be made in the context of this chapter. In the first place, Shakespeare sometimes turns the traditional alternation between blank verse and prose into a fine barometer of his villains' duplicity. The little epilogue at the end of I.i leaves Regan and Goneril alone on stage for the only time in *King Lear*. Consequently, they speak at length in prose – also for the only time in the play – and so confirm our suspicions about their earlier speeches to Lear. The well-balanced blank verse was, like all their later speech, meant for public consumption; this prose that begins with a hiss ('Sister, it is not little I have to say of what most nearly appertains to us both') bares for a brief moment the fangs of the real Regan and Goneril – these adders, as Edmund calls them (V.i.56-7). Conversely, Edmund seems to use prose as a cloak, and opens his true self to us in blank verse, as befits someone with his social aspirations. He soliloquizes in poetry at the start of I.ii, then switches to prose to ingratiate himself with Gloucester and Edgar, and ends the scene back in blank verse with us. He repeats this last switch with Gloucester at III.iii, and later feigns to Cornwall in prose (III.v) and tells us the truth in blank verse (V.i).

In addition to such alternation, Shakespeare indicates deception through the diction of his two wicked sisters. He makes them speak a language of circumlocution, even when alone together: 'then must we look from his age, to receive not alone the imperfections of long-engraffed condition, but therewithal the unruly waywardness that infirm and choleric years bring with them.' The only time they have no trouble coming to the point is at Gloucester's arraignment: 'Hang him instantly,' 'Pluck out his eyes.' The terseness of these lines is so unexpected, given their usual verbosity and euphemism (Goneril poisons Regan with 'medicine'), and yet it is so in character that it shocks us. They speak from the heart only to be bestial because they are 'dog-hearted,' as Kent tells us (IV.iii.46). Kent himself uses a high-flown style only to parody his hypocritical betters, not to ape them like Oswald, and reveals himself in honest prose. His speech to Cornwall is a biting *reductio* of the two love-test responses:

> KENT Sir, in good faith, in sincere verity,
> Under th' allowance of your great aspect,
> Whose influence, like the wreath of radiant fire
> On flick'ring Phoebus' front, –
> CORN.   What mean'st by this?
> KENT To go out of my dialect, which you discommend
> so much. I know, sir, I am no flatterer. (II.ii.106-11)

Returning to the initial impressions made by these characters, we can see the polarization of the first scene continuing into the second, and thus into the subplot. No sooner have Regan and Goneril made their exit than Edmund enters, in meaningful proximity to them. He picks up the implications of their prose and versifies them. From the first line, his soliloquy leaves no doubt about his moral nature. His speech recalls the Vice's announcement, as we found in Chapter 3, and it echoes the self-advertisements of such Elizabethan villains as Marlowe's Barabas, Dekker's Eleazar, Jonson's Sejanus, and Shakespeare's own Iago – all of whom lose no time in baring their wicked souls to us. Edmund then puts his ideals into 'practice,' setting up the machinery to dupe Gloucester and Edgar. 'I do serve you in this business,' he tells his brother.

Critics have often observed how Edmund's 'service' in *King Lear* mocks and testifies to the true service of a character like Kent,[11] but they have not noted the play on words that reinforces this contrast. Surrounding Kent's promises of service to Lear in I.iv are Edmund's vows to Edgar and, in II.i, to Cornwall: 'I shall serve you, Sir' (116). In these two instances, may we not suspect Shakespeare of using 'serve' in the sense of 'to play (one) a *trick*' or 'To treat in a specified (usually unpleasant or unfair) manner,' usages of which the *Oxford English Dictionary* records three other clear examples in Shakespeare?[12] Since Edmund's first vow of service comes on the heels of both his iconoclastic soliloquy and his mocking of father and brother, such usage would at any rate complement its context. Following the vow and ending the second scene is a more direct kind of revelation, as Edmund gives us a short character sketch of his brother, 'a brother noble,/ Whose nature is so far from doing harms/ That he suspects none; on whose foolish honesty/ My practices ride easy!'

All of these initial impressions are of course substantiated by the characters' later conduct, and there are several conventional ways in which Shakespeare strengthens the lines of moral opposition that emerge through the action. Sometimes he highlights a character's nature simply by associating him with others of the same disposition, as when a knight tells Lear, 'Since my young Lady's going into France, Sir, the Fool hath much pined away' (I.iv.77-8), or when Regan inquires about Edgar:

> REG. Was he not companion with the riotous knights
> That tended upon my father?
> GLOU. I know not, Madam; 'tis too bad, too bad.
> EDM. Yes, Madam, he was of that consort. (II.i.94-7)

Since none of Lear's knights – unlike those of Peter Brook – has impressed us as 'riotous,' Edgar's association with them ranks him with those who oppose the moral anarchy of Regan, Goneril, and Edmund.

Edmund's rebellious soliloquy exemplifies another convention of characterization, one widely used on the Elizabethan stage. Frequently, playwrights would condition audience response by having their characters voice positive or negative views on contemporary moral concerns. Thus, in Wilkins' *The Miseries of Enforced Marriage* (1606), Will Scarborrow inspires approval when he counters the raucous antifeminist views of his friends. He tells them that he construes more divinely of the opposite sex, and that women 'are the stems on which do Angels grow.'[13] By this same stroke, his friends' opinions establish them as potentially evil, prefiguring their later betrayal of him. Conversely, in Dekker and Middleton's *The Roaring Girl* (1608), Moll directs sympathy and moral approval to both herself and the young couple whose romance she has furthered, after Sebastian thanks her for helping them:

> SEB. Thou hast done me a kind office, without touch
> Either of sinne or shame, our loues are honest .
> MOLL. I'de scorne to make such shift to bring you together else.[14]

Shakespeare advances presentation of character in *King Lear* by making similar associations. His characters' attitudes towards old age, for instance, emerge along the moral lines established in the opening scenes. Regan, Goneril, and Edmund have no respect for their aged parents, and refer to age in terms of derision and contempt. Edmund goes so far as to seek his father's life, and he signs Lear's death warrant. By blinding Gloucester, Cornwall reveals himself as cut from the same cloth. On the other hand, Edgar and Cordelia revere and care for their parents; and even on the heath, Kent calls the mad old man nothing less than 'my Lord.' Similarly, when Cordelia affirms that she can 'out-frown false Fortune's frown' (V.iii.6), she reveals her contempt for the fickle goddess whom Edmund thinks he has at his command ('Briefness and Fortune, work!'). The characters' sexual standards illustrate the same distinction. Cordelia and Edgar are above sexual passion, while Regan, Goneril, and Edmund are increasingly caught in a web of lust and adultery. And the fact that Cordelia's 'Obey you, love you, and most honour you' paraphrases the marriage vow can only serve to bring her closer to the audience.

Lear and Gloucester stand apart from both groups in the first act. Their conduct is hardly commendable, but it is more deluded than depraved. Both act from blind rage, when their better judgment has been clouded (purposely, in Gloucester's case), rather than from the calculating self-interest that marks the actions of their evil children. But after the first act both begin to attract our sympathy, and by the end of the play we group them with their kinder offspring and servants. Bradley was deeply touched by Lear's regeneration, and viewed it as one of the play's glories: 'There is nothing more noble and beautiful in literature than Shakespeare's exposition of the effect of suffering in reviving the greatness and eliciting the sweetness of Lear's nature ... Should we not be at least as near the truth if we called this poem *The Redemption of King Lear*?' (pp. 284-5). With equal justice one might think of the subplot as 'The Redemption of Gloucester,' who advances from anxious timeserving to philosophic resignation.[15]

With both characters it is mainly, as Bradley noted in Lear's instance, their suffering that wins our affection and admiration. Lear begins to suffer before the first act is over, striking his head in remorse for having misjudged Cordelia (I.iv.280). The retainers incident causes him further pain, and issues in the unbearable torments of the heath. Edgar's reaction is ours: 'O thou side-piercing sight!' (IV.vi.85). In the last scene, the pain of ingratitude is replaced by the infinitely greater pain of loss, and the wonder is that Lear endures so long. Gloucester wins our approval even before his ordeal, by compassionately asking that Kent not be put in the stocks (II.ii.140-54) and by selflessly relieving the miseries of his king (III.iv and vi). His blinding is the greatest atrocity in major Shakespearean tragedy, and makes us share Edgar's pity for him. In Pauline terms, Lear and Gloucester must both put off the 'old man' within themselves, and put on the new man. The symbolic climax of this process is reached at Gloucester's 'suicide,' which kills the old Gloucester, and through Lear's madness and subsequent change to 'fresh garments.'

Physical or spiritual humiliation of a basically good character results in pathos in the Aristotelian sense; and the kind of pathos elicited by Lear and Gloucester (or Kent in the stocks, or the First Servant killed by Regan) was a common experience in popular drama, especially where characterization encouraged deep moral and emotional involvement in the fortunes of its characters. Even Ben Jonson evokes pathos, during the courtroom scene of *Volpone*. The action proceeds with methodical brutality, as Volpone and his confederates turn the judicial process into an enormous slander. Celia swoons and Bonario protests, but the judges remain unmoved:

> AVO. 1 Let her o'recome. What witnesses haue you,
> To make good your report? BON. Our consciences.
> CEL. And heauen, that neuer failes the innocent.
> AVO. 4 These are no testimonies. (IV.vi.15-18)

The scene wins sympathy for Volpone's helpless victims, and helps the audience to feel that his own final humiliation is justified when it comes at the end of the play. Especially in domestic tragedies Elizabethan drama abounds in such scenes, ranging from the touching to the horrifying. The entire process requires from Jonson's art a lack of self-consciousness seldom achieved elsewhere in his comedies.

Elizabethan playwrights sometimes furthered their conventional characterization by creating scenes that depict a member of the highest class performing a beneficent gesture for less fortunate figures. Such magnanimity always creates a favourable impression of the highborn character, who is to be admired for his condescension. In Part I of Heywood's *If You Know Not Me You Know Nobody* (1604), for instance, Princess Elizabeth's servants weep because their mistress suffers when her household is broken up on Queen Mary's orders. Elizabeth is touched, cheers them, and divides the last of her money among them. The lesson she gives them might be summed up by Edgar's words: 'When we our betters see bearing our woes,/ We scarcely think our miseries our foes.'

(III.vi.105-6). In *King Lear*, France shows a magnanimity like Elizabeth's when he accepts Cordelia without a dowry, in refreshing contrast to the niggling quantification of Burgundy ('will you tender less') and Lear ('her price is fallen'). He appeals to us by affirming a comforting maxim often voiced on the Elizabethan stage, that virtue is the only true nobility. Magnanimity also helps to redeem Lear and Gloucester in our eyes. On the heath, Lear sees that he has 'ta'en/ Too little care of this,' and vows to 'shake the superflux' to those who are less privileged (III.iv.32-5). Gloucester, blind and groping his way to Dover, wishes that 'distribution should undo excess,/ And each man have enough' (IV.i.70-1). A true dramatic alchemist, Shakespeare manages to use this rather heavy-handed convention without being obvious or awkward. He artfully makes the gesture one of many stages fitting naturally into the development of his characters.

Thus, the strong moral impressions made by characters' initial speeches and actions in *King Lear* are supplemented by Shakespeare's skilful use of a number of dramatic conventions. There is one other convention, however, that is not merely adapted by Shakespeare, but is transformed radically to accord with the nature of the *Lear* world. Shakespeare weaves this convention into the story of Kent. Like the other older aristocrats in *King Lear*, Kent suffers immensely. The *Lear* world is no place for old men.[16] Kent undergoes the humiliation of banishment, disguise, and then the stocks, and he endures the chilling, stormy night on the heath without complaint. But his greatest suffering comes at the end. He had thought to delay revealing his disguise to Lear 'Till time and I think meet' (IV.vii.11), and now Lear is too overwrought to comprehend him. In spite of his repeated efforts to explain, 'All's cheerless, dark, and deadly.' Kent's failure involves the reversal of a disguise convention found mainly in domestic dramas.

According to this convention, the casting off of a disguise would coincide with the proclaimed reformation of a morally errant character. The disguise is assumed near the beginning of a play, after a close friend or relative has been spurned by a reprobate; concerned about the wayward man's welfare, the friend dons a disguise so that he can remain close enough to help him. So both Orlando in Part II of Dekker and Middleton's *The Honest Whore* (1605) and old Flowerdale in *The London Prodigal* (1604) assume disguises in order sur- reptitiously to observe and guide their children on the road to moral rectitude. In *The London Prodigal* young Flowerdale's wife also disguises herself and helps in the reformation. *The Fair Maid of Bristow* (1604) features two such disguises. In the subplot, Harbert disguises himself as the servant Blunt to follow and help redeem his friend Sentloe. This action is paralleled in the main plot, where Challener masquerades as Doctor Julio and aids in his friend Vallen- ger's reclamation from prodigality. (The subplot parallel in *King Lear* is Edgar's disguised redemption of Gloucester; but like Kent's disclosure, Edgar's goes tragically awry.) Both the statement of repentance and the unmasking usually occur together in the last scene of each play, so that this dramatic convention gives symbolic emphasis to the idea of immoral conduct as an eclipse of one's real nature. Perhaps this is the 'made intent' that Kent and Edgar never explain. Whatever their intent, it is as out of place in 'this tough world' as Cordelia's silence was.

In the reversal of these plans, the *Lear* world asserts itself over the characters who populate it. Yet, paradoxically, it is the nature of those characters that contributes greatly to defining the outlines of this world and that reinforces its effect on us. At this point, we can conclude discussion of the characters' delineation by summarizing their role in that effect. First, as Bradley intimated, the characters' starkly antithetical nature confirms 'that feeling which haunts us in *King Lear*, as though we were witnessing something universal, – a conflict not so much of particular persons as of the powers of good and evil in the world' (pp. 262-3). Shakespeare takes a traditional kind of character presentation and exaggerates it in order to convey the vast universal associations of a play-world detached from mundane realities. His characters become titans, people whose natures are defined at awesome extremes. Wiped out are all of the softening mundane features of the source play – Ragan's remorse, Leir's feebleness, Cordella's flirtation. Regan and Goneril are literally wolves, while Cordelia is described in terms of the sacrificial Lamb. We feel that these characters are working out a universal allegory – as Kent himself seems to feel when he says, 'It is the stars,/ The stars above us, govern our conditions;/ Else one self mate and make could not beget/ Such different issues' (IV.iii.33-6).

Thus Shakespeare's character presentation enhances the effect of a primarily Jacobean trait, the creation of an isolated, extreme world. Yet we never think of Shakespeare's characters as mere vivified concepts, the abstract projections of a theoretical world, because the compelling nature of his characterization keeps us attached to the characters by emphasizing the basic human capacities for joy and for suffering that we share with them. Nor does the 'allegory' distance us, for it is one that we partake of just by living. *King Lear* is not a drama written to expound a particular doctrine; rather, the *Lear* world dramatizes that timeless and placeless confrontation of good and evil that involves every man in his journey through *this* world. To invert Goethe's line, '*Ein König Lear ist stets ein alter Mann*' (King Lear is always any old man, or young man for that matter).

Shakespeare's version of this tradition of characterization also enhances the strong scenes that *King Lear* has in common with other Jacobean plays, since every meeting of characters becomes an explosive confrontation of antitheses. Edgar's nobility pits itself against Edmund's baseness, Kent's true service against Oswald's false, the First Servant's pity against Cornwall's heartlessness. It is the nature of Shakespeare's characterization that perhaps contributes most to the 'pattern of pugnacity' that Maynard Mack finds running through the tragedy from beginning to end, creating the 'remarkably passionate collisions' of its strong scenes (p. 88).

Finally, the kind of characterization Shakespeare employs in *King Lear* coincides perfectly with one of the play's major themes. In presenting his characters in order to involve us continually with them and their struggles, he gives us opportunities to act out the compassion for which his play so frequently argues the need. We come to *feel* the necessity of the love that Lear rejects in I.i, a love that manifests itself when Kent offers Lear 'service/ Improper for a slave,' when the First Servant and the Old Man put themselves in jeopardy for the sake of a blinded old man, and when Cordelia and Edgar minister to their parents later in the play. Shakespeare makes it impossible to be a spectator who 'will not see/ Because he does not feel' (IV.i.68-9). He involves us totally in the appreciation of feeling above form that Edgar finally arrives at when he vows to 'Speak what we feel, not what we ought to say.'

II

Among the *données* of public-theatre dramaturgy, traditional features for which Shakespeare had to make allowance in the course of writing, stood the clown. Over twenty years of theatrical supply and demand had established his presence as nearly indispensable, and actors like Tarlton, Kempe, and Armin had demonstrated the role's extraordinary potential. The clown lacked the stature of a serious protagonist, yet he filled out the thinnest drama with familiar substance and the depth of a spirited personality, drawing audiences to him. In addition to dispensing verbal wit and buffoonery, he could – being ineffaceably both a character and 'the clown' at the same time – turn his position of detachment into a channel of rapport between play and audience. The clown could comment on the action, divulge its secrets to us, and so pull us into it.

Shakespeare had realized this potential long before he came to write *King Lear*, and had expanded the role into such memorable characters as Bottom, Falstaff, Jaques, Touchstone, and Feste. But the Fool in *King Lear* surpasses all his predecessors in that Shakespeare manages here to make the clown a vital component of a great tragedy, without either diminishing the play's seriousness or altering the clown's role out of recognition. To remove him from the play would in Bradley's eloquent image 'spoil its harmony, as the harmony of a picture would be spoiled if one of the colours were extracted' (p. 311). However, it will become evident that the Fool's special hue not only colours his own person, but also radiates outward to shine through most of the other characters as well, forming its own harmony within the larger one. For Shakespeare puts him at the centre of a Renaissance tradition, the *moriae encomium*, and this tradition figures largely in defining our response to the *Lear* world. Before its workings can be discussed, there is a need to define more specifically both the Fool's role in *King Lear* and the nature of the *moriae encomium* tradition.

Enid Welsford's description of the fool in Continental Renaissance drama also fits the position he held in English public-theatre drama:[17] 'He is a licensed critic of the action, a link between the stage and the auditorium. In this respect the rôle of the fool resembles that of the Greek chorus, but unfortunately the full possibilities of the part were never realized.'[18] *King Lear* realizes these possibilities and adapts them to fulfil unique dramatic requirements. Like the classical chorus, the Fool voices a commonplace wisdom that the hero rises above; and the Fool also stands outside the action, like the chorus, and comments on it without full involvement. Far from being mere aesthetic archaisms, however, these two aspects of the Fool's role satisfy particular needs in *King Lear*. His speeches, all variations on the theme of 'look out for Number One,' advocate a wisdom that is plain prudence. By understatement, their limited moral perspective throws into high relief the moral enormities of Lear's situation. The Fool taunts Lear for violating a code that is inadequate for the *Lear world*, so inadequate that we and Lear come to appreciate the worth of those much higher standards abandoned in Act I. His wisdom acts as a foil, then, an alternative itinerary by which we can gauge both the length and the necessity of Lear's spiritual journey.

His choric commentary performs a similarly pivotal function. In the scenes that follow upon the love-test, Shakespeare needs a source of objective criticism to underline the error of Lear's conduct and so bring him to some realization of its magnitude. An objective viewpoint cannot emerge from any of the active participants in the *Lear* world, because they are so completely polarized that a critical statement (such as Goneril's to Regan at the close of I.i) makes us look as much for the motive behind it as at its applicability to Lear, and because Lear himself would – as we well know – never brook such opposition. But the Fool is 'all-licens'd,' a touching crackbrain whose antic disposition is tolerated because he obviously lacks the wherewithal to mount a real threat. Lear clamours to be treated to the Fool's raillery, and we too can listen to it without having to search for malicious motives – or, indeed, without even having to relate the Fool's speeches to a human presence beneath them. As a result, our attention focuses on how those speeches relate to Lear, and we watch him suffer and change under the scrutiny of (with apologies to Shakespeare and Frye) a natural's perspective.

The same licence that allows Lear's Fool to speak with impunity also figured largely in the *moriae encomium* tradition. Folly could climb up to her platform and say the most outrageous things because her pronouncements were, after all, only the babblings of a fool. Erasmus and praisers of folly before and after him took great satiric advantage of this protective coloration. They also took advantage of a teasing ambiguity in the word 'fool.' As Enid Welsford observes, a fool could on the one hand be 'the actually worthless character that lurked beneath [a] veneer of wealth, learning, and respectability,' someone who 'was neglecting his true, ultimate [and therefore spiritual] self-interest, and what could be more ridiculous than that?' Alternatively, a fool was 'the "sage-fool" who could see and speak the truth,' a 'truth-teller whose real insight was thinly disguised as a form of insanity.'[19]

Both usages had already worked their way into Tudor drama. In the moral interlude called *Mundus et Infans* (1508), the Vice is called Folye, and is friend to the seven deadly sins and enemy to Conscience. Similarly, 'Moros' is the worldly hero of Wager's *The Longer Thou Livest the More Fool Thou Art* (1559), a play in which God's Judgment tells us:

> We do not only them fools call here
> Which have not the perfect use of reason,
> Innocents whereof be many far and near
> In whom discretion is geason [i.e., scanty],
> But those are the greatest fools properly
> Which disdain to learn sapience
> To speak, to do, to work all things orderly
> And as God hath given intelligence;
> But contrary to nature and God's will
> They stop their eyes through wilful ignorance.[20]

Conversely, wise fools appear in such later works as Greene's *Friar Bacon and Friar Bungay* (1589), Rowley's *When You See Me You Know Me* (1604), and of course Shakespeare's *As You Like It* and *Twelfth Night*. Especially note-worthy here is *James IV* (1590), where Greene incorporates the ambiguity itself by creating two fools: Slipper is a corrupted knave who betrays his equally nefarious master, while Nano is percipient and good-hearted.

In *King Lear* Shakespeare goes a step farther than Greene. Besides giving his wise fool an unprecedented part in the tragedy, he scatters the seeds of both kinds of folly through all his major characters. He associates folly with the villains, who are oblivious to their ultimate best interests, and also with charac-ters who are so virtuous that they neglect the call of prudence. He seems to subscribe to the logic, and dramatize the examples, of a work like Erasmus' *The Praise of Folly*.[21] Mainly through comparison with Erasmus' work, best-known of its kind, the rest of this chapter will follow the traces of a 'great stage of fools' who make up the carefully constructed *moriae encomium* that is em-bedded in *King Lear*. In referring to *The Praise of Folly*, I am no more attempt-ing to argue for direct influences from a 'source' than in referring to contem-porary Elizabethan plays. It will become clear that Shakespeare was in fact familiar with the tradition of *moriae encomium*, but the primary concern of this study is with his use of that tradition (along with more exclusively dra-matic traditions) to shape our response to the play.

Specifically, Shakespeare uses the tradition to support a process of character-ization involving intense moral oppositions; he creates a pattern of references to fools and folly that reinforces these oppositions. Involved in our experience of *King Lear* is an Erasmian anatomy of humanity, a distillation of mankind into those who are wise fools and those who are vicious fools. As we witness the characters of *King Lear* repeatedly referring to each other as fools or behaving in traditionally 'foolish' ways, we learn to distinguish between the two kinds of folly, and we come to appreciate the value and even the necessity of the more noble kind that Erasmus himself espoused. The *moriae encomium* tradition thus gives Shakespeare a method of intensifying the moral polarization that distinguishes character presentation in *King Lear*; and it also brings together the play's diverse characters and actions by catching them up in a single perspective that entails an ultimate moral judgment on life in the *Lear* world. Shakespeare makes us share in that judgment; for by the end of the play the sufferings of the wise fools have made us apprehend both the immediate futility of their conduct and its ultimate worth.

When Lear bends over Cordelia's body and cries, 'my poor fool is hang'd!' his terror sees truth. Cordelia has unmistakably played the fool, in the best Erasmian sense. 'For truly it hath euer best lyked me to speake streight what so euer laie on my tongues ende,'[22] says Folly, 'For in me (ye must thynke) is no place for settyng of colours, as I can not saie one thyng, and thynke an other: but on all sydes I dooe resemble my selfe' (p. 10). In the first scene, Regan and Goneril summon up all the colours of rhetoric to paint over their real feelings; but Cordelia imprudently says what is on her mind, lacking 'that glib and oily art/ To speak and purpose not.' She finds it impossible to say one thing and think another. Her plain speaking is the most conspicuous attribute of the more noble kind of fool, and it leads to disaster: 'Let pride, which she calls plainness, marry her,' responds Lear, looking for flattery rather than for her plain statement of the crucial commutual bond. The context of the love-test turns Cordelia's honesty to sheer folly, for 'nothing can be more foolisshe than wisedome out of place' (p. 38).

Her claim to value deeds over words ('what I well intend,/ I'll do 't before I speak') is verified by her self-sacrificing conduct later in the play, but it cannot possibly succeed here, 'so is mans mynde framed, as muche more it deliteth in thynges to the shew, than in suche as are in deede' (p. 63). In coming to her defence, Kent too emphasizes the difference between the 'hollowness' of flattery and the 'plainness' of true honour; but it is a distinction that Lear will be brought to recognize only through suffering. When she is dead in his arms, he will recall that her voice was 'ever soft,/ Gentle and low,' and will realize that this was 'an excellent thing.' Now, he rejects the 'low sounds' for which Kent tries to apologize.

Yet according to Folly, Cordelia's foolish championing of deed over word in face of such opposition places her in hallowed company: '*For who so semeth* (saieth [St Paul]) *to be wise amonges you, let him become a foole, to the ende he be wise in deede*' (p. 116). In fact, Shakespeare's later references to 'The holy water' in 'her heavenly eyes' (IV.iii.31) and her redemption of nature 'from the general curse' (IV.vi.207), as well as her own reference to the 'dear father' whose 'business ... I go about' (IV.iv.23-4), group Cordelia with those who '*are become fooles for Christes sake*' (p. 116). This kind of folly entailed renouncing earthly gains for spiritual values, thereby achieving a position of detachment from which one could out-frown false Fortune's frown. As Erasmus' Folly took no end of delight in pointing out, it was a foolishness much advocated by the New Testament, and involved patterning one's life after that of Christ, who himself, says Folly, 'became yet a maner foole.'[23] As Lear holds her dead body in his arms, Cordelia completes this pattern emblematically.

The other virtuous characters join Cordelia in her folly. Neither Kent nor Edgar nor the Fool comes as close to being an archetypal Christian fool as she does, but they all exhibit aspects of the virtuous fool's demeanor. Kent is a fool for sharing Cordelia's frankness: '*A foole speaketh like a foole* (id est) **plainely**. For what soeuer he hath in his thought, that sheweth he also in his countinaunce, and expresseth it in his talke' (p. 49). The predilection gets Kent into trouble twice. First, he rebukes his king for bowing to flattery, calling Lear a 'mad ... old man.' As he says later, he can 'deliver a plain message bluntly' (I.iv.35-6). Kent justifies his outbursts by arguing that when so much is at stake, 'To plainness honour's bound.' Lear does not see his conduct in the same light, and banishes him. Kent's lot resembles that of the enlightened man who returned to Plato's cave, in a story told by Folly: '*For wheras he like a man of wisedome and experience seemed to pitie their madnesse and great blindnesse in mistakyng so of thynges, thei on the other side did potte at him, and thrust him out of their companie, for a frantike foole*' (p. 123).

Kent's second misfortune comes as a result of his confrontation with Oswald in II.ii. He sees Oswald's nature for what it is and tells him so, earning Oswald's ridicule (as shown by Kent's 'Smoile you my speeches, as I were a Fool?') and Cornwall's displeasure; and then he compounds the offense by voicing dissatisfaction with Cornwall's physiognomy. Kent's justification might be lifted directly from Folly's self-portrait: 'Sir, 'tis my occupation to be plain,' he says, and gets thrust into the stocks. Cornwall speaks wiser than he knows when he derisively characterizes Kent as 'An honest mind and plain, [who] must speak truth.' He also repeatedly calls Kent a 'knave' (70, 102, 127), a term that Regan also applies to Kent at line 137, and that the Elizabethans often used interchangeably with 'fool.' Cornwall and Regan recognize his folly but are incapable of seeing its value.

Although the two virtues are related, it is Kent's fidelity rather than his frankness that reminds one of the Christian fool. He imprudently follows a great wheel as it runs downhill, selflessly serving Lear through the ravages of storm and madness. He refuses to smile as the wind sits, and therefore the Fool says 'Let me hire him too: here's my coxcomb' (I.iv.100), offering Kent the cap of a professional fool as a badge of office. The gesture gives us graphic proof of Kent's election to an office whose isolation and whose nobility we are coming to recognize. 'Sirrah, you were best take my coxcomb,' the Fool urges, 'for taking one's part that's out of favour,' and he calls Kent a Fool again at II.iv.87. But Kent perseveres, and we last see him preparing to follow his master even on that final journey into the unknown.

By the time the Fool sees a kindred spirit in Kent, we have already heard Edmund describe Edgar as a brother 'on whose foolish honesty/ My practices ride easy' (I.ii.188-9). The adjective applies to more than Edgar's honesty, which in itself would proclaim him a virtuous fool in a world where 'Robes and furr'd gowns hide all.' Since Erasmus repeatedly shows how folly and madness are two sides of the same coin, each a kind of the other, Edgar's protective disguise as poor Tom turns him into a physical emblem of folly; and when he

defends the disguise as a choice of madness over nothing ('Poor Turlygod! poor
Tom!/ That's something yet: Edgar I nothing am'), he echoes the Fool's choice
of folly over Lear's condition: 'I am better than thou art now; I am a Fool,
thou art nothing' (I.iv.201-2). Edgar even seems to take over one of the Fool's
customary rituals at the end of III.iv, when he delivers a prophecy (the Fool
had given one two scenes earlier):

> *Child Rowland to the dark tower came.*
> His word was still: *Fie, foh, and fum.*
> *I smell the blood of a British man.*

With chilling immediacy, Cornwall enters at once to fulfil it: 'I will have my
revenge ere I depart his house.'

Edgar and the Fool choose wisely, according to Erasmus' Folly: quoting
Cato, she remarks that '*It is most wysedome for a man, in place to countre-
faicte Folie*' (p. 105). Although Lear's folly is not counterfeited, his madness
also recognizes the wisdom of Edgar's, as he calls poor Tom a 'Noble philosopher' and vows to 'keep still with my philosopher' (III.iv.176-80). Yet when
Edgar is called upon to perform before his own blinded father, the wise fool
realizes that even this occupation has its hazards: 'Bad is the trade that must
play the fool to sorrow' (IV.i.38). In his 'mad' monologues, Edgar in fact
identifies himself with the sufferings of two other fools, Lear's Fool and Kent,
when he talks of being 'whipp'd' and 'stock-punish'd' (III.iv.137-8). Here and
at other places, we are encouraged as spectators to see the play's wise fools as a
group: Kent defends Cordelia's plainness with his own, and both are exiled; the
Fool pines away at Cordelia's banishment; Edgar and Cordelia have been
spurned by their parents; Kent and Edgar resort to disguises; and even as we
recognize their like nature, the consequences of their behaviour become increasingly tragic.

So, as Edgar proceeds from the foolery of the Dover Cliffs scene to the folly
of his delayed revelation to Gloucester, the torment that was earlier only a part
of his play becomes a spiritual reality: the foul fiend follows and vexes him
indeed. We come to perceive that Edgar's madness stands midway between the
Fool's harmless lunacy (harmless to himself, that is) and Lear's psychic tor-
ture – the two types of madness recognized by Folly:

> But ye must vnderstande, that there be two kyndes of madnesse. One is that rage, whiche
> the **Furies** of hell, beyng punisshers of the wicked, doe bringe with them ... whan those
> **Furies** do trouble, and vexe the giltie conscience of a man, with the pricke of dredefull
> furiousnesse. But there is an other kynde of madnesse, farre vnlike the former, whiche
> procedeth from me wholy, and most is to be embraced. As often as a certaine pleasant
> rauing, or errour of the mynde, deliuereth the herte of that man, whom it possesseth,
> from all wonted carefulnesse, and rendreth it dyuers waies, muche recreated with new
> delectacion. (p. 52)

Increasingly dark clouds engulf the *Lear* world, forcing Edgar from an assumed innocuous raving associated with 'deliverance' of heart to genuine spiritual turmoil.

This deepening of mood helps to account for the complete disappearance of the fourth and titular member of the play's wise group, the Fool. All we need do to dismiss Bradley's charge that the Fool's exit is due to Shakespeare's 'haste and carelessness' (p. 315), is to try picturing the Fool breathing the sombre air of Act V. He is totally out of place in a world where 'All's cheerless, dark, and deadly,' for his very presence symbolizes the hope that makes even bitter laughter possible. His presence would also be superfluous because, as we come to see, so many other characters have assumed the prerogatives of his role. The cold night turns them all to fools and madmen. Of these characters, the three just discussed are the ones who have assimilated nuances of this Fool's character as well as of his role. For Lear's Fool is a virtuous one. He may preach a doctrine of prudent self-service, but in practice he rejects 'court holy-water in a dry house' in favour of shivering on the heath with his master – a choice that is, from a worldly perspective, as foolish as Kent's loyalty or Cordelia's plainness. From a higher perspective, he too is a fool in show '*to the ende he be wise in deede*' (p. 116).

Both perspectives emerge from Shakespeare's play on the word 'knave' as applied to the Fool. Enid Welsford has found the same wordplay in Erasmus, and her observation that it stems from a common ambiguity in meaning can provide a key to its usage in *King Lear*: 'the words "fool" and "knave" were constantly coupled together, but not always in quite the same way; for sometimes they were treated as synonyms, sometimes emphasis was laid on the distinction between them' (pp. 236-7). 'Knave' could thus be used with affectionate approbation or with contempt. Lear speaks affectionately when he says, 'Poor Fool and knave, I have one part in my heart/ That's sorry yet for thee' (III.ii.72-3). In quite another frame of mind, Goneril distinguishes between the two terms: 'You, sir, more knave than fool, after your master,' she snaps at him (I.iv.324). The Fool makes the same distinction in his jingle, but places himself (correctly, we feel) on the other side of the dichotomy:

> That sir which serves and seeks for gain,
>   And follows but for form,
> Will pack when it begins to rain,
>   And leave thee in the storm.
> But I will tarry; the Fool will stay,
>   And let the wise man fly:
> The knave turns Fool that runs away;
>   The Fool no knave, perdy. (II.iv.78-85)

Juggling meanings with Erasmian dexterity, the last two lines make 'knave' the constant and 'Fool' the variable. As with the Fool's counterpart in *Twelfth Night*, a sentence (or a word) is but a chev'ril glove to a good wit.

The earlier part of the Fool's ditty, besides prophesying his loyalty and the storm, makes a traditional distinction between wise man and fool. This too works in handy-dandy fashion. From one angle – that of a Fool – a wise man is that cunning fellow who packs up and runs; from another, the Fool who stays behind displays true wisdom. Lear in his madness recognizes this wisdom when he addresses the Fool as 'sapient sir' (III.vi.22), and Kent perceives it too: 'This is not altogether Fool, my Lord' (I.iv.157). Another *topos* from the *moriae encomium* tradition crops up in the Fool's rejoinder to Kent's line, when he deliberately misinterprets 'not altogether' to mean 'not the only' rather than 'not entirely': 'No, faith, lords and great men will not let me,' he remarks, 'if I had a monopoly out, they would have part on't: and ladies too, they will not let me have all the fool to myself; they'll be snatching.' Erasmus' Folly had reached the same view: 'These are thynges as foolisshe as can be, to laugh wherat one Democritus suffiseth not ... This verie branche of Folie buildeth citees, foundeth states, headrulers, religions, counsaile motes, iudgementes' (p. 35). After surveying all the notable activities of mankind, she concluded that 'all this worlde is in maner of a temple most goodly (as I take it) vnto me' (p. 67).

I shall again take up the *topos* following this discussion of particular 'fools,' and shall consider its applicability to the whole *Lear* world; but I want now to complete this examination of the Fool by looking at his relationship with Lear, since that relationship embodies Shakespeare's most moving use of both the *moriae encomium* tradition and the stock theatrical figure of the clown.

Most of the Fool's traditional *topoi* and witticisms come in I.iv, and in fact that scene gives rise to a sustained *moriae encomium*. For half the scene, the Fool takes a central position and applies his wit in turn to Kent, Lear, and Goneril, bantering and calling attention to their folly in rhyme and in song. Lear bears the brunt of the Fool's ridicule. He tolerates much more stinging insubordination than that for which he disinherited Cordelia and banished Kent. One might account for this tolerance partly in terms of the Fool's 'licence,' as expounded for us by Folly:

> Now so it is in deede, trueth (for the most part) is hatefull to princes. And yet we see, that of fooles oftetymes, not only true tales, but euin open rebukes are with pleasure declared. That what woorde comyng out of a wise-mans mouthe were an hangyng mattier, the same yet spoken by a foole shall muche delight euin hym that is touched therwith. (p. 50)

However, Lear's communion with the Fool goes beyond the traditional indulgence. He strikes one of Goneril's gentlemen for chiding the Fool, and at the beginning of scene iv beckons for the Fool with a persistence that bespeaks great mental preoccupation with him. In fact, early in the scene he voices two demands: 'Dinner, ho! dinner! Where's my knave? my Fool? Go you and call my Fool hither' (45-6). The Fool seems to be as necessary to him as food; and since he calls for him three more times, we may assume that Lear's need for the

Fool is actually more pressing. Could this need spring from a tacit identification that Lear makes between the Fool and Cordelia? He would have several objective reasons for associating the two of them: both are plain speakers whose loyalty manifests itself in deed rather than word, both have held positions of intimacy and dependence towards Lear, and the pair were evidently in close sympathy with each other: 'Since my young Lady's going into France, Sir, the Fool hath much pined away' (I.iv.77-78), the Knight reveals.

Having exiled Cordelia, then, Lear tries to fill the gap in his heart ('I lov'd her most') with the Fool. He deliberately subjects himself to the Fool's lacerating taunts, and perhaps he welcomes them because they satisfy a deep and growing need to suffer for what he did to Cordelia:

> FOOL Thou canst tell why one's nose stands i' th' middle
> on's face?
> LEAR No.
> FOOL Why, to keep one's eyes of either side's nose, that
> what a man cannot smell out, he may spy into.
> LEAR I did her wrong. (I.v.19-24)

The *moriae encomium* of I.iv is thus a comparatively mild anticipation of the punishment that Lear embraces on the heath, and Shakespeare has skilfully incorporated the genre into the spiritual development of his hero. But the human relationship of Lear and the Fool, besides giving a generic tour de force deep emotional resonance, continues beyond I.iv. The bond becomes closer as the Fool awakens his master's charity on the heath ('In, boy; go first'), and the association of antic and daughter remains quiescent beneath Lear's consciousness until it surfaces in the anguished climax to both relationships: 'my poor fool is hang'd!'

As intimated earlier, the villains in Shakespeare's piece are fools in the sense that they neglect their ultimate welfare for ephemeral earthly gains – just how ephemeral, *King Lear* shows us. The lot of them may be seen as falling under the censure of God's Judgment in *The Longer Thou Livest*: 'They seek to slay, to prison, to poll, to pill/ Only for their own furtherance./ Of all fools indeed this is the worst kind' (lines 1881-3). Shakespeare groups them together and displays their collective nature by letting them turn variations on a practice described by Folly: 'The vnkyndest kynde of men liuyng, who beyng in deede the verie standerdbearers of my bande, woulde seeme yet afore folke to be so ashamed of my name, as not seldome they cast it in others teethe for a great reproche' (p. 10). Or, in words that she quotes from Ecclesiastes, *'a foole ... that walketh in the strete, beyng hym selfe vnwise, supposeth all men to be fooles as he'* (p. 109). The villains in *King Lear* have a penchant for labelling others as 'fools': Edmund calls Edgar foolish at I.ii.188; Cornwall calls Kent a knave repeatedly through II.ii, and Regan concurs at II.ii.137. But Goneril takes the prize. She calls Lear a fool at I.iii.20, and castigates his 'folly' again at II.iv.293; calls the Fool a knave at I.iv.323; and refers to Albany as a fool five times during IV.ii. Yet when her plans go awry, she herself can think only of the desperate folly of suicide.

In addition to wearing this common motley, each villain displays his own distinct kind of folly. Edmund sounds perhaps the strongest note during his manifesto at the start of I.ii: 'Why brand they us/ With base ... / Who in the lusty stealth of nature take/ More composition and fierce quality/ Than doth, within a dull, stale, tired bed,/ Go to th' creating a whole tribe of fops,/ Got 'tween asleep and wake?' he asks. He is echoing Folly. For Folly is herself a bastard, who also flaunts her shameful origins with pride. Her father Plutus, she boasts, was not 'at the tyme of my begettyng clogged with the heauie yoke of wedlocke ... but rather mixed in loue (as my Homere saieth) whiche I take to be a copulacion not a little more pleasant than the other is' (p. 12). Furthermore, she would have us understand 'that **Plutus** begatte me not in his olde daies, whan he was blynde, and skarce able to goe for age ... but in his prime yeres, whan as yet he was sounde, and full of hote bloudde' (p. 12). Edmund, then, is a 'natural' in two senses of the word, by virtue of both his bastardy and his kinship to a fool. It is understandable that he takes Nature as his goddess and binds his services to her law, because the traditional Folly recommends this course of action as a sure recipe for happiness: 'So are those men most happie, who ... folow **Nature** onely for theyr guide and maistres' (p. 46).

Edmund's soliloquy shows that he has taken lessons from Folly. Given this set of credentials, he sets off on the road from whoreson to near-king. 'Briefness and Fortune, work' (II.i.19), he commands, and they obey. His meteoric rise is only to be expected, for Folly tells us that '**Fortune** hir selfe, the guidresse of all worldly chaunces, is so muche bent on my syde, as euer for the moste part she is heauie maistresse, and contrarious to these wysemen, wheras to fooles on the other syde she dealeth hir giftes so largely, as if she crammed the same into theyr mouthes whiles they are slepyng' (p. 103). Her wheel turns and raises Edmund up, while Kent's fortune 'grow[s] out at heels' (II.ii.157) and Edgar finds himself the 'lowest and most dejected thing of Fortune' (IV.i.3).

Of course, Edmund does not owe his success to Fortune alone. He is also a self-made man, and works hard to put a carefully developed strategy into practice; his role as stage-managing 'servant' is not a passive one. Yet even his strategy has been borrowed from folly. More than any other character in *King Lear*, Edmund exemplifies in his career the self-seeking policies advanced by Shakespeare's own Fool, many of whose wryly spoken maxims reflect directly upon him. Edmund is one of those who 'serves and seeks for gain,/ And follows but for form' (II.iv.78-9), a counsel that the Fool 'would have none but knaves follow' (76). The knave who does follow it never repeats the generous errors that the Fool chides Lear for making, and Edmund always speaks less than he knows, lends less than he owns. In this way, the Fool's prudent counsellings are a central point of reference in the *Lear* world: the villainous fools follow his advice to the letter, while the wise fools (including the Fool himself) prove by their actions that they subscribe to a completely opposite moral code. Thus it comes as no surprise to spectators who recognize Edmund's folly for what it is that he winds up, in Goneril's words, 'cozen'd and beguil'd' (V.iii.154), finally fooled by Edgar.

Edmund's two paramours are also villainous fools, but they manifest their folly in a different way. Instead of feigning service to others, they rise to the top through flattery and pretended affection. Their conduct during Lear's love-test interlude is recommended by Folly, who says that 'to dissemble ... is the right plaiying of the pageantes of this life' (p. 39). Like the maxims of Shakespeare's Fool, Folly's disquisition frequently and ironically points out the merits of flattery, and the success of those who 'ar *double tounged*, as the aforesaied **Euripides** telleth vs, with the one of whiche they speake the trueth, with the other, thynges mete for the tyme and audience. Theyr propretee it is to chaunge blacke into white, and out of one mouthe to blow bothe hote and colde: and thynke vnhappeliest in their hertes, whan they speake smotheliest with their tounges' (pp. 49-50). Regan and Goneril have that glib and oily art that Cordelia lacks, and so majesty falls to folly. Lear should have listened not to the advice of Folly, but to that of Ecclesiastes (another voice that reverberates throughout *King Lear*): '*It is* better to hear the rebuke of the wise, than for a man to hear the song of fools' (7:5).

These fools' henchman, Oswald, displays yet another, similar kind of folly. Erasmus devotes an entire section in *The Praise of Folly* to courtiers like Oswald, calling them 'fawnyng' and 'seruile,' and observing that 'theyr faces lyke visers will blusshe at nothyng: and finally that in bourdyng, and in flyryng, thei can flatter pleasauntly' (94). This sounds like Kent's denunciation of Oswald as one of the smiling rogues who

> smooth every passion
> That in the natures of their lords rebel;
> Being oil to fire, snow to their colder moods;
> Renege, affirm, and turn their halcyon beaks
> With every gale and vary of their masters,
> Knowing nought, like dogs, but following. (II.ii.76-81)

Edgar agrees, calling Oswald 'a serviceable villain;/ As duteous to the vices of thy mistress/ As badness would desire' (IV.vi.254-6). Such courtiers, says Folly, care more about clothing their bodies than their minds, garnishing themselves 'with golde, with gemmes, with silkes' (p. 94); again, Kent calls Oswald a 'glass-gazing' barber-monger, a knave made by a tailor (II.ii.16-55). (Like Edgar Kent also seems to have assumed the natural fool's gift for prophecy, since he refers to Oswald as 'one that wouldst be a bawd in way of good service,' II.ii.18-19.) As this minor satellite gains ascendancy during *King Lear*, we can imagine him going through the reverse of Lear's purgation, putting on rich clothes and jewellery as Lear removes them.

If none of these indictments has convinced us that Oswald is one of the villainous fools, Shakespeare brings the message home through several ironic theatrical juxtapositions. Near the beginning of I.iv – that miniature *moriae encomium* – Lear gives the order to 'call my Fool hither' (46). Immediately after his command comes the stage direction, '*Enter* OSWALD.' This fool babbles three words and exits, and several lines later Lear commands an attendant once more to 'call hither my Fool.' Oswald re-enters, dutifully on cue, to go through a series of slapstick knockabouts with Kent. After Oswald has been slapped and tripped, Kent asks him, 'have you wisdom?' In reply Oswald exits. By the end of the scene even Goneril seems to have caught on to her servant's real identity, as her words indicate:

> GON.   ... What, Oswald, ho!
> [*To the Fool.*]   You, sir, more knave than fool. (323-4)

As with the moral dichotomy discussed in the first section of this chapter, there are three characters here who do not consistently display either virtuous or villainous folly. Rather, they shift from one side to the other. Lear and Gloucester are transformed from reprehensible fools to wise fools, and Albany emerges from limbo to claim his place as a wise fool. Shakespeare begins the play by showing that Folly's cap sits on the greatest of them, King Lear. Almost the first words from Lear's mouth reveal his folly: ''tis our fast intent/ To shake all cares and business from our age,/ Conferring them on younger strengths' (I.i.38-40). Folly numbers among her band those princes, 'whiche through my procurement, remittyng all care and charge hereof to the goddes, dooe for the most parte onely tende theyr owne pleasure' (p. 93), and she speaks of 'my good dotardes ... [who] rest vacant and discharged of all suche cares and anxieties, wherwith wisemen of fressher sprites are wrongen continually' (p. 18). Lear then compounds the foolishness by rewarding flatterers and rejecting wise counsellors; he 'falls to folly' (149), as Kent observes in words emphasizing that this is a departure from Lear's previous disposition. Thus, princes become 'right miserable,' warns Folly, because they 'are faine ... to take flattrers for their friendes' (p. 50). Sure enough, Lear is soon striking his head in anguish: 'O Lear, Lear, Lear!/ Beat at this gate, that let thy folly in' (I.iv.279-80).

The Fool prompts Lear's recognition of his enormous folly. He calls Lear a fool many times (I.iv.113-15, 148-54, 184-5; I.v.39), as well as harping constantly on the folly of what Lear has done. It is having to face this recognition, as well as the conduct of Regan and Goneril, that drives Lear into the analogous condition of madness. 'O Fool! I shall go mad,' he cries (II.iv.288), connecting the two states much as he had done earlier:

> FOOL If thou wert my Fool, Nuncle, I'd have thee beaten
> for being old before thy time.
> LEAR How's that?
> FOOL Thou should'st not have been old till thou hadst
> been wise.
> LEAR O! let me not be mad, not mad, sweet heaven;
> Keep me in temper; I would not be mad! (I.v.42-8)

Unlike the Fool's madness, Lear's belongs to the type described by Folly as 'whan those **Furies** do trouble, and vexe the giltie conscience of a man, with the pricke of dredefull furiousnesse' (p. 52). In this state, Edgar replaces the Fool as Lear's tutor, since the foul fiend also vexes poor Tom.

Through madness Lear makes the transition from erring fool to virtuous fool, discovering '**Charitee**, whose poinct perseth into the inwarde partes of mans hert' (p. 113). He exhibits his election to the ranks of the virtuous fools by tearing off his clothes, like Tom, thus imitating what the first Christian fool told his apostles to do as a means of setting their minds on charity: 'that they not onely shoulde set no store by shoes, nor by vitailyng bagges, but should cast awaie theyr cotes also' (pp. 112-13). Lear experiences the night that pities neither fools nor wise men, and finally recognizes that he is 'even/ The natural fool of Fortune' (IV.vi.192-3). Sanity and an awareness of his errors come to Lear together when, in the reunion scene, he tells Cordelia 'I am a very foolish fond old man' (IV.vii.60) and bids her 'Pray you now, forget and forgive: I am old and foolish' (84). He has joined Cordelia in spirit as well as in physical presence, and his repetition of 'foolish' here emphasizes his election to her noble group.

Lear's awakening also reminds one of the reformed morality hero's moment of regeneration – as in *Mundus et Infans*, when Perseverance comes to Manhood (now Age) and gives him a new name, Repentance. Lear's experience is the opposite of the damned Moros' reaction in *The Longer Thou Livest*, although it is expressed in remarkably similar terms. Moros says (lines 1823-6):

> Am I asleep, in a dream, or in a trance?
> Ever methink that I should be waking.
> Body of God! this is a wonderful chance;
> I cannot stand on my feet for quaking. [*Fall down.*]

Lear *awakens*, appropriately, and asks:

> Where have I been? Where am I? Fair daylight?
> I am mightily abus'd. I should e'en die with pity
> To see another thus. I know not what to say.
> I will not swear these are my hands: let's see;
> I feel this pin prick. Would I were assur'd
> Of my condition! (IV.vii.52-7)

His is the folly of the redeemed fool rather than of Moros and his descendants in the *Lear* world.

Gloucester begins his career in Moros' kind of folly, and soon commits himself to it even more deeply. In the first scene, Lear and Gloucester are depicted to resemble those two strong champions of Folly that war against reason: '**Anger**, raignyng in the fortresse of the hert: and **concupiscence**, whiche euin to the lowest part of the bealy, dooeth occupie a large possession' (p. 23). Gloucester boasts of the 'good sport' that brought Edmund into the world, and in scene ii he adds superstition to lechery by heeding a prognostication based on 'late eclipses.' Folly says that among her votaries are two astrologically minded groups of people: first, there are those men 'that take vpon theim by lokyng on the sterres, and planetes, to tell vs aforehand, what shall happen ... Declaryng by theyr **Prognosticacions**, the successe of certeine wonderous accidentes' (pp. 77-8); and then there are 'men, who of theyre singular grosnesse geue credence also to this their so plaine illusion' (p. 78). 'This is the excellent foppery of the world,' remarks Edmund of his father's superstition, perhaps placing Gloucester in the ranks of those who are 'fools by heavenly compulsion.' In this same scene, Gloucester places himself with the wicked fools by heeding Edmund's combination of calumny and subserviency, and on the flimsiest evidence branding his innocent son a 'villain' (he shouts the epithet five times in as many lines).

His folly rages longer than Lear's. Even on the heath, he is still convinced of Edgar's guilt: 'I had a son,/ Now outlaw'd from my blood; he sought my life' (III.iv.170-1). As a result, says Gloucester, his own condition resembles Lear's: 'I am almost mad myself' (170). Folly would remove the 'almost' from Gloucester's speech, and would diagnose that he has been mad for some time, certainly since before 'The grief hath crazed [his] wits' (174). For, she says, 'he that not onely erreth in his senses, but is deceiued also in iudgement of the mynde, and that extraordinarely, and of custome, he (I saie) maie well be holden madde, and out of his right mynde' (p. 53). Folly notes that this widespread madness is 'peculier to me' (p. 53), and that it is therefore a kind of folly. But unlike Lear's folly-madness, Gloucester's does not disillusion him or put him on the road to charity. It takes the terrible physical torment of the blinding to bring him to his senses. Then, awareness of his error comes in a flash, along with the impulse towards charity: 'O my *follies*! Then Edgar was abus'd./ Kind Gods, forgive me that, and prosper him' (III.vii.90-1, italics mine). Soon, he is echoing Lear in urging that 'distribution should undo excess,/ And each man have enough' (IV.i.70-1) – the rallying cry of an altogether different kind of folly.

Slowest to wake up to the nature of his own wife, Albany is appropriately the last character to be touched by Folly's bauble. But like Lear and Gloucester, he acquires the title of 'virtuous fool' at the instant that he makes a definite commitment to goodness. When Oswald informs Goneril of her husband's 'chang'd' attitude (IV.ii.3), she responds by telling Edmund that 'My Fool usurps my body' (28). Faced with Albany's denunciation of her cruelty, she sneers 'No more; the text is foolish' (37). Albany's rejoinder singles out the two types of conduct that characterize all the virtuous fools in the *Lear* world, and indicates why that world rejects their conduct as folly: 'Wisdom and goodness to the vile seem vile.' In a land of lunatics, sanity is madness. Only Fools pity those villains 'who are punish'd/ Ere they have done their mischief' (54-5), says Goneril, her topsy-turvy morality proclaiming the novel judicial theory that the punishment should precede the crime. She then gives Albany an unintended compliment on his new identity, dubbing him a 'moral fool' (58), and at the same time she anticipates the worldly failure of his mission by calling him a 'vain fool' (61). Her anticipation proves correct. Just when he is pronouncing a comfortable benediction over the play's final moments ('All friends shall taste/ The wages of their virtue, and all foes/ The cup of their deservings'), Lear's death pulls him back into the world of tragedy: 'Our present business/ Is general woe.' Or, as Lear had said earlier, 'we cry that we are come/ To this great stage of fools' (IV.vi.184-5).

Shakespeare has indeed presented us with a great stage of fools in *King Lear*. His *moriae encomium* complements the play's affinity to a tradition of morally polarized characters, and reinforces its effect by defining that opposition from another perspective. Shakespeare has thus taken another feature of contemporary drama, the clown, and made him the centre of his version of a Renaissance literary tradition; and he has shaped his *encomium* to underline the characterization that emerges through more inherently dramatic means. Moreover, this *encomium* may be seen to unfold along the lines of the character-centred Marlovian structure mentioned in Chapter 2: just as Lear proceeds from knavish fool to mad fool, so the play's references to folly are coupled with allusions to knavery in the early acts (see I.iv and II.ii especially), and to madness later on (III.iv, III.vi, IV.vii). Lear stands at centre stage in Shakespeare's pageant of fools,[24] which illuminates the tragic figure of this foolish king through an arrangement of reflecting mirrors. Thus, Shakespeare literalizes and dramatizes the intimations of mortal folly that all great tragedy summons up in us.

In doing so, he breaks out of the controlling vision of the *moriae encomium*, for Erasmus' and similar satires are based on the premise that '*diyng to this worlde is the beginnyng of a better life, wheras this here, is but a maner death as it were*' (p. 38). Shakespeare leaves us with no such comforting assurance, and so he checks Folly's ultimately unperturbed laughter; as Folly herself says, her pageant 'is dooen vnder a certaine veile or shadow, whiche taken awaie ones, the plaie can no more be plaied' (p. 38). For similar reasons, the conduct of someone like Oswald can be censured repeatedly as 'folly' in the play, but that of Regan and Goneril is less frequently assailed from this perspective; what they are and what they do belongs largely outside the scope of the *moriae encomium*'s ultimately gentle philosophical consolation.

The last act of *King Lear* takes away the 'veile'; or, to use its own language, it introduces us to the quality of nothing – a realm from which Shakespeare very properly excludes the Fool. Nothingness has lurked in the shadows of the *Lear* world right from the beginning, in the ironic, unintentional prophecies of Lear that 'Nothing will come of nothing' (nothing *does* finally issue from Cordelia's reply), and of Gloucester that 'if it be nothing, I shall not need spectacles.' Edgar and the Fool seemed to recognize the power of nothing, and they chose folly and madness instead (I.iv.201-2; II.iii.20-1). But in Act V, the *Lear* world wears out to nothing, and changes everything; Edgar's earlier words to Gloucester may be applied ironically to his experience and to ours: 'In nothing am I chang'd' (IV.vi.9). Chapter 5 will attempt to explore the nature of this change, the act that follows Shakespeare's play of fools.

5

The Rack of This Tough World

The last scene of *King Lear* has a long history of inspiring Kent's reaction in its audiences: 'Is this the promis'd end?' Spectators have felt shocked by the deaths of Lear and Cordelia, and outraged that neither finds the happiness – or even the survival – that both so undeniably deserve. It was this reaction that made two centuries of audiences and critics grateful to Nahum Tate. Bradley voiced their objection to Shakespeare's ending when he wrote that 'this catastrophe, unlike those of all the other mature tragedies, does not seem at all inevitable. It is not even satisfactorily motived. In fact it seems expressly designed to fall suddenly like a bolt from a sky cleared by the vanished storm' (pp. 252-3). This chapter will study the ending of *King Lear* with an eye to discovering how it is indeed 'expressly designed' to shock and overwhelm us. First, the discussion will pay attention to points of convergence between *King Lear* and the conventions of the Elizabethan theatre, to see how Shakespeare uses his dramatic heritage to help define our experience in another area of the *Lear* world. I shall look first at those features of the play which feed our expectation of a more congenial denouement, and then at the strong signs of total disaster which converge upon us at the same time. In isolating these two aspects for discussion, however, it must be remembered that Shakespeare unites them in our experience of the play, so that they interact to keep us suspended between hope and despair. Finally, I shall discuss the kinds of assistance that Shakespeare gives us when he forces us to come to grips with the import of this most powerfully devised ending, so provocative to our sense of theatre and our sense of life. At that point the discussion will, like *King Lear* itself, leave the traditions behind as we explore more solitary regions of the *Lear* world.

Mrs Lennox long ago called attention to the aspect of *King Lear* which, in the minds of most spectators, augurs a less brutal conclusion. Deploring Cordelia's death by hanging, she termed it 'a very improper Catastrophe for a Person of such exemplary Virtue.'[1] Cordelia's virtue, along with the regeneration of Lear, makes us expect something better. Cordelia has proved as good as her word, and through his sufferings Lear has won an enlightened soul and the sympathy of his audience. To be sure, we always hope against hope that any tragic hero will survive; but unlike Hamlet, Othello, or Macbeth, these two characters have no unpaid debts to settle. Shakespeare has tested their mettle through agonizing trials, shown us how worthy they are, and brought us to the point where we bring no sense of futility to our anticipation of their prosperity. Then, he denies them the rewards that he has made us consider their due.

But the spectacle of unrewarded virtue – perhaps residing as much in Mrs Lennox's standards of propriety and our standards of justice, as in Shakespeare's play – is not the only reason for our outrage. Just before the catastrophe, as Bradley perceived, we are given reason to believe that the worst of the storm may be over. Several incidents in the last two acts have nurtured this faint but discernible hope, which we feel even after Edmund has sent the Captain on his grim errand. First, there was Gloucester's 'miracle' at Dover. Edgar saved his father's life, and since so many other subplot incidents in *King Lear* have prefigured those in the main plot, we can conceive of Cordelia completing the design by rescuing Lear. Her reclamation of him from madness encourages us to think so. Early field reports from the battle in Act V give equal cause for hope: the two forces appear to be well matched, and neither side anticipates Lear's defeat. After the battle, our hopes are still encouraged. 'Come, let's away to prison,' Lear says, and conjures up a vision of peace and contentment during their future confinement. He seems to have fulfilled a pattern as old as human myth – that of separation, wandering, and final reunion. Besides playing so large a role in Greek and biblical legend, the pattern had worked its way into the religious drama of the Middle Ages and the early Renaissance, as well as the dramatic romances of the Elizabethan stage.[2] Since *King Lear* has incorporated innumerable other motifs from earlier literature, it would be fitting for the play to end with the complete fulfilment of this venerable one.

We can still hope during the interminable moments that follow, as the duel between Edmund and Edgar takes place. Edmund's suppressed confession ('This speech of yours hath mov'd me,/ And shall perchance do good; but speak you on') tantalizes us with the faint possibility of rescue, a possibility that seems to shatter at once when a Gentleman enters with a bloody knife:

> GENT. Help, help! O, help!
> EDG.   What kind of help?
> ALB.   Speak, man.
> EDG. What means this bloody knife?
> GENT.   'Tis hot, it smokes;
> It came even from the heart of – O! she's dead.
> ALB. Who dead? speak, man.

'Cordelia' leaps to our minds, since a 'sword' (V.iii.33) had been dispatched to kill her, and Shakespeare puts us on the rack by delaying the revelation that the knife came rather from the heart of Goneril – a judgment that touches us not with pity but with renewed expectation. After the false alarm, the sight of his

mistresses' bodies causes Edmund to tell all, and our hopes quicken when the
Officer is sent out to stop the murders. Even after Lear enters with Cordelia's
body in his arms, there is still that brief flutter that catches our breath: 'This
feather stirs; she lives!' But the moment turns out to be breathless indeed, and
all goes dark forever.

Not just these flickerings of the candle throughout Act V, however, but the
very shape of the play as it has evolved before then, encourages our wary
expectations. Lear's sufferings have not been at the centre of our attention for
some time. Unlike the heroes of Shakespeare's other tragedies, he suffers greatly during the first two-thirds of the play, and unlike them he *learns* from his
agonies. Throughout *King Lear*, in fact, suffering has been presented as something to be learned from, as opposed to its purely catastrophic function in the
other tragedies. Lear's torments on the heath teach him to 'Expose thyself to
feel what wretches feel,/ That thou mayst shake the superflux to them'
(III.iv.34-5), and Gloucester's blindness transforms him from one 'that will not
see/ Because he does not feel' (IV.i.68-9) to a more charitable and noble being.
In this respect *King Lear* resembles Shakespeare's last plays more than it does
Hamlet, Othello, or *Macbeth.* The heroes of those last plays, especially Leontes
and Prospero, are subjected to ordeals that begin well before each play is half
over, as if they (like Lear) were being put on trial. The punishments they suffer
bring about a transformation of spirit within each hero, and at journeys' end
seemingly irretrievable losses are restored to them. In *King Lear* Shakespeare
has departed from his normal tragic construction to place Lear on this path,
and the play's treatment of suffering points us to something closer to the last
plays' happy endings than to the terrible conclusion that awaits us here.

As in the last plays, too, the impetus seems to have passed to a new, more
innocent generation. We mentioned above that, as we come to V.iii, Lear's
sufferings have not been at the centre of our attention for some time. What has
replaced them is the emergence of Edgar. In fact, the 1608 Quarto telescopes
the play's movement in its title: 'True Chronicle Historie of the life and death
of King LEAR and his three Daughters. *With the vnfortunate life of* Edgar,
sonne and heire to the Earle of Gloster, and his sullen and assumed humor of
TOM of Bedlam.' Edgar claims our attention by taking over both the Fool's
role as sympathetic choral interpreter and Edmund's as chief stage manager,
and as the play progresses we see more and more of its events through his eyes.
He witnesses and approximates Lear's madness on the heath, and deals with
Gloucester's blind despair on Dover Cliffs. Edgar is the only one of the three
noble sufferers who establishes a direct relationship with the audience through
soliloquies and asides, and he faithfully tries to reckon with the play's actions
and help us to comprehend the *Lear* world.

Moreover, Edgar demands a central position in *King Lear* through his own
actions as well as through our relationship with him. In Act II he had set out as
nothing but a poor, bare, forked animal, but by stages he progresses from
madman to rustic ('Methinks you're better spoken' says Gloucester at IV.vi.10)
to knight in armour ('thy outside looks so fair' [V.iii.142], observes Edmund)

to Lear's successor as king. Edgar is most emphatically not a tragic figure: he answers the Gentleman's confused cries for help with a pragmatic 'What kind of help?' (V.iii.222), and constantly tries to put the best light on every setback. His journey reverses Lear's tragic fall, and directs our attention away from it. Anticipating *The Winter's Tale*, then, *King Lear* seems to some degree to have taken us from the catastrophic saga of one generation to the more successful, auspicious story of the next. But suddenly in the last scene, Lear's tragedy ('Great thing of us forgot!') thrusts itself forward to monopolize our thoughts, obliterating first Edgar's triumph and then Albany's restoration of order.[3] Edgar does have the last word (although even this achievement depends on which version of the play we accept), but he speaks as no more than a stunned spectator.

In Bradley's words, 'It is Shakespeare's wish to deliver a sudden and crushing blow to the hopes which he has excited' (p. 253n). For Shakespeare's original audience, these hopes would have been excited not only by incidents in the play, but by the story's heritage as well. Every previous version of the popular Lear story had ended happily. At the end of *The History of King Leir*, Leir was restored to the throne. There was not a single casualty on either side in the last-scene battle, and Cordella lived happily ever after with her husband Mumford (i.e., France). Holinshed depicted Leir regaining his kingdom, and Cordeilla reigning as Queen after her father's death two years later. As in *The Faerie Queene*, Holinshed's heroine is said to have hanged herself only long after the throne had been regained from her evil sisters. Nothing in Shakespeare's sources, therefore, gave reason to anticipate the tragic ending of his play.

Yet despite the straws that Shakespeare gives us to cling to, the tragic end of *King Lear* has been promised us. Those apocalyptic forecasts in the first act, following hard upon Lear's breaking of the bond, prophesied a chain of ineluctable catastrophes. Everything they predicted has so far come true, and they envisioned a tragedy that is unmitigated. As if in compliance with these omens, the Fool has taken leave of the *Lear* world. His sudden disappearance portends as much sorrow for *King Lear* as the sudden appearance of Autolycus portends joy for *The Winter's Tale*: the Fool has taken the possibility of laughter with him. Shakespeare has also prepared us for the play's final, pitiful tableau by associating Cordelia with Christ: the mortal result of 'my father's business' was the best known fact of Renaissance spiritual life. In the play's action, too, several irreversible turns have taken place before the last act. Cornwall and the First Servant have been killed during the blinding of Gloucester, and Edgar's ministrations can never restore Gloucester's eyes. Such irreparable disasters to major characters, and such profound suffering, violate the spirit of tragicomedy and belong only to the genre of tragedy.

It is during those moments following Edmund's command to the Captain, however, that we are made to realize that no other end is possible. No matter how strongly we feel that enough suffering has occurred, every other action closes another door on our hopes. The scene is superbly constructed to keep us on the rack of the *Lear* world. At first, the stage action seems excruciatingly periph-eral to the fate of Lear and Cordelia. The love triangle of Edmund, Regan, and Goneril issues in heated conflict. 'That's but a trifle here,' we feel as our suspense mounts and we grow increasingly uneasy about the destiny of those characters who are closest to us. Then comes the duel and the mortal wounding of Edmund, another irreversible turn. When Edgar reveals that Gloucester is dead, it becomes only too evident how the main action can complete the structural pattern by echoing the subplot. The deaths of Regan and Goneril and Edmund are announced, and each report breaks upon us with the force of Sophocles' messenger in *Oedipus Rex*. When Kent is finally denied the meagre pleasure of communicating his faithfulness to Lear, we must view the *Lear* world as one calling for the deaths of Lear and Cordelia. They too are de-stroyed by a final assertion of this hostile environment. Bradley has described the effect with great sensitivity:

> This sudden blow out of the darkness, which seems so far from inevitable, and which strikes down our reviving hopes for the victims of so much cruelty, seems now only what we might have expected in a world so wild and monstrous. It is as if Shakespeare said to us: 'Did you think weakness and innocence have any chance here? Were you beginning to dream that? I will show you it is not so.' (p. 271)

This tragic assertion of the play's world has also been forecast by a series of similar assertions during the last two acts. There, Shakespeare creates an em-blematic pattern that conveys the perversity of the *Lear* world − a place where intentions are unremittingly thwarted. A series of incidents, all involving Edgar, counterpoints abstract statements with theatrical tableaux that negate rather than fulfil the statements. In each case, the emblem contradicts its motto; the *Lear* world ironically crushes every one of his hopes as soon as he voices them. At the start of Act IV, for instance, Edgar accepts his poor lot: he has experi-enced the worst possible buffetings, he says, and owes nothing to Fortune. Immediately Gloucester enters, blinded and bleeding. Edgar cries out appropri-ately, 'World, world, O world!' and learns from the wretched tableau that 'the worst is not/ So long as we can say "This is the worst." ' Then, after he saves Gloucester from suicide in scene vi, he gives his father this stoical advice: 'Bear free and patient thoughts.' Mad Lear enters at once, decked in wild flowers, and the apparition forces Edgar to betray his own injunction: 'O thou side-piercing sight!' When Lear has finished his pitiful spectacle, Edgar volunteers to lead his father to shelter. 'Hearty thanks,' Gloucester replies, 'The bounty and the benison of Heaven/ To boot, and boot!' Oswald enters immediately and, with sword drawn, follows up Gloucester's wish for 'bounty' with an ironic counterpoint: 'A proclaim'd prize! Most happy!' Finally, during the battle in Act V, Edgar leaves Gloucester with these words: 'If ever I return to you again,/ I'll bring you comfort.' He returns almost at once, a picture of appre-hension: 'Away, old man! give me thy hand: away!/ King Lear hath lost, he and his daughter ta'en.' Edgar is being schooled in the *Lear* world. His hopes are crushed as ours will be in the last scene, during *our* education.

Behind Edgar's kind of education, this pitting of an emblem against its motto, stands a dramatic convention. Many Jacobean plays feature scenes that abrasively counterpoint philosophical positions with a conflicting dramatic world, though not in such a thoroughly emblematic manner. Marston's *The Dutch Courtesan* (1604) is structured in this way, as is part of Barry's *Ram-Alley* (1608): Boucher, like Malheureux in *The Dutch Courtesan*, meets passion with speeches of extreme puritan confidence and strictness which are defeated by a probative situation. When the coquettish widow Taffeta makes advances to him, he proudly affirms: 'I yet am free and reason keepes her seate,/ Aboue all fond affections yet is she fayre.'[4] 'Yet' – like Malheureux, he is only passionate man in his slight play, and in this scene he turns to putty in the widow's able hands. The tragedies of Chapman and Marston execute more serious variations on the technique, achieving a forceful effect by similar counterpointing to exploit the gap between philosophy and the play's reality. Senecan stoicism is so tested in Act II of *Antonio's Revenge* (1600), for instance, when Antonio enters dressed in black and reading Seneca's *De Providentia*. He reads out a Latin excerpt, and then dismisses the tranquil counsel with a single line: 'Pish, thy mother was not lately widowed.'[5] But no other playwright realizes the technique's formidable thematic implications as fully as Shakespeare does. In *King Lear*, the series of contradicted emblems becomes itself emblematic of the play's relentlessly hostile world.

Shakespeare also contributes to our sense of the *Lear* world as ineluctably tragic by overturning a less sophisticated convention. This convention, sustained by the popular teleological view of history, postulated a harmonious relationship between the struggles of virtuous characters and the workings of a divine order: the triumph of the good and the punishment of the bad in each play were thus presaged and accompanied by invocations that showed such events to be of divine origin. When Caradoc sees the body of a traitor in *The Valiant Welshman* (1612), for instance, he proclaims immediately that the event manifests 'heauens justice.'[6] Similarly, in *A Warning for Fair Women* (1599), the mortally wounded John Beane lives on long enough to point an accusatory finger at his assassin, causing his fellow characters to marvel at the 'wondrous worke of God,' and to cite other instances of the strange ways in which heaven maintains justice.[7] As sophisticated a playwright as Ben Jonson turns to the convention in *Volpone* (1606): his chaste heroine, appropriately named Celia, cries out for help from 'iust God' (III.vii.266) when Volpone tries to rape her, and in response Bonario (another ticket name) enters and saves her just when Volpone starts to say that she calls on God in vain. Later, ''Fore god, my left legge 'gan to haue the crampe;/ And I apprehended, straight, some power had strooke me/ With a dead palsey' (V.i.5-7), notes Volpone as, unknown to him, Mosca's web begins to tighten around him. When justice finally does catch up with him ('How ready is heau'n to those, that pray!' observes Celia at V.xii.5, echoed by Bonario at line 98: 'Heauen could not, long, let such grosse crimes be hid'), Volpone finds his premonition confirmed in the judge's sentence: 'Thou art to lie in prison, crampt with irons,/ Till thou bee'st sicke, and lame indeed' (V.xii.123-4).

King Lear seems designed to illustrate Volpone's truncated comment that God is invoked in vain, for whenever characters in the *Lear* world call for divine intervention, they meet with either silence or hostility. We have already seen how Gloucester's wish for 'The bounty and the benison of heaven' ushers in Oswald, with sword in hand. Earlier, Gloucester had proclaimed, 'I shall see/ The winged vengeance overtake such children' (III.vii.64-5), but Cornwall accurately responded, 'See 't shalt thou never.' Other characters encounter similar misfortunes. Lear goes raging mad shortly after he implores the Heavens for patience (II.iv.273), and his petition that 'the great Gods' should 'Find out their enemies now' (III.ii.49-51) comes crashing back on the heads of Lear and his noble followers. 'The Gods defend her!' Albany prays, a split second before Cordelia's limp body is carried in by her desolate father. A prayer from Kent seems twice to be the kiss of death: for Cordelia, he bids that 'The Gods to their dear shelter take thee, maid' (I.i.182), and is finally answered with crushing literalism; to Gloucester, he wishes that 'The Gods reward your kindness' (III.vi.5), and Gloucester's eyes are gouged out in the next scene. 'By the kind Gods, 'tis most ignobly done' (III.vii.35), says Gloucester with unconscious ambiguity. For awhile, it looks indeed as if the gods are standing up for bastards, as if they too are being stage-managed by Edmund. But the truth is even worse. When Edmund and his comrades in evil also find themselves thrown from Fortune's wheel, we are faced with a world for which the gods do not even care enough to 'kill us for their sport' (IV.i.37). If the gods invoked by these characters do exist, they move about in complete indifference to the *Lear* world. Shakespeare has broken the Elizabethan dramatists' teleological link between the play's world and a beneficent divine order, and in doing so he has set the *Lear* world terrifyingly adrift. Thunder and lightning threaten the wrongdoers in *The History of King Leir*, and virtuous characters walk under a mantle of supernatural protection, but not in Shakespeare's version. By the time we reach the reversals and casual slaughters of Act V, we have been conditioned for them by a chronicle of divine indifference. Kent's early words to Lear have tapped a major fault line running through the play's core: 'Thou swear'st thy Gods in vain' (I.i.161).

I have treated separately the two threads of hope and despair that Shakespeare weaves together to create the denouement of *King Lear*. The very fact that there are two threads, however, marks a departure from the usual kind of closure in Shakespearean tragedy. None of the other tragedies tantalizes us with even the possibility of hope. Shakespeare clearly sets Hamlet, Othello, Macbeth, Antony, and Cleopatra on incontrovertibly tragic courses that are well established by the time the last act of each play begins. *King Lear* breaks away from this straightforward closure by cultivating an atmosphere of turnabout, thus introducing a potential for reversal. The potential is neither so vast nor so visible as in tragicomedy, but it is pronounced enough to reveal a distinct similarity in construction between *King Lear* and Shakespeare's late tragicomedies. In both, the 'two threads' weave through a series of last-act situational turns to create an effect that is, in Harold S. Wilson's words, 'profoundly true and right, and yet not logical or inevitable at all.'[8] By lessening our sense of inevitability, Shakespeare invites a kind of double perspective: we follow the action as it progresses towards both its actual and its possible conclusions, and we wait with some anxiety for the final stroke that will determine the shape of the whole. This is, of course, the perspective that was also to be demanded by Fletcherian tragicomedy; and scholars have often disputed which play inaugurated the tragicomic vogue, *Cymbeline* or *Philaster*. But *King Lear* points towards them both, and towards all their progeny. Had Shakespeare smoothed out those few irreversible turns and satisfied our intimations of a happy ending by bringing Cordelia back to life, the result would be something like (an admittedly grim) tragicomedy. Similar denouements were being created just before *King Lear* was written, and it was on the early Jacobean stage that the double perspective was first developed.[9] Indeed, a similar denouement crowns Shakespeare's own *The Winter's Tale*, when Hermione comes back to life; and the same construction is also evident in Tate's *King Lear*, a less graceful exercise in the Fletcherian mode. Perhaps what moved Tate to transform Shakespeare's play into tragicomedy was not only a dissatisfaction with the ending, but a realization that the potential for tragicomedy had always been there, 'unpolisht' he would say. He undoubtedly would have found the job more difficult with the other tragedies.

Bradley also sensed that the spirit of Shakespeare's *King Lear* was close to that of his late tragicomedies. Wishing for a more skilful version of Tate's happy ending, Bradley wrote: 'I believe Shakespeare would have ended his play thus had he taken the subject in hand a few years later, in the days of *Cymbeline* and the *Winter's Tale*,' and he said that his own feelings called for such an ending (p. 252). Few of us would agree with those feelings, although we can appreciate the fact that his response was not rooted in mere eccentricity: combined with Bradley's undramatic view of character (which enabled him to conceive of Lear and Cordelia in a different conclusion) was a very definite lessening of inevitability on Shakespeare's own part, as we have seen. Yet none of us would wish to imagine the poor, shrivelled thing that a tragicomic *King Lear* would be. It has not been the purpose of this line of discussion to argue for such a creation. I have instead argued that in *King Lear* Shakespeare introduces a kind of dramatic closure that keeps the hope of reversal alive in our minds, and that this technique – resembling developments on the private stage – anticipates the denouements of Shakespeare's later tragicomedies.

We should also observe how this kind of closure, unprecedented in Shakespearean tragedy and perhaps for that reason untragic to Bradley, contributes greatly to the white-hot tragic intensity of the last act. By holding out the remote possibility of turnabout, instead of making the fates of Lear and Cordelia a foregone conclusion, Shakespeare involves us more intensely with them. As Act V begins we feel that, since Lear and Cordelia have already suffered so much, they *should* survive; Shakespeare constructs Act V so that it alternately offers and jeopardizes the chance that they *will* survive. Their condition becomes more immediate to us because we can share fully the other characters' hopes and anxieties about them. There is no unmistakable, inevitable drift strong enough to place us in a position of greater awareness and therefore of relative detachment. Thus, Shakespeare has once again employed a technique mainly associated with Jacobean drama as a means of enhancing the strong emotional identification that was part of a broader Elizabethan heritage.

We accept this denouement of 'Reversals, recognitions, challenges, confessions ... the gamut of dramatic effects,'[10] partly because of another characteristic that *King Lear* shares with Shakespeare's tragicomedies and with those of Beaumont and Fletcher. All of these works turn to romance rather than to historical or realistic narrative for the framework of their play-worlds. The affinities between *Philaster* or *The Winter's Tale* and romance have long been recognized, but those between *King Lear* and romance have largely been overlooked, perhaps because we usually tend to confine the range of our comparisons to the other tragedies. Yet Shakespeare opened the door to such inquiries when he turned to Sidney's *Arcadia* for his subplot story several years before Beaumont and Fletcher began dramatizing Arcadian romance;[11] and the similarities between *King Lear* and romance extend far beyond the subplot.

Most of the *Lear* world's attributes as described in Chapter 1 – extreme characters, illogical actions, spatial and temporal discontinuities – not to mention wicked sisters, a fairy prince, and ubiquitous castles: these find their home in romance. Like *Pericles, The Tempest,* or numerous narrative romances, *King Lear* takes us to a remote setting and invites us into a world where mundane logic is frequently left behind, a world that makes us accept its *own* logic. The places we visit are highly expressive of themes and of the characters and actions depicted in them, and the weather and topography act on the characters anthropomorphically. What goes on in the *Lear* world is also redolent of romance: spiritual wandering, the testing of patience, the opposition of court and country, brothers waging mortal combat against each other, and the separation and reunion of loved ones. By the time we reach Act V, this romance atmosphere has prepared us to accept the exciting denouement of turn and counterturn which also belongs to romance.

What does not belong to romance is tragedy. As one recent interpreter of the genre has written, 'In the romance nothing is ever abandoned past recovery; resurgence is always possible.'[12] Not for Lear and Cordelia, whose deaths are doubly shocking because they rend apart the fabric of romance in *King Lear*. Yet, the way Shakespeare has treated his romance material all along should warn us that this is no ordinary romance. In the opening scene Lear, an eighty-year-old ruler like Sidney's Basilius, has followed Basilius' foolish course and renounced the responsibilities of his office; but instead of being tested by long adversity and finally finding her reward according to the usual formula, Lear's virtuous daughter has been recognized and rescued by her prince before the first scene is over. Too good to be true, this suspicious development sets the pace for a chain of later inversions of romance elements. With France's exit, for instance, the romance phenomenon of innocent young love disappears from the *Lear* world, to be replaced by the sordid triangle of Edmund and his para-mours; lust and hatred have been substituted for selfless affection, as if Lear has banished the latter from his world by his conduct in I.i. Similarly, the storm-swept heath, where 'for many miles about/ There's scarce a bush' (II.iv.303-4), replaces the lush arcadian retreat of pastoral romance.

Perhaps the most important difference, in terms of the play's effect on our feelings, resides in the treatment of time. In romance, and especially in Shake-speare's romances, time the destroyer is time the redeemer: even in the charac-ters' worst trials, a great expanse of time lets us conceive of an hour other than the present, and therefore we can conceive of an end to present suffering. Misery and even evil are buried beneath the sands of time. But *King Lear* takes place in a world without clocks, where there is no sense of time passing – not even the ocean journeys of *Othello* and *Hamlet*. Instead, everything is always *now*, unmitigated and unredeemed. In the light of these crucial departures from romance, the overturned reunions of Lear and Cordelia, Edgar and Gloucester, and Kent and Lear are only to be expected, along with the final inversion. In *King Lear*, Shakespeare visits the country of romance only to conquer it.

One aspect of romance, however, works hand in hand with Shakespeare's tragic design. The romance hero seems frequently to be at the mercy of titanic, inscrutable forces, which manifest themselves through chance, through the ele-ments, and through the machinations of evil characters. As Bertrand Evans has written of Shakespeare's tragicomic romances, 'They are worlds too large for their puny inhabitants, who become displaced and lost.'[13] In *King Lear*, all of the good characters join Lear as he 'Strives in his little world of man to out-storm/ The to-and-fro conflicting wind and rain' (III.i.10-11) of his hostile universe. They all feel the power of Fortune's blows, and are left reeling. Like Pericles tossing on the waves or Imogen lost in the wilderness, they cry out for their gods to intervene in a world that seems more wildly out of control than that of the other tragedies. 'Seems' is, of course, the operative word in the romances, where the inscrutable powers eventually show themselves (literally, in *Cymbeline*) as benevolent. But as we have seen, the *Lear* world denies its characters this metaphysical consolation. It even denies them a place of tem-porary refuge, that Bohemia or island retreat that complements the more terri-ble aspect of the romance universe. In scene i, Shakespeare's characters talk of such a sanctuary: Kent says that 'Freedom lives hence' in 'a country new,' and France promises Cordelia 'a better where.' But none of them ever escapes. Shakespeare maintains a remorselessly steady focus on one side of the romance Janus, and so puts romance to the service of a more awesomely malevolent power than is found even in the other tragedies.

Just as *King Lear* takes hold of the romance tradition only to overturn it and – along with the *moriae encomium* tradition discussed in Chapter 4 – to underline its inadequacy as a final means of reckoning with the *Lear* world, so the play holds up a number of other perspectives only to reject them in the last scene. As we explore how that last scene reflects the *Lear* world, and begin the task of coming to grips with its meaning, it might be helpful to enumerate some of these blind alleys so that we ourselves may avoid them. Here we can profit from the experiences of Shakespeare's characters, many of whom are actively involved in this process of sifting and winnowing. Indeed, in no other Shakespearean tragedy do so many characters tend to search for and reflect on the meaning of their world – a process that in itself testifies to a unique, complex play-world.

We have already touched on the passive role that the gods play in *King Lear*, and we may observe here how the play rejects the possibility of looking to those gods for an explanation of the *Lear* world. Several characters come to this realization in Act V. Albany must give up the facile teleological perspective through which he viewed his world earlier: 'This shows you are above,/ You justicers, that these our nether crimes/ So speedily can venge' (IV.ii.78-80), he had proclaimed when informed of Cornwall's death. But the holocaust of Act V, bringing in Cordelia's death on the heels of his plea that the gods defend her, makes him abandon his statement of even an earthly quid-pro-quo justice: the neat distribution of rewards and punishments begun at V.iii.300 dissolves into a stunned recognition of 'general woe.' Similarly, the deaths of Lear and Cordelia mock Edgar's assertion that 'The Gods are just' (V.iii.170), and leave him with no more consolation than the awareness of suffering and finitude which he expresses in the play's last lines. Even Edmund's sardonic hope that the gods 'stand up for bastards' has surrendered to a colder, more mechanistic view of the universe: 'The wheel is come full circle; I am here' (V.iii.174). We can read a lesson in the discoveries of these characters. They teach us that if there is a key to the *Lear* world, it is not to be found in that world's metaphysics.

Nor can we find it in any character's *sententiae* – neither in the Fool's prudent proverbs, nor Kent's conventional moralisms, nor Gloucester's cries from the heart, nor Edgar's stoic counsels. Even though Shakespeare gives an extraordinary number of *sententiae* to the characters of *King Lear*[14] – more than he gave to even the prodigiously sententious figure of Polonius – none of them can deal satisfactorily with the events of Act V. We cannot even begin to account for the final humiliation of Lear and Cordelia by reciting how 'Fortune, that arrant whore,/ Ne'er turns the key to th' poor' – the gap between adage and experience is ludicrous. We cannot tell Lear that 'It is the stars,/ The stars above us, govern our conditions,' or console him with the maxim that 'our mere defects/ Prove our commodities,' or that 'The worst returns to laughter.'[15] So many speeches in *King Lear* invite us to view them as distillations of the whole, the *Lear* world in a grain of sand, but in fact none is. Shakespeare throws out a large collection of *sententiae*, both optimistic and gloomy, which – depending on our predilections – we can choose among for epigraphs; but the play itself resists such summary treatment. Nowhere is this more evident than in the final moments of Act V when Shakespeare asserts the absolute primacy of his irreducible dramatic reality. We, like Edgar, can only throw away our *sententiae* as inadequate to the moment, and 'Speak what we feel, not what we ought to say.' The last scene of *King Lear* is the supreme victory, in Shakespeare, of experience over formula. It decimates attempts at reduction.

Not just *sententiae*, but all of the conventional symmetries and ceremonies of closure are rejected by the last scene. *King Lear* does not, for instance, follow the other tragedies (and histories) by directing us to a solid new political order in its last lines. Instead of transcending the play's chaos and suffering, Edgar's speech emphasizes them, delivering a prophecy of impending death rather than one of continuity. Similarly, we have noted above that Albany's 'O! see, see!' breaks another closural pattern; and in Chapter 4 we observed how the last-scene unmaskings of Kent and Edgar also go awry, overturning a traditional public-theatre ending that emphasizes the reformation of a morally errant hero.

The crises of the last scene, therefore, are not to be resolved in the hope of a future concord bringing political or spiritual renewal. Nor are they subsumed under the convention of a cyclical return to a happier beginning. The play's last scene does resemble the first: trumpets sound once more, and the royal party again groups itself around Lear. But Shakespeare denies any sense of purpose to the particular elements that make up this general resemblance. Carol L. Marks is undoubtedly justified in stressing the importance of Edgar's duel as the 'first ceremonial occasion since the opening scene,'[16] for instance, but the pressure of action immediately shunts this event to the background, and the revived concept of ceremony is itself soon rejected in Edgar's own final speech. Albany echoes the opening scene when he gives up the throne, and this gesture meets with the same fate as Edgar's. As John Shaw has observed, even though Albany's speech 'stands in neat and symmetrical relationship to Lear's first speech of the play,' 'the symmetry turns out to be a false one and is dissolved by the last twenty lines.' [17]

Apparently, then, the last scene's terrible fulfilment of the *Lear* world does not provide us with an answer to that world. Its gods fail to give it an ultimate meaning, and its characters cannot account for it through either their words or their actions. Shakespeare depicts a tragic experience that his characters cannot comprehend, an experience untempered by the consolations of philosophy or convention. To be sure, he softens the shock by distancing us somewhat from Lear's final moments. Instead of sharing directly in Lear's condition and outlook, as we did on the heath, we view his last agony from the vantage point of more detached spectators: as the trio of Gloucester, Kent, and Edmund played the distancing chorus in I.i, so Albany, Kent, and Edgar assume that role at the end. As mentioned above, we look especially through the steady eyes of Edgar, who has come forward to the centre of our attention and won our close empathy during the last two acts. Yet even Edgar's experience emphasizes that the *Lear* world at its most terrible is not to be reckoned with through formulas that insulate us from its terror. Physically, he has abandoned his succession of protective disguises, and now faces reality in his own person; philosophically, he has been schooled by the series of overturned stoic mottoes discussed earlier, and the fruit of his learning emerges in his final admonition to meet the experience of 'this sad time' head-on, without recourse to pat answers – neither optimistic stoic ones, nor pessimistic ones that view us as flies to wanton boys.

If we conclude that Edgar's vision brings us to the ultimate meaning of the *Lear* world, then we should agree with John D. Rosenberg's description of that world as 'neither a sublime affirmation nor a grotesque denial, but a savage and beautiful confrontation of the ambiguity of human experience.'[18] But would a writer living in the seventeenth century have created such a world? Would Shakespeare have created such a world, given the unambiguous themes and assumptions that run through all his other works, early and late? One should avoid the line of criticism that turns every artist into a prisoner of his zeitgeist, but surely we must also beware of making Shakespeare over in our own image. 'The ambiguity of human experience' is a theme of the twentieth-century writer, but not of his Elizabethan predecessors. For them, human experience was sometimes confusing, always mutable and complex, but never ultimately ambiguous. Any interpretation that advances the prospect of ambiguity as the final meaning of *King Lear* must therefore be looked on with extreme scepticism. Rather than accept such an interpretation unhesitatingly, we should perhaps take another look at the *Lear* world to see if it directs us to any meaning beyond Edgar's vision.

Shakespeare certainly takes pains to establish that Edgar's vision and the world that it confronts are thoroughly pagan, so that we cannot view the events of *King Lear* as taking place under a Christian aegis. The play is set in pre-Christian Britain, and a constant flow of references to Hecate, Apollo, and other pagan deities keeps that setting fresh in our minds. Thus, we cannot say that the tragic sacrifice of Lear and Cordelia demonstrates either the failure or the success of the Christian ontology. But although *King Lear* does not *expound* Christian doctrine, it definitely points us to it: *King Lear* directs us to a realm of meaning that exists outside the *Lear* world. Such direction comes primarily from the association of Cordelia with Christ. The verbal allusions noted earlier, and the plangent tableau that follows her ignominious death, encourage us to see mirrored in Cordelia's trials those of another 'poor fool' who 'redeems nature from the general curse.' This is not to say that Cordelia portrays or represents Christ. Rather, it is to say that the import of her suffering – the complete and undeserved forgiveness, the unqualified self-sacrifice, the awful and irreparable injustice – reminds us of the import of Christ's suffering. As Rosemund Tuve has written of such parallels in allegorical romance, 'It is the meanings that recur' rather than the outward circumstances: 'the characters do not equate, [and therefore] their stories need not echo each other, but merely meet where [their] meanings touch.'[19] Like the Erasmian parallels that support it, this pattern of sympathetic vibrations presumes less, but says far more, than any simple identification of Cordelia with Christ. It directs us to the significance of the Christian myth rather than to its accidentals.

Other features of the *Lear* world point us in the same direction. Shakespeare's treatment of good and evil, for instance, underlines the Christian humanist idea that man has within him the seeds of both bestiality and sanctity. In Pico della Mirandola's words: 'Thou shalt have the power to degenerate into the lower forms of life, which are brutish. Thou shalt have the power, out of thy soul's judgment, to be reborn into the higher forms.'[20] Thus, the extremes of good and evil in the *Lear* world are literally generated from the flesh of Lear and Gloucester. Lear has fathered Cordelia's virtue and the beastly natures of Regan and Goneril, and Gloucester's life has borne similar fruit. Both old men finally come to acknowledge their responsibility for their evil offspring, and are then spiritually reborn. The process of their spiritual regeneration, especially Lear's, also acts out an essential part of the Christian life. They undergo a deprivation of worldly goods, a relentless stripping-away of rank, servants, riches, clothing, and even the comforts of their senses. Such total ascesis embodies the most profound Christian attitude towards the things of this world. Material goods are fetters, and the body a husk to be discarded so that the fruit can be reached, or – in a popular iconographic image – a cage that imprisons the singing bird of the soul. Perhaps Shakespeare had this emblem in mind when he made Lear say to Cordelia, 'Come, let's away to prison;/ We two alone will sing like birds i' th' cage' (V.iii.8-9). At any rate, the soul is finally liberated when Lear completes the process of ascesis in V.iii: 'Pray you, undo this button.'

It is a brutal liberation, 'A condition of complete simplicity/ (Costing not less than everything),' as Eliot describes the end of the Christian journey in *Four Quartets*. But then, *King Lear* has never promised us anything else from its very beginning. In fact, the first and last scenes of *King Lear* are mutually illuminating, and work together in pointing us to the Christian vision beyond the *Lear* world. Edgar's desire to 'Speak what we feel, not what we ought to say,' for instance, shows that he has recognized the great value that resides in Cordelia's plainness, as opposed to her sisters' pleasing surfaces; and his words bring us to the same recognition. Similarly, the spectacle of unrewarded virtue in the last scene should remind us of the pageant in I.i. In her reaction to the love-test, Cordelia emphasizes that true virtue is never 'mingled with regards' – that it has nothing to do with tangible reward. Lear tries in error to mix them, and Burgundy would too; but Cordelia will not have this, and France sees the riches of her poverty. Significantly, he voices his discovery in a series of paradoxes, a fit language for truths that transcend the logic of the *Lear* world and of ours: 'most rich, being poor,' 'Most choice, forsaken,' 'most lov'd, despis'd,' 'from their cold'st neglect/ My love should kindle to inflam'd respect,' 'Thy dowerless daughter ... / Is Queen of us,' 'this unpriz'd precious maid' (I.i.250-9).

France's paradoxy points us towards the same truths that Lear learns later, and towards the values that the rest of the play will affirm. For *King Lear* constantly proclaims that love, service, and virtue – the three are always intertwined – are their own reward. Only the Regans, Gonerils, Edmunds, and Oswalds try to mix reward, or 'bounty,' with their service. By the end of *King Lear*, we should see that Cordelia possesses everything that is genuinely worth having. Such was Bradley's final appraisal of the last scene: 'The extremity of the disproportion between prosperity and goodness first shocks us, and then flashes on us the conviction that our whole attitude in asking or expecting that goodness should be prosperous is wrong; that, if only we could see things as they are, we should see that the outward is nothing and the inward is all ... some such thought as this ... is really present through the whole play' (p. 326). We protest so strongly against Cordelia's death because we are not of her world (nor is Lear, try as he does to reach it): we cannot, in fact, value virtue more than life, although we can look up to such a value as an ideal. We are more like Edgar, who compromises and clings to life.

Edgar, then, does not embody the ultimate vision of *King Lear*, but he provides us with a perspective on it. We look through his eyes, as Gloucester did, and we gauge the distance between ourselves and that ultimate vision. Edgar is our Virgil, the well-meaning guide who can take us only to the threshold of the highest truth. But Cordelia has always lived beyond that threshold; she has always rejected absolutely the prudent counsellings of the Fool, nowhere more genuinely fool than when he advocated a policy of worldly wisdom. Looking again at the first scene through the lens of the last, we can say that to ask Cordelia to be diplomatic in I.i, as some critics have done, is to ask her to compromise and show a more pleasing surface; and diplomacy is hardly a heroic virtue.

But of course we are denied the advantage of such hindsight when we experience I.i; and, in fact, Shakespeare seems to have made it easy for us to misinterpret Cordelia's actions. Unlike her prototype in *The History of King Leir*, this Cordelia is not presented to us in a sympathetic scene before the love-test begins, and so we are not predisposed to judge her conduct favourably. Shakespeare simply puts us down in the love-test and asks us to judge Cordelia, as Lear does, solely on the basis of her performance there. Cordelia's two asides win pity for her dilemma, but the emblematic way she acts makes her much less likable than such similarly righteous figures as Chaucer's patient Griselda or Dekker's dramatized version of Griselda (in *Patient Grissil*, 1600). Could it be that Shakespeare deliberately lets us attribute some blame to Cordelia, so that we actually experience a minor variant of Lear's error? The dramatic advantages of such a technique would be prodigious, since we would feel something of the horror that Lear comes to feel when he sees catastrophe issuing from a seemingly casual action – what one critic has described as 'such an act of self-indulgence as any citizen might commit.'[21]

But even if we discount this conjecture, our feelings at Cordelia's death bring us closer to an experience of her ideal, for *we feel* – much more than we would if *King Lear* had been set in a Christian world – the irreparable nature of what has been lost; and we find that we too must reject the conventional courtesies (dramatic, in our case) as unsatisfactory, in favour of a response that simply speaks what we feel. Shakespeare has made such a response in the last scene of *King Lear*, transcending both the *Lear* world and the world of dramatic convention to create a conclusion that is as powerful as the ideal that it affirms and the feelings that it portrays.

Notes

INTRODUCTION

1 *Ben Jonson*, ed. C.H. Herford, Percy and Evelyn Simpson (Oxford, 1925-52), Vol. IV, V.i.129-30. The two further quotations from *Poetaster* are also taken from this edition, lines 134-5 and 136-8.

2 Denis Donoghue, ed. *W.B. Yeats: Memoirs* (London, 1972), p. 165

3 See R.W. Babcock's classic study, *The Genesis of Shakespeare Idolatry, 1766-1799* (Chapel Hill, 1931), and Earl R. Wasserman, 'Shakespeare and the English Romantic Movement,' in *The Persistence of Shakespeare Idolatry: Essays in Honor of Robert W. Babcock,* ed. Herbert M. Schueller (Detroit, 1964), pp. 77-103. S. Schoenbaum enumerates many of the important sources of this tradition in 'Shakespeare the Ignoramus,' in *The Drama of the Renaissance: Essays for Leicester Bradner*, ed. Elmer M. Blistein (Providence, R.I., 1970), pp. 154-64.

4 T. W. Baldwin, *William Shakspere's Small Latine and Lesse Greeke,* 2 vols. (Urbana, Ill., 1944); Theodore Spencer, *Shakespeare and the Nature of Man* (New York, 1942)

5 Kenneth Muir, *Shakespeare's Sources I* (London, 1957 [rpt. 1965]), p. 96. For the full complement of sources, see Geoffrey Bullough, *Narrative and Dramatic Sources of Shakespeare*, 8 vols. (London and New York, 1957-74). Studies referred to above are: G. Pellegrini, 'Symbols and Significances,' in *Shakespeare Survey*, 17 (1964), 180-87, and Russell A. Fraser, *Shakespeare's Poetics in Relation to 'King Lear'* (London, 1962); C. L. Barber, *Shakespeare's Festive Comedy* (Princeton, 1959); Carol Gesner, *Shakespeare and the Greek Romance* (Lexington, Ky., 1970); Brian Vickers, *The Artistry of Shakespeare's Prose* (London, 1968); Rosalie L. Colie, *Paradoxia Epidemica* (Princeton, 1966). esp. pp. 461-81.

6 *The Resources of Kind: Genre-Theory in the Renaissance* (University of California, 1973), esp. pp. 114-15

7 As demonstrated by Gerald Eades Bentley, *Shakespeare and Jonson: Their Reputations in the Seventeenth Century Compared* (Chicago, 1945), I, 109, 137

8 Maynard Mack's *'King Lear' in Our Time* (Berkeley and Los Angeles, 1965) cogently summarizes and discusses the play's stage history, pp. 1-41. Mack's extremely suggestive book also shows how *King Lear* reinterprets elements of earlier literary and dramatic traditions. Other recent studies that stress the play's formal inclusiveness are: Katherine Stockholder, 'The Multiple Genres of *King Lear:* Breaking the Archetypes,' *Bucknell Review*, vol. 16, no. 1 (1968), 40-68; Colie, *The Resources of Kind,* pp.

122-28, and *Shakespeare's Living Art*
(Princeton, 1974), pp. 302-16, 351-61;
and many of the essays in *Some Facets of
'King Lear': Essays in Prismatic Criticism,*
ed. Rosalie L. Colie and F.T. Flahiff
(Toronto, 1974).

9 Kenneth Muir, ed. *King Lear* (Arden ed.,
London, 1957), p. xxiv. All references to
King Lear are to this edition and will be
cited in the text.

10 For dramatic conditions at Court, see
E.K. Chambers, *The Elizabethan Stage*
(Oxford, 1923), I, 1-234 and III, 1-46;
G.E. Bentley, *The Jacobean and Caroline
Stage,* VI(Oxford, 1968), 255-9; Glynne
Wickham, *Early English Stages,* Vol. II,
pt. 2 (London, 1972), 148-65. Philip J.
Finkelpearl explores the literary and
dramatic milieu of the Inns in *John
Marston of the Middle Temple* (Cam-
bridge, Mass., 1969), pp. 3-80.

11 Peter Saccio, in *The Court Comedies of
John Lyly* (Princeton, 1969), shows how
Lyly's art gradually developed under such
pressure.

12 The private theatres operated between
1576 and 1584, and again from 1599
onwards, then attracting many more
playwrights and much more attention. It
is estimated that public theatres such as
the Globe or the Fortune could accommodate about 2500 spectators, while the
private theatres at Blackfriars or White-
friars could certainly hold no more than
about nine hundred. Further information
on theatres and audiences may be found
in Alfred Harbage, *Shakespeare and the
Rival Traditions* (New York, 1952), the
work that first established that each type
of theatre produced a different kind of
drama. It is now generally agreed that
Harbage's study failed to take account of
the complex ways in which both theatres
developed and interacted, and that it
overstated the moral and aesthetic differences of the two theatres: see R.C.
Bald's incisive review in *Modern Philology,* vol. 51, 1954, 278-81. In Chapters
Four and Six of *The Shakespearean
Stage: 1574-1642* (Cambridge, 1970),
Andrew Gurr has culled the relevant
information on theatres and audiences
from Chambers' *The Elizabethan Stage*
and Bentley's *The Jacobean and Caroline
Stage*, and has summarized it in
eminently readable form. For more information on early seventeenth-century
theatres, see Wickham, *Early English
Stages*, pp. 101-38. William A. Armstrong
has also assembled valuable information
in 'The Audience of the Elizabethan
Private Theatres,' *Review of English
Studies,* NS 10, 1959, 234-49, and in *The
Elizabethan Private Theatres: Facts and
Problems*, The Society for Theatre
Research Pamphlet Series No. 6 (London,
1958). For more recent discoveries about
private theatres, see Michael Shapiro,
'Three Notes on the Theatre at Paul's,
c.1569 – c.1607,' *Theatre Notebook*,
vol. 24, 1970, 147-54, and 'What We
Know About the Children's Troupes and
Their Plays,' *Shakespearean Research and
Opportunities,* nos. 5-6, 1970-1, 34-45.
Shapiro's forthcoming study of private-
theatre drama should settle many long-
standing questions.

13 In Andrew Gurr's words, 'the rich went
to public and private theatre alike, the
poor more exclusively to the public' *(The
Shakespearean Stage*, p. 143).

14 See R.A. Foakes, 'John Marston's Fan-
tastical Plays: *Antonio and Mellida* and
Antonio's Revenge,' *Philological Quarterly*, vol. 41, 1962, 229-39; also
Reibetanz, 'Hieronimo in Decimosexto:
A Private-Theatre Burlesque,' *Renaissance Drama,* NS 5, 1972, 89-121.

15 *Endeavors of Art: A Study of Form in
Elizabethan Drama* (Madison, Wisc.,
1954), pp. 3-23, 370-6. I am greatly
indebted to Doran's comprehensive work.

16 Marco Mincoff, 'Shakespeare and Lyly,'
Shakespeare Survey, vol. 14, 1961,
15-24; C.L. Barber, *Shakespeare's Festive
Comedy*, pp. 87-162. See also Norman
Sanders, 'The Comedy of Greene and
Shakespeare,' in *Early Shakespeare,* ed.

John Russell Brown and Bernard Harris, (London, 1961), pp. 35-53.

7 Nicholas Brooke, 'Marlowe as Provocative Agent in Shakespeare's Early Plays,' *Shakespeare Survey*, vol. 14, 1961, 34-44; F.P. Wilson, *Marlowe and the Early Shakespeare* (Oxford, 1953)

8 Eleanor Prosser, *Hamlet and Revenge* (Stanford, 1967); Fredson Bowers, *Elizabethan Revenge Tragedy* (Princeton, 1940), pp. 3-118

9 Finkelpearl, *John Marston*, pp. 19-80. He notes that 'any serious Elizabethan writer must have thought of the Inns as the home of his prime judges, a Court of Critics' (p. 79). See also R.A. Foakes, *Shakespeare: The Dark Comedies to the Last Plays* (London, 1971), pp. 7-62; Robert Kimbrough, *Shakespeare's 'Troilus and Cressida' and its Setting* (Cambridge, Mass., 1964).

20 For *Pericles*, see F.D. Hoeniger's fine introduction to the Arden edition (London, 1963), pp. xix-xxiii, lxxi-xci. The first study to look at Shakespeare's late plays in the context of private-theatre dramaturgy was G.E. Bentley's 'Shakespeare and the Blackfriars Theatre,' *Shakespeare Survey*, vol. 1, 1948, 38-50. See also R.A. Foakes, *Shakespeare: The Dark Comedies to the Last Plays*, pp. 94-172; Arthur C. Kirsch, '*Cymbeline* and Coterie Dramaturgy,' *ELH*, vol. 34, 1967, 285-306, and *Jacobean Dramatic Perspectives* (Charlottesville, Virginia, 1972), pp. 64-74.

21 In referring to these plays, I have sought to avoid the problem of direct influence *on them* by choosing my examples, wherever possible, from works not known to have been influenced by *King Lear*; thus, I have generally avoided reference to Tourneur and Webster, on whose work *King Lear* had a noticeable effect. My task has been made easier by the fact that, as mentioned above, *King Lear* seems not to have been among Shakespeare's most popular plays.

22 Sources for these five observations are: *Coleridge's Shakespearean Criticism*, ed. Thomas Middleton Raysor (London, 1930), I, 59; Bradley, *Shakespearean Tragedy* (London, 1956), p. 263; James, *The Dream of Learning* (Oxford, 1951), p. 117; Mack, '*King Lear*' in Our Time, pp. 4-5; Nowottny, 'Some Aspects of the Style of *King Lear*,' *Shakespeare Survey*, vol. 13, 1960, 49.

23 Notably L.C. Knights, *Drama and Society in the Age of Jonson* (London 1937); F.P. Wilson, *Elizabethan and Jacobean* (Oxford, 1945); Brian Gibbons, *Jacobean City Comedy* (Cambridge, Mass., 1968)

24 G.E. Bentley, *The Profession of Dramatist in Shakespeare's Time* (Princeton, 1971), pp. 29-37

25 Or perhaps also because they found themselves controlling so much of the final shape of their plays: since many of them wrote for the newly re-opened private theatres, they could exert more control over their boy actors than they could over experienced, strong-willed adults.

26 Una Ellis-Fermor, *The Jacobean Drama: An Interpretation* (London, 1935); Robert Ornstein, *The Moral Vision of Jacobean Tragedy* (Madison, Wisc., 1960); M.C. Bradbrook, *The Growth and Structure of Elizabethan Comedy* (London, 1955), pp. 148-96; Millar MacLure, *George Chapman: A Critical Study* (Toronto, 1966), pp. 83-157; Finkelpearl, *John Marston*; Eugene M. Waith, *The Pattern of Tragicomedy in Beaumont and Fletcher* (New Haven, 1952); Clifford Leech, *The John Fletcher Plays* (London, 1962).

CHAPTER 1

1 *Shakespearean Tragedy* (London, 1956), p. 256. All further quotations from Bradley are taken from this edition and will be cited in the text.

2 *The Malcontent*, ed. M.L. Wine (London, 1965), S.D. before I.i. All further quotations from *The Malcontent* are taken from this edition and will be cited in the text.

3 *The Plays of John Marston*, ed. H. Harvey Wood (Edinburgh, 1939), Vol. II, p. 20

4 *John Marston of the Middle Temple* (Cambridge, Mass., 1969), p. 243. Compare also R.A. Foakes's description of the world of Jonson's *Sejanus* (1603): 'It is a savage world, in which nothing redeems the viciousness of the central figures, and the good are limited to expressing their feelings in their moralizing or satirical commentary ... The world of the play is a dark and cruel one, in which the good are shown as impotent; it anticipates in some ways the "gloomy world" of Webster's plays, and the assumption of corruption as the norm in Middleton's tragedies' (*Shakespeare: The Dark Comedies to the Last Plays*, London, 1971, pp. 80-1). Foakes's reference to 'moralizing or satirical commentary' brings to mind the choric observations of Kent, Edgar, and the Fool in *King Lear*.

5 *Bussy D'Ambois*, ed. Nicholas Brooke (London, 1964), I.ii.27. All further quotations from *Bussy D'Ambois* (first performed in 1604) are taken from this edition and will be cited in the text.

6 As one character describes conditions in Chapman's *The Widow's Tears* (1605), ed. E.M. Smeak (Lincoln, Neb., 1966), V.i.375

7 Though these plays have long been singled out for their 'realism,' Brian Gibbons shrewdly notes that it is not realism but rather a mannered manipulation of concrete details that characterizes their art (*Jacobean City Comedy*, Cambridge, Mass., 1968, esp. pp. 15-18), and he describes the essential genius of Jonson as 'the invention of his own supremely lively, artificial world' (pp. 206-7). For examples of such a world, see *Epicoene* (1609) or *The Alchemist* (1610). Some Middleton plays that also illustrate this characteristic are *A Trick to Catch the Old One, Your Five Gallants* (both 1605), *A Mad World, My Masters,* and *Michaelmas Term* (both 1606).

8 I am, of course, not alone in emphasizing the unique, artificial world of *King Lear*. Some of the more notable works viewing that world from other perspectives are: G. Wilson Knight, 'The *Lear* Universe,' in *The Wheel of Fire* (London, 1949), pp. 177-206; Moody E. Prior, *The Language of Tragedy* (New York, 1947), pp. 74-93; Harold S. Wilson, *On the Design of Shakespearian Tragedy* (Toronto, 1957), pp. 182-204; Maynard Mack 'Action and World,' in *'King Lear' in Our Time* (Berkeley and Los Angeles, 1965), pp. 81-117; and Bernard McElroy, *Shakespeare's Mature Tragedies* (Princeton, 1973), pp. 145-205.

9 *Samuel Johnson on Shakespeare*, ed. W.K. Wimsatt, Jr. (New York, 1960), p. 96

10 *The Complete Works of John Webster*, ed. F.L. Lucas (London, 1927), IV, 42

11 A notable exception to this statement is Dekker's *The Whore of Babylon* (1606), a public-theatre allegory of the conflict between Queen Elizabeth and Mary Stuart.

12 *The Allegory of Love* (Oxford, 1936), p. 358

13 'I do not mean to imply, by writing this note, that I believe in the hypotheses suggested in it. On the contrary I think it more probable that the defects referred to arose from ... other causes' ('Note T: Did Shakespeare Shorten *King Lear?*' p. 448).

14 *The History of King Leir*, prepared by W.W. Greg and checked by R. Warwick Bond, Malone Society Reprints (Oxford, 1907), line 19. Ragan's speech comes at lines 111-12.

15 For a concise summary of Tate's 'improvements' in this area, see Mack, *'King Lear' in Our Time*, pp. 11-12.

6 *Prefaces to Shakespeare* (Princeton, 1946, rpt. 1965), II, 53. Further references will be cited in the text.

7 *Coleridge's Shakespearean Criticism*, ed. Thomas Middleton Raysor (London, 1930), I. 59. Further references will be cited in the text.

8 Lyly, like many Jacobean playwrights, wrote for the children's companies; and his artifice, like theirs, often seems to have arisen in response to the skills and the limitations of the child actors. For an interesting essay arguing that *Love's Labour's Lost* may in fact have been written for performance by one of the children's companies, see Alfred Harbage, 'Love's Labour's Lost and the Early Shakespeare,' *Philological Quarterly*, vol. 41, 1962, 18-36.

19 Often much less subtle than Shakespeare's. At the start of Heywood's *The Royal King and the Loyal Subject* (1602), the King gives a biographical character sketch of his loyal subject, Heywood's hero, while the two villains reveal their jealousy in asides. The Earl opens Heywood's *The Four Prentices of London* (1600) by explaining to his daughter how Fortune has thrown them from nobility to the London citizenry, as if she did not already know. See also *The Blind Beggar of Bednal Green* (1600) by Chettle and Day, Dekker's *The Shoemaker's Holiday* (1599), and the anonymous *A Larum for London* (1599). Earlier antecedents and more accomplished examples of this kind of discursive opening are found in both parts of Marlowe's *Tamburlaine* (1587) and in Greene's *James the Fourth* (c. 1590).

20 The relationship is confirmed by Edmund's words as he is dying: 'Yet Edmund was belov'd.' The 'Yet' indicates his feeling that this experience outweighs the catastrophic reversal and even the mortal wound he has suffered. By placing so much value on love, he reveals a need as intense as that expressed by Lear in I.i. Edmund and Lear have each brought about a series of tragic events through what has emerged as each one's perverse attempt to satisfy a hunger for love.

21 An analogous structural pattern is displayed by a distinct group of plays roughly contemporaneous with *King Lear*: the 'disguised ruler' plays consist of Marston's *The Fawn* (1605), Middleton's *The Phoenix* (1604), and Shakespeare's own *Measure for Measure* (1604). At the start of each play, a ruler sets off an extended series of actions by pretending to go on a long trip, but remains present in disguise to view and expose the humours of his inferiors. When the resulting situations have run their course, the ruler ends the play by revealing his disguise. Unlike King Lear these rulers remain in control of the chain of events that their initial actions precipitate.

22 The reader might object that the particular examples I have given in these two paragraphs come from plays written after *King Lear*. However, we shall see that the general structural bias to which these plays and *King Lear* all conform had numerous precedents. Like any artist whose work grows out of a response to living traditions, Shakespeare was simultaneously a follower and a leader.

23 For an illuminating discussion of the many kinds of emblematic techniques used by Shakespeare and his contemporary dramatists, see Dieter Mehl, 'Emblems in English Renaissance Drama,' *Renaissance Drama*, NS 2, 1969, 39-57. Further emblematic conformations in *King Lear* will be explored below and in Chapters 2 and 5, and have been brought together in an essay, 'Theatrical Emblems in *King Lear*,' *Some Facets of 'King Lear'*: *Essays in Prismatic Criticism*, ed. Rosalie L. Colie and F.T. Flahiff (Toronto, 1974), pp. 39-57.

24 'Introduction' to his edition of the play (Lincoln, Neb., 1966), p. xvii

25 Some of the incidents mentioned above have also been referred to as trials, and have been treated from a different per-

spective in Dorothy C. Hockey, 'The Trial Pattern in *King Lear,*' *Shakespeare Quarterly,* vol. 10, 1959, 389-95.

26 See p. 328n, where Bradley lists the references elaborated here.

27 Such symbolic regrouping may be observed in other Jacobean plays. In *Amends for Ladies* (1611), for instance, the three ladies whose debate initiated the dramatic action come forward once again at the end, to demonstrate that the process in which they were involved has come full circle. Similarly, parallel speeches by Freevill emphasize fulfilment of the pattern behind Marston's *The Dutch Courtesan* (1605): Freevill's long condemnation of prostitutes in Act V stands in revealing contrast to his equally long praise of them in Act I, and rounds off the evolution traced by the play.

28 *This Great Stage: Image and Structure in 'King Lear'* (Seattle, 1963), p. 126

29 *'King Lear' in Our Time,* p. 100. Aspects of this 'bond' have also been explored by Jonas A. Barish and Marshall Waingrow in their pioneering article, ' "Service" in *King Lear,*' *Shakespeare Quarterly,* vol. 9, 1958, 347-55, and by William R. Elton in *'King Lear' and the Gods* (San Marino, 1966), pp. 75-82.

30 I use the Folio punctuation, rather than Muir's in the Arden edition. We should note how Edmund also follows in his father's footsteps, later, by pursuing his course of adultery with Regan and Goneril; and Heilman notes that they, in turn, are later associated with their father through the pervasive animal imagery (*This Great Stage,* p. 98).

31 For other correspondences between *King Lear* and the late romances, see Chapter 5 below.

32 As noted by L.A. Beaurline in the 'Introduction' to his edition of the play, p. xv

33 *Elizabethan and Jacobean Poets* (London, 1964), p. 119

34 For an attempt to interpret our response here, see the second-last paragraph of Chapter 5.

35 'Introduction' to his edition of *King Lear* (New York, 1963), p. xxxi

CHAPTER 2

1 *King Lear,* ed. Kenneth Muir (London, 1957), p. xliii

2 It becomes a building block of Restoration drama; for an important study linking this and other aspects of Jacobean playwriting to later drama, see Joseph W. Donohue, Jr., *Dramatic Character in the English Romantic Age* (Princeton, 1970). Philip Edwards has written perceptively on the strong scenes of Fletcherian drama in 'The Danger Not the Death: The Art of John Fletcher,' in *Jacobean Theatre,* ed. John Russell Brown and Bernard Harris (London, 1960) .pp. 159-77.

3 *'King Lear' in Our Time,* p. 95

4 See, for instance, Edward A. Block, *King Lear: A Study in Balanced and Shifting Sympathies,*' *Shakespeare Quarterly,* vol. 10, 1959, 499-512; Sigurd Burckhardt, *Shakespearean Meanings* (Princeton, 1968), pp. 237-59; and, of course, Heilman's *This Great Stage.*

5 *From 'Mankind' to Marlowe* (Cambridge Mass., 1962), pp. 207-8

6 See his *Principles of Art History* (New York, 1950), pp. 155-95.

7. Felix E. Schelling, one of the first scholars to study the chronicle history, found it characterized primarily by a deep interest in the story for the story's sake (*The English Chronicle Play,* New York, 1902, p. 16). More recently, Madeleine Doran has observed that in these plays 'Only too often the dramatists do nothing except to select enough striking incidents from a reign to fill up the time of a play and set them down as they come' (*Endeavors of Art: A Study of Form in Elizabethan Drama,* Madison, Wisc., 1954, p. 114). If one leaves aside the results of the alchemy by which Marlowe and Shake-

speare managed to transform this unpromising genre, little worthwhile drama remains. Some typical examples staged at about the same time as *King Lear* are: Heywood's *If You Know Not Me, You Know Nobody*, a two-part drama of 1604-5; Dekker and Webster's *Sir Thomas Wyatt* (1604); or *Sir John Oldcastle* (1599), on which Drayton, Hathaway, Munday, and Wilson collaborated.

8 For other early examples of this tendency, see Marston's *What You Will* (1601), Middleton's *Your Five Gallants* (1605), and Jonson's *Poetaster* (1601).

9 See Peter Saccio, *The Court Comedies of John Lyly* (Princeton, 1969), esp. pp. 1-10; also Michael R. Best, 'Lyly's Static Drama,' *Renaissance Drama*, NS 1 (1968), 75-86. *Campaspe* and *Gallathea*, in particular, display many structural affinities with private-theatre plays of the early 1600s; and one of the latter, *The Maid's Metamorphosis*, was at one time attributed to Lyly and appears in R. Warwick Bond's 1902 edition of Lyly's works.

10 Philip Edwards, 'The Danger Not the Death,' p. 173

11 *Dramatic Character in the English Romantic Age*, p. 28. The narrative drama from which this tradition departs has been described and interpreted by Patricia Russell, 'Romantic Narrative Plays: 1570-1590,' in *Elizabethan Theatre* (London, 1966), pp. 107-29.

12 Compare also the Governor who emerges to give a final bizarre turn to the 'topsy-turvy world' of Chapman's *The Widow's Tears* (1605); Phego, the gentleman usher who pops out of nowhere to enliven Act II of Mason's *The Turk* (1607); Nilo, who enters to deface a temple in Act I of Beaumont and Fletcher's *Cupid's Revenge* (1607-8) and then disappears; or the schoolmaster who brings four students for a brief visit to Act II of Marston's *What You Will* (1601).

13 *Ben Jonson*, ed. C. H. Herford, Percy and Evelyn Simpson (Oxford, 1925-52), IV, 398

14 In his book on *Antony and Cleopatra* (*The Pillar of the World*, Columbus, Ohio, 1968), Julian Markels agrees that 'Shakespeare has begun to evolve here [in *King Lear*] a new technique of discontinuity' (p. 121). Markels also finds a plethora of unmotivated, gratuitous actions in *King Lear*, but he adduces from their presence a new, discontinuous world outlook on Shakespeare's part, the existence of which remains unproved for me.

15 *Renaissance Drama*, NS 2 (1969), 39-57

16 This is not to say that *King Lear* contains no emblems of the kind that Mehl describes. Henry Green noticed some of the first type a century ago in his *Shakespeare and the Emblem Writers*, (London, 1870); see esp. his list on p. 540. Those of the third type also occur: Kent, the 'good man' in the stocks at II.ii.157; Lear kneeling at II.iv.156; blind Gloucester epitomizing the world's 'strange mutations' for Edgar at IV.i.11; and poor Tom, pointed to by Lear ('Is man no more than this? Consider him well') at III.iv.105-6. Granville-Barker recognized the emblematic quality of this last scene when he wrote of it: 'Here is a volume of argument epitomized as only drama can epitomize it, flashed on us by word and action combined' (*Prefaces to Shakespeare*, II, 33).

17 'Some Emblems in Shakespeare's Henry IV Plays,' *ELH*, vol. 38, 1971, 517

18 See Mehl, as well as Jocelyn Powell, 'Marlowe's Spectacle,' *Tulane Drama Review*, vol. 8, 1964, 195-210. Powell, however, applies the term 'emblem' to a wider range of images than I feel it can appropriately describe.

19 *This Great Stage*, pp. 67-87. In particular, Heilman shows how Lear's redemptive experience is manifested in a succession of tableaux relating to Lear's headgear: the king goes from crown to bare head to

crown of weeds (or thorns). In an essay on 'The Clothing Motif in *King Lear'* (*Shakespeare Quarterly*, vol. 5, 1954, 281-6), Thelma Nelson Greenfield expands on Heilman's observation and relates Lear's experience to other, more ambiguous usages of clothing imagery in the play; especially, she demonstrates how the contrast between gorgeousness and nakedness is less simple in *King Lear* than in an earlier play like Medwall's *Nature* (c. 1495): nakedness, for instance, can point to both Lear's purgation and Regan's lust (p. 285). The essay provides another instance of how Shakespeare renews and reinterprets the many traditions behind *King Lear.*

20 For examples of this emblem, see pp. 110-12 of Russell A. Fraser, *Shakespeare's Poetics in Relation to 'King Lear'* (London, 1962), a book that comprehensively explores many other sources of Shakespeare's verbal and pictorial imagery.

21 I am aware that this scene direction ('*Enter* LEAR, *fantastically dressed with wild flowers'*) does not appear in the Quarto or Folio texts. But the scene directions on Elizabethan dramatic texts are usually far from complete realizations of original performance conditions, and of course neither Quarto nor Folio of *King Lear* provides us with an authorial text. Consequently, I feel it justifiable as well as convenient to agree with later theatrical and editorial tradition, and to say that it seems most *likely* that Lear would enter dressed in this manner, given the earlier description of him. We have been prepared for this 'side-piercing sight,' as Edgar has not been.

22 This and later references to *Bussy D'Ambois* are taken from the Revels Plays edition, ed. Nicholas Brooke (London, 1964).

23 I am indebted for this observation to Nicholas Brooke's excellent introduction to his edition, p. xxix.

24 As formulated in the stimulating essay, 'Engagement and Detachment in Shakespeare's Plays,' in *Essays on Shakespeare and Elizabethan Drama in Honour of Hardin Craig*, ed. Richard Hosley (London, 1963), pp. 275-96

25 *Images and Themes in Five Poems by Milton* (Cambridge, Mass., 1967), p. 17

26 ' "Speak What We Feel": The End of *King Lear,' ELN*, vol. 5, 1967-8, 165. The D.G. James quotation, cited by Marks, comes from *The Dream of Learning* (Oxford, 1951), p. 113.

27 *The Dramatic Works of Thomas Heywood*, ed. R.H. Shepherd (London, 1874, rpt. New York, 1964), II, 175

28 *The Dramatic Works of Thomas Dekker,* ed. Fredson Bowers (Cambridge, 1953-61), I, lines 22-23

29 *The Complete Plays of Christopher Marlowe*, ed. Irving Ribner (New York, 1963), p. 51. Further references to Marlowe's plays are to this edition.

30 J.P. Brockbank, 'The Frame of Disorder — *Henry VI,'* in *Early Shakespeare*, ed. John Russell Brown and Bernard Harris (London, 1961), p. 75. Brockbank's essay gives a fine interpretation of Shakespeare's structural principles in the trilogy.

31 Madeleine Doran *Endeavors of Art*, pp. 150, 291, as cited by R.B. Parker in his Revels edition of the play (London, 1969), p. xlii. In *The Multiple Plot in English Renaissance Drama* (Chicago and London, 1971), Richard Levin takes issue with this appraisal, rightly affirming a 'special significance' (p. 202) for the love story; but this significance manifests itself through symbolic contrast with the play's satirical plots, rather than through our involvement in the narrative.

32 Paul V. Kreider, *Elizabethan Comic Character Conventions as Revealed in the Comedies of George Chapman* (Ann Arbor, Michigan, 1935), p. 155

33 The actions of later Jacobean tragedies such as Tourneur's *The Revenger's Tragedy* (1606), Beaumont and

Fletcher's *The Maid's Tragedy* (1610), or Webster's *The White Devil* (1612) may be seen to evolve in similarly anti-narrative ways. John Russell Brown's comment about Webster's play is applicable to a great deal of Jacobean tragedy: *'The White Devil* presents its characters in flashlight moments' ('Introduction' to his edition, London, 1966, p. xlvi). For a sensitive appraisal of the relationship between character and background in *The Maid's Tragedy*, see Arthur C. Kirsch, *Jacobean Dramatic Perspectives* (Charlottesville, Va., 1972), pp. 42-7.

34 *Reality and the Heroic Pattern* (Chicago, 1967), p. 60
35 *Religion and Literature* (London, 1971), p. 75. Further quotations, ibid., p. 74
36 *Shakespeare's Dramatic Heritage* (London, 1969), p. 22
37 See Wickham, pp. 28-9.

CHAPTER 3

1 It might be objected that such 'impediments' are an inevitable characteristic of Elizabethan drama, since similar breaks in action and concentration result from the typically Elizabethan alternation of plot and subplot. I do not deny this. But as Richard Levin observes, 'The multiple plot is apparently more effective in comedy than in tragedy, as some of the better playwrights recognized,' since 'the tragic effect is by its very nature more homogeneous and more concentrated than that of comedy' *(The Multiple Plot in English Renaissance Drama*, Chicago and London, 1971, p. 221). Like the multiple plot, the structural attributes mentioned above usually foster a detachment that is more appropriate to comedy than to tragedy. *King Lear* is all the more remarkable for managing to incorporate both these attributes and a double plot into its tragic design.
2 For discussion of the distancing effects of Jacobean drama, see: Arthur C. Kirsch,

'Cymbeline and Coterie Dramaturgy,' *ELH*, vol. 34, 1967, 285-306, and *Jacobean Dramatic Perspectives* (Charlottesville, Va., 1972), esp. for Beaumont and Fletcher, Middleton, Webster, and Ford; and Brian Gibbons, *Jacobean City Comedy* (Cambridge, Mass., 1968), esp. pp. 61-82 (for Jonson and Chapman) and 105-33 (Middleton).
3 Line 638 of *Mundus et Infans* (1508), in *Specimens of the Pre-Shakespearean Drama*, ed. J.M. Manly (Boston, 1897), Vol. I. Also cited by Spivack, p. 153. Compare as well Edmund's words to Edgar, 'I do serve you in this business' (I.ii.185), with those of Covetousness to Worldly Man in *Enough Is as Good as a Feast* (1560): 'About your affairs I have business this way' (ed. R. Mark Benbow, Lincoln, Neb., 1967, line 1114).
4 See Spivack, pp. 346-57.
5 *Shakespeare's Dramatic Heritage*, p. 22
6 *Religion and Literature*, p. 74
7 T.M. Parrott noted long ago that such displays are so frequent in *An Humourous Day's Mirth* 'that it seems no unfair assumption to suppose that the play was written mainly for their sake' *(The Plays of George Chapman: The Comedies*, London, 1914 [rpt. New York, 1961], II, 687). Paul V. Kreider agrees that these humourous scenes predominate over story: 'There is a slight, barely traceable plot, but there are numerous scenes which have not even the most indirect connection with it' *(Elizabethan Comic Character Conventions as Revealed in the Comedies of George Chapman*, Ann Arbor, Mich., 1935, p. 151). Similarly, Herford and Simpson have remarked that in the humours plays Jonson made exhibition of humours the sole function of plot *(Ben Jonson*, Oxford, 1925-52, I, 343). To agree with this view is not, however, to argue that display of humours is the 'sole function' of the humours plays. If we look at these plays through another perspective, that of comical satire for instance, it is clear that display of

humours is by no means their only aim (see O.J. Campbell, *Comical Satyre and Shakespeare's 'Troilus and Cressida,'* San Marino, California, 1938; also Gibbons, *Jacobean City Comedy*, pp. 61-82, and R.A. Foakes, *Shakespeare: The Dark Comedies to the Last Plays*, London, 1971, pp. 31-7). But such displays seem to have played a larger role than any other factor in shaping the *structure* of the humours comedies. Foakes makes a valuable distinction between the commentary of Mitis and Cordatus, which is 'designed to answer possible objections and to explain the way satire works' in *Every Man out of His Humour*, and what actually goes on in the play: 'The dramatic action in fact *displays* an entertaining and engaging group of 'humourous' characters ... courtier and citizen, student and countryman, are all *displayed* in their affectations and folly' (p. 36; italics mine).

8 *An Humorous Day's Mirth*, I.ii.18-19, in *The Plays of George Chapman: The Comedies*, ed. Alan Holaday (Urbana, Ill., 1970)

9 This device was perhaps already implicit in those humours comedies that, like Jonson's, featured commentators: to a degree, the intriguer is a commentator who has renounced some of his passivity. Some notable humourous intriguers from the early private-theatre plays are: Planet, in Marston's *Jack Drum's Entertainment* (1600); Lodovico, in Chapman's *May-Day* (1602); Rinaldo, in Chapman's *All Fools*; Vandome, in his *Monsieur D'Olive*; Hercules, in Marston's *The Fawn*; and the eponymous hero of Middleton's *The Phoenix* — the latter four plays all produced c. 1604-5.

10 Private-theatre plays written just after *King Lear* continue this practice, and the mock poisoning of *Satiromastix* (1601) finds its parallel in the machinations of Edward Sharpham's Fleer, whose invention animates the last act of the 1606 play named after him. Demetrius is the main stage manager in Day's *The Isle of Gulls* (1606), as his disguises and intrigues thrust characters in and out of a chain of contrived situations; but, of course, the same is true of the stage-managing of Volpone and Mosca, in Jonson's 1606 *Volpone*, written for the Globe. In associating the stage-managing intriguer with private-theatre comedy, I have not meant to imply his total absence from public-theatre comedy: the relationship between playwriting at the two types of theatre was a fluid one, and no such rigid dichotomy exists. But the stage manager appears so frequently in private-theatre comedy at this period as to be typical of it, whereas he is found much more rarely in the extant public-theatre comedies of these years.

11 Shakespeare was brilliantly successful in mixing genres. In *Othello* as in *King Lear*, the stage-managing intriguer seems to owe as much to contemporary comedy as to the traditional Vice (Iago's masterful use of the handkerchief finds parallels in comedy rather than in the moralities); and jealous husbands, cuckolds, and scheming wives (putative or otherwise) are the commonplaces of Jacobean comedy. Shakespeare himself was creating a comic stage manager at about the same time he used the figure in these tragedies: Duke Vincentio stage-manages many of the actions in *Measure for Measure* (1604), especially the powerfully tragicomic final scene.

12 Chambers applied the phrase to the play in *King Lear* (Glasgow, 1940), p. 48.

13 'Intrigue in Elizabethan Tragedy,' in *Essays on Shakespeare and Elizabethan Drama in Honour of Hardin Craig*, ed. Richard Hosley (London, 1963), p. 41

14 John D. Rosenberg, 'King Lear and His Comforters,' *Essays in Criticism*, vol. 16, 1966, 142. Alan C. Dessen also finds that Shakespeare encourages the audience (mainly through Gloucester's impressions) to view the fall as a very obvious fiction, right from the start of the scene:

see 'Two Falls and a Trap: Shakespeare and the Spectacles of Realism,' *English Literary Renaissance*, vol. 5, 1975, esp. 301-7.

5 *The Plays of George Chapman: The Tragedies* (London, 1910 [rpt. New York, 1961]), II, 598

6 Finkelpearl, *John Marston of the Middle Temple*, pp. 157, 160. The further quotation is from p. 259.

17 This difference between Jacobean and earlier Elizabethan structure seems to constitute the basic difference between two of Eugene M. Waith's 'herculean heroes,' as we can see by comparing Waith's statements about each of them in light of the structural distinction. Of Tamburlaine, he writes: 'The figure is vast. The very structure of the play conveys this impression, for the succession of scenes ... stretching over great expanses of time and space, *presents the man* in terms of the places he makes his and the time which at the last he fails to conquer ... There is a forward movement of the play in unfolding not only the narrative but the full picture of the hero' (*The Herculean Hero*, London, 1962, pp. 63-4). But he writes of *Bussy D'Ambois* that 'this *world* of court intrigue which Bussy opposes, yet the only *world* in which he can act, is his fate. Clermont, too, falls victim to this *world* in the end'; and he notes that *Bussy D'Ambois* presents us with 'the moving dilemma of a great-spirited man who attempts to live by a heroic code in a *world* dominated by Machiavellian policy' (pp. 110, 111), a dilemma not too distant from that faced by the great-souled Lear. (All italics in the Waith quotations are mine.) Tamburlaine's world takes the shape of his character; Bussy's world is arranged to provoke and frustrate his character's every feature.

18 Horace Howard Furness, ed., *King Lear*, *A New Variorum Edition of Shakespeare*, Vol. V (Philadelphia and London, 1880), p. 449

19 'Recognition in *King Lear*,' in *Some Facets of 'King Lear*,' pp. 114-15

20 Joseph W. Donohue, Jr., *Dramatic Character in the English Romantic Age*, p. 28.

21 *Shakespeare Survey*, vol. 13, 1960, 49. Inga-Stina Ewbank comes to a similar conclusion after examining Lear's speech to Cordelia at IV.vii.45. She finds the speech 'related to the whole poetic quality of *King Lear*,' in that instead of playing 'as a kind of decoration over the dramatic situation, Lear's [poetry] *is* the situation ' ('Shakespeare's Poetry,' in *A New Companion to Shakespeare Studies*, ed. Kenneth Muir and S. Schoenbaum, Cambridge, 1971, p. 110).

22 'Introduction' to his Revels Plays edition of *Philaster* (London, 1969), p. lxxi

23 These quotations are located at, respectively, I.ii.119, III.ii.48-49, III.ii.50, and IV.i.10-11.

24 For other instances see *Arden of Feversham* (1591), *The London Prodigal* (1604), Heywood's *If You Know Not Me You Know Nobody: Part II* (1605), or his *The Fair Maid of the West: Part I* (1610), and *A Yorkshire Tragedy* (1606). The practice was widely followed, and this list is intended to provide only a sampling.

25 *Prefaces*, II, 21. 'Shakespeare had, besides, to carry us into strange regions of thought and passion, so he must, at the same time, hold us by familiar things' (p. 20).

26 In Richard Levin's perceptive and wide-ranging study of *The Multiple Plot in English Renaissance Drama* (Chicago and London, 1971), p. 221

27 See Bevington, *From 'Mankind' to Marlowe*, pp. 170-98, for a full discussion of these early developments.

28 Heywood's *A Woman Killed with Kindness* (1603) and Middleton and Rowley's *The Changeling* (1622) are two notably successful tragedies. See the fine discussion of Heywood's plotting in R.W. Van Fossen's edition of the play (London, 1961), pp. xxxvi-xli.

29 To take only one example, in Marston's 1604 *The Dutch Courtesan*, (ed. M.L. Wine, London, 1965), Cocledemoy's praise of bawds (I.ii.29-54) is designed to parallel and echo Freevill's praise of prostitutes in lines 92-127 of the previous scene. See also Chapman's *Monsieur D'Olive* (1604), Field's *A Woman Is a Weathercock* (1609), and just about any comedy by Middleton. Richard Levin's study of how the multiple plot works in Middleton's *The Family of Love* (1602) provides a fine, detailed instance of such usage (*The Multiple Plot in English Renaissance Drama*, pp. 59-66) in a poor but representative play. I am indebted to Levin's discussion for the example from *The Family of Love* cited later.

30 *The Works of Thomas Middleton*, ed. A.H. Bullen (Boston, 1885 [rpt. New York, 1964]), Vol. III (V.iii.390-7)

31 As Blissett notes in 'Recognition in *King Lear*,' p. 109. Paul J. Alpers observes that the subplot in effect overtakes and passes the main plot in Act IV, and what Gloucester learns first, Lear himself then comes to terms with ('*King Lear* and the Theory of the "Sight Pattern," ' in *In Defense of Reading: A Reader's Approach to Literary Criticism*, ed. Reuben A. Brower and Richard Poirier, New York, 1962, pp. 144-51).

32 'Prose is used for most of the scenes where Gloucester and Edmund appear together, thus providing us with a kind of stepping-stone to the more remote plane on which Lear's affairs are conducted' (*Shakespeare's Tragedies*, London, 1961, p. 64). In a fascinating essay in *Some Facets of 'King Lear,'* Bridget Gellert Lyons observes that 'the subplot simplifies the central action, translating its concerns into familiar (and therefore easily apprehensible) verbal and visual patterns. The subplot is easier to grasp because its characters tend to account for their sufferings in traditional moral language; it also pictorializes the main action, supplying interpreted visual emblems for some of the play's important themes' (p. 25). As we found in Chapter 2, visual emblems are not confined to the subplot; but Lyons' basic point about differences in complexity does seem to apply to the two plots. Formulas, she notes (ibid.), are less applicable in Lear's world than in Gloucester's; and her essay distinguishes Edmund's patent bastardy (an emblem of his parents' sin) from the less accountable evil of Regan and Goneril, Edgar's feigned madness from Lear's real madness, and the trial by combat from Lear's speech on justice.

33 'The Music of Poetry,' in *On Poetry and Poets* (London, 1957), p. 32

34 For examples, see Heywood's *How a Man May Choose a Good Wife from a Bad* (1602) and his *The Wise Woman of Hogsdon* (1604); Wilkins' *The Miseries of Enforced Marriage* (1606); *The Fair Maid of Bristow* (1604); *The London Prodigal* (1604); and Part II of Dekker and Middleton's *The Honest Whore* (1605) — all popular at about the time *King Lear* was written.

35 *Patient Grissil*, written in 1600 by Dekker, Chettle, and Haughton; Part I of Dekker and Middleton's *The Honest Whore* (1604) — each part of which thus provides a different type of domestic drama; and a play written later than *Lear*, Heywood and Rowley's *Fortune by Land and Sea* (1609).

36 I might note here that I do not consider the differences between Lear and Gloucester as being primarily that distinction pointed out by Sigurd Burckhardt, between one who trusts words too much and one who does not trust them at all. Burckhardt oversimplifies when he says that 'It is false to ascribe to him [Lear in scene one] a despot's greed for praise or fawning submission; he makes a fearful mistake, but the mistake is the regal one of taking people *at their word* in the most radical and literal sense' (*Shakespearean Meanings,* Princeton, 1968, p. 239). One

might ask why Lear does not also take Kent at his word. I find Burckhardt's entire theory about the double plot an engaging one, but one unsupported by my own experience of the play.

7 Bevington, p. 161

8 Shakespeare makes another bold departure from the norm in the prominence he gives to the subplot. Richard Levin notes that 'in most of the multi-plot tragedies ... the causation only proceeds "downward" — that is, the main action alters the course of the subplot, but is not altered by it' (*The Multiple Plot in English Renaissance Drama*, p. 221). Yet in *King Lear,* many of those 'seeds of action' that the subplot sows take root in the main plot: Edmund introduces the ambitious betrayal and contempt for custom that Regan and Goneril pick up in their confrontations with Lear; Edgar first images the theme of madness; and Gloucester's recovery prefigures that of Lear, as does his death.

CHAPTER 4

1 Edmund's apparent mellowing in Act V comes significantly at the end of his career, and seems at best a mild version of the conventional last-minute reversal that M.C. Bradbrook describes as 'frankly artificial' (*Themes and Conventions of Elizabethan Tragedy*, Cambridge, 1935, p. 62). Otherwise, Edmund reveals not a glimmer of conscience.

2 *Themes and Conventions* p. 61

3 Villains whose characters are drawn according to the outlines of this convention include: Bagot, in *Thomas Lord Cromwell* (1600); Codigune, in *The Valiant Welshman* (1612); Wolsey, in Rowley's *When You See Me You Know Me* (1604); Eleazar, in *Lust's Dominion*, written in 1600 by Dekker, Day, and Chettle; and Roderigo Borgia, in Barnes's *The Devil's Charter* (1607). Exemplars of virtue include: Gresham, in Part II of Heywood's *If You Know Not Me You Know Nobody* (1605); the title character of *Sir John Oldcastle,* a 1599 play by Drayton, Hathaway, Munday, and Wilson; Henry VIII, in Rowley's *When You See Me You Know Me* (1604); Cicero, in Jonson's *Catiline* (1611); the Marshal, in Heywood's *The Royal King and the Loyal Subject* (1602); and of course Grissil, in the 1600 *Patient Grissil* written by Dekker, Chettle, and Haughton. With its emphasis on morally antithetical figures, this convention of characterization was perhaps another vestige of an earlier dramatic tradition: like these popular plays, the moralities defined their characters along rigid moral lines, and have picked up their name as a result.

4 *The Revenger's Tragedy* ed. R.A. Foakes (London, 1966), II.i.35-39

5 'Cymbeline and Coterie Dramaturgy,' *ELH*, vol. 34, 1967, 287. Compare also the discontinuous and indecorous characterization of: Iachimo, in Marston's *What You Will* (1601); Justiniano, in *Westward Ho*, written by Dekker and Middleton in 1604; or Antonio, in Marston's *Antonio's Revenge* (1600).

6 Charles A. Hallett arrives at a fine interpretation of *Volpone* by examining the place and presentation of Celia in the work ('Jonson's Celia: A Reinterpretation of *Volpone*,' *Studies in Philology*, vol. 68, 1971, 50-69). In doing so he fills out this paradigm, for the techniques of characterization that he describes Jonson using in the play are those of the tradition under discussion here. Also, the importance that Hallett attaches to Celia's silence, as one of the hallmarks of a virtuous woman (pp. 58, 65), leads one to make inevitable comparisons with the presentation of Cordelia in I.i.

7 *Ben Jonson*, ed. C.H. Herford, Percy and Evelyn Simpson (Oxford, 1925-52), Vol. V (III.vii.267-75). Further references to *Volpone* are to this edition and will be cited in the text.

8 *The History of King Leir*, ed. W.W. Greg, Malone Society Reprints (Oxford, 1907), lines 253-4, 273-4

9 Cf. Sir John Oldcastle, in the 1599 play of that name by Drayton, Hathaway, Munday, and Wilson; Momford, in Chettle and Day's *The Blind Beggar of Bednal Green* (1600); the Marshal, in Heywood's *The Royal King and the Loyal Subject* (1602); and Cromwell, in the 1600 *Thomas Lord Cromwell*.

10 For instance: Winifred M.T. Nowottny, in 'Some Aspects of the Style of *King Lear*,' *Shakespeare Survey*, vol. 13, 1960, 49-57; Sheldon P. Zitner, in '*King Lear* and Its Language' *Some Facets of 'King Lear,'* pp. 3-22; and Granville-Barker's fine comments in his *Preface* (41-66)

11 See Jonas A. Barish and Marshall Waingrow, ' "Service" in *King Lear*,' *Shakespeare Quarterly*, vol. 9, 1958, 347-55; also William R. Elton, *'King Lear' and the Gods* (San Marino, Calif., 1966), pp. 286-7.

12 Not to mention the kind of service Edgarpoor Tom performed when he 'serv'd the lust of [his] mistress' heart' (III.iv.86-7), a usage that anticipates the 'woman's services' that Goneril thinks are due to Edmund (IV.ii.27) when she makes herself his *'Affectionate servant'* (IV.vi.271) and gives Oswald the chance to become 'a serviceable villain;/As duteous to the vices of [his] mistress/ As badness would desire' (IV.vi.254-6). These references allude to such 'servicing' as a bull performs for a herd of cows — with bestial overtones quite appropriate for Goneril.

13 *The Miseries of Enforced Marriage*, ed. Glenn H. Blayney, Malone Society Reprints, (Oxford, 1963), line 160

14 *The Dramatic Works of Thomas Dekker*, ed. Fredson Bowers (Cambridge, 1953-61), Vol. III (IV.i.38-40)

15 At the time *King Lear* was first produced, the regeneration of scapegraces was an especially popular dramatic motif, running through such plays as: Heywood's *How a Man May Choose a Good Wife from a Bad* (1602) and his *The Wise Woman of Hogsdon* (1604); Part One of Dekker and Middleton's *The Honest Whore* (1604); and two anonymous plays also produced in 1604, *The Fair Maid of Bristow* and *The London Prodigal*.

16 Disguised as Caius, Kent gives his age as 48. But in II.ii Oswald calls him an 'ancient ruffian' and refers to his grey beard (62-3), and Cornwall calls him 'old fellow' (86) and 'ancient knave' (127). Certainly Kent's final speeches in Act V also gives us an impression of a much older man.

17 The clown never appears on the private stage, perhaps because his role required the talents of an experienced adult actor, and perhaps also because the private theatres' more consciously literary playwrights resented the improvisational liberties that clowns notoriously took with texts (see Hamlet's complaint at the start of III.ii).

18 *The Fool* (London, 1935), p. 248. Welsford discusses the Fool in *King Lear* on pp. 253-70. See also William Empson's chapter on 'Fool in Lear,' in *The Structure of Complex Words* (London, 1951), pp. 125-57. For examples of the Fool's stepping out of the action in *King Lear* to address the audience, see his speeches at the end of I.v and III.ii.

19 All quotations ibid., p. 237

20 Ed. R. Mark Benbow, (Lincoln, Neb., 1967), lines 1871-80. Further quotations from this edition will be cited in the text.

21 For further evidence that Shakespeare was well acquainted with the Erasmian tradition, see Thelma N. Greenfield's discussion of its presence in one of the comedies: '*A Midsummer Night's Dream* and *The Praise of Folly*' *Comparative Literature*, vol. 20, 1968, 236-44.

22 Sir Thomas Chaloner, tr., *The Praise of Folie*, ed. Clarence H. Miller, Early English Text Society (London, 1965), p. 9. All further quotations from Erasmus are taken from this edition and will be cited in the text.

3 P. 118. Folly also notes 'that **Christian Religion** seemeth to haue a certaine sybship with simplicitee, and deuoute foolisshenesse, in nothyng agreyng with worldly wysedome' (p. 120).

4 In structuring his *encomium* this way, perhaps Shakespeare took his cue from one of Erasmus' variations on the 'stage of fools' *topos*, where Erasmus also rests his focus on a king — a very similar focus: 'So likewise, all this life of mortall men, what is it els, but a certaine kynde of stage plaie? wheras men come foorthe disguised one in one arraie, an other in an other, eche plaiyng his parte ... as who before represented a kynge, beyng clothed all in purpre, hauyng no more but shyfted hym selfe a little, shoulde shew hym selfe againe lyke an woobegon myser' (p. 38).

CHAPTER 5

1 Horace Howard Furness, ed., *King Lear, A New Variorum Edition of Shakespeare*, Vol. V (Philadelphia and London, 1880), p. 392

2 See David M. Bevington, *From 'Mankind' to Marlowe* (Cambridge, Mass., 1962), pp. 190-8.

3 John Shaw has propounded the fascinating idea that Albany's speech unfolds as the traditional closing speech of a Shakespearean tragedy, but that — to Albany's shock and our own — Lear's agony interrupts the final couplet towards which Albany is heading. See 'King Lear: The Final Lines,' *Essays in Criticism*, vol. 16, 1966, 261-7.

4 *Ram-Alley*, ed. Claude E. Jones, (Louvain, 1952), lines 312-13

5 *Antonio's Revenge*, ed. G.K. Hunter (London, 1965), II.ii.50. Shakespeare's Edgar might well echo Antonio's words after another such situation, later in the play: 'Man will break out, despite philosophy' (IV.ii.69). And he does, after Lear's death: 'The weight of this sad time

we must obey;/Speak what we feel, not what we ought to say.'

6 *The Valiant Welshman*, ed. Valentin Kreb (Erlangen and Leipzig, 1902), IV.iii.16. Popular playwrights thus imposed the teleological convention on pre-Christian times as well as on their own; so also in the final lines of Heywood's *The Rape of Lucrece* (1607), the triumphant soldiers 'March on to *Rome, Ioue be* our guard and guide,/That hath in us, veng'd Rape, and punisht Pride' (ed. Alan Holaday, Illinois Studies in Language and Literature, Vol. 34, Urbana, 1950, lines 2988-9).

7 *A Warning for Faire Women*, ed. Richard Simpson, *The School of Shakespeare* (London, 1878), Vol. II, Act II, lines 1052 ff. Beane's killer is convicted on the basis of this deathbed testimony, and thus the thought that he had voiced just after enacting the deed has been confirmed: that Beane's wounds gaped unto the skies and called for vengeance (II.525-26). Compare also the reflections of divine purpose that characters see in the wicked Bagot's downfall, in II.ii of *Thomas Lord Cromwell* (1600).

8 *On the Design of Shakespearian Tragedy* (Toronto, 1957), pp. 185-6

9 For instance, a tragic denouement seems inevitable in Chapman's *The Gentleman Usher* (1602). Margaret, the heroine, has rubbed her face with disfiguring ointment at the report that her lover is dead. But the report turns out to be false, a Doctor Benevemus enters and cures Margaret almost at once, and the discovery that Medice was really Mendice sets everything right again. This turnabout also occurs in Marston's *Jack Drum's Entertainment* (1600), where another heroine is saved from facial disfigurement. In such plays, a Benevemus always waits in the wings to right the ostensibly irreversible situation. More serious outcomes are reversed in other early plays. Poisonings occur in the last acts of Dekker's *Satiromastix* (1601) and Day's *Law Tricks*

(1604); but when the resulting histrionics have run their course, each 'poison' turns out to have been only a sleeping potion. Both of these plays withhold the ruse from the audience until the situation is almost over, fostering that double perspective discussed above, and keeping us in suspense until the final decisive turn.

10 Wilson, *On the Design of Shakespearian Tragedy*, p. 185

11 Shakespeare seems to have been the first playwright to see the possibilities, in the *Arcadia*, for a new kind of dramatic romance, more aesthetically coherent and philosophically profound than such early Elizabethan theatrical romances as *Clyomon and Clamydes* (c. 1570) or *Common Conditions* (1576). Beaumont and Fletcher began mining the *Arcadia* only in 1607-8 (at least two years after *King Lear*) for the tragedy of *Cupid's Revenge*, and wrote their first tragicomic romance, *Philaster*, in 1609. Even John Day's comic treatment of Arcadian material, in *The Isle of Gulls* (1606), postdates *King Lear* by over a year.

12 Gillian Beer, *The Romance* (London, 1970), p. 38. Beer also observes that 'The happy ending has remained typical of romance ... Romance is an inclusive mode. It offers comedy; it includes suffering. Yet it does not have ... the finality of tragedy. It celebrates — by the processes of its art as much as by the individual stories — fecundity, freedom and survival' (p. 29).

13 *Shakespeare's Comedies* (Oxford, 1960), p. 220

14 See Martha Andresen, ' "Ripeness is All": Sententiae and Commonplaces in *King Lear*,' in *Some Facets of 'King Lear,'* pp. 145-68; also Russell A. Fraser, *Shakespeare's Poetics in Relation to 'King Lear'* (London, 1962).

15 The four precepts are applied by, respectively, the Fool at II.iv.52-3, Kent at IV.iii.33-4, Gloucester at IV.i.20-1, and Edgar at IV.i.6.

16 ' "Speak What We Feel": The End of *King Lear*,' *English Language Notes*, vol. 5, 1967-8, 165

17 '*King Lear:* The Final Lines,' 265, 266

18 'King Lear and His Comforters,' *Essays in Criticism*, vol. 16, 1966, 146

19 *Allegorical Imagery* (Princeton, 1966), pp. 405, 404

20 'Oration on the Dignity of Man,' tr. Elizabeth Livermore Forbes, in *The Renaissance Philosophy of Man*, ed. Ernst Cassirer, Paul Oskar Kristeller, and John Herman Randall, Jr. (Chicago and London, 1948), p. 225

21 Julian Markels, *The Pillar of the World* (Columbus, Ohio, 1968), p. 103

Index

Alpers, Paul J. 134
Armin, Robert 23, 93

Baillie, Joanna 38
Baldwin, T.W. 3
Barker, Harley Granville. *See* Granville-
  Barker
Barry, Lording 113
Beaumont, Francis 8; *The Knight of the
  Burning Pestle* 17
Beaumont and Fletcher 20, 21, 22, 25,
  38, 47, 56, 71; *Cupid's Revenge* 20,
  23, 24, 69; *The Maid's Tragedy* 20,
  24, 69, 83; *Philaster* 24, 115, 116;
  The Woman Hater 13, 20
Beaurline, L.A. 25
Beer, Gillian 116n
Bevington, David 35, 73, 79
Biblical descriptions 26
Blissett, William 70, 77n
Bradbrook, M.C. ix, 82
Bradley, A.C.
  HIS APPROACH: its affective nature
  34, 35-6, 72, 89, 109, 111; its merits
  9, 36, 38; narrative expectations 21,
  .35, 46-7, 51, 53-4, 77; limitations 4,
  16-17, 34-6, 47, 115
  ON KING LEAR: characterization 8,
  65, 67, 70, 76, 81-2, 115; 'defects'
  11-12, 33-4, 34, 40, 41, 46, 47, 52,
77, 99, 108; extreme aspects of 16,
  22, 25, 29, 30, 92; opening scenes 11,
  19, 21; unity of play's world 14, 15,
  26, 29, 92, 93, 112, 121-2
Brown, John Russell 56-7
Browne, Sir Thomas 15
Brecht, Bertolt 21
Burckhardt, Sigurd 135
Byron, George Gordon, Lord 77·

Chambers, R.W. 66
Chapman, George 5, 8, 13, 14, 22, 25,
  29, 37, 56, 74, 113; *Bussy D'Ambois*
  13, 21, 24, 25, 27, 41, 44, 45, 46,
  50-1, 68, 71; *The Conspiracy and
  Tragedy of Charles, Duke of Byron*
  38, 44, 68; *The Gentleman Usher* 50,
  138; *An Humourous Day's Mirth* 37,
  60-1; *May-Day* 36; *The Revenge of
  Bussy D'Ambois* 68; *Sir Giles Goose-
  cap* 50; *The Widow's Tears* 13n, 21,
  24, 27
Charney, Maurice ix
Chaucer, Geoffrey 31, 122
Chettle, Henry 59
Clyomon and Clamydes 49
Coleridge, Samuel T. 8, 11, 20, 22
Colie, Rosalie L. 4, 6
Common Conditions 49
Cooke, Katharine 9

Danby, John F. 31
Day, John: *The Isle of Gulls* 12, 21, 23, 132; with Dekker, Thomas, and Haughton, William: *Lust's Dominion* 88; with Rowley, William, and Wilkins, George: *The Travels of the Three English Brothers* 17;
Dekker, Thomas 8; *Old Fortunatus* 48, 49; *Patient Grissil* 31, 122; *Satiromastix* 61; *The Shoemaker's Holiday* 50, 72; *The Whore of Babylon* 126; with Middleton, Thomas: *The Honest Whore* 91, *The Roaring Girl* 17, 89; with Webster, John: *Westward Ho* 41. *See also* Day, John
Donne, John 71
Donohue, Joseph W., Jr. 38, 70n
Doran, Madeleine 6, 128-9
dramatic emblems 24, 42-3, 44-5, 127-8. *See also* Shakespeare, *King Lear*

Eliot, T.S. 48, 78, 121
emblems. *See* dramatic emblems
Erasmus 95-107 *passim*
Evans, Bertrand 117

Fair Maid of Bristow, The 91
Field, Nathan 21, 23, 24, 25, 128
Fielding, Henry 56
Finkelpearl, Philip 13, 68-9n
Fletcher, John 8, 27. *See also* Beaumont and Fletcher
Foakes, R.A. 126
Fraser, Russell 32

Gardner, Dame Helen 54-5, 60
Gibbons, Brian 126
Goethe, J.W. von 92
Gombrich, E.H. ix
Granville-Barker, Harley 20, 21, 22, 52-3, 73
Greene, Robert 5, 8; *Friar Bacon and Friar Bungay* 95; *James IV* 6, 95
Greenfield, Thelma Nelson 130

Grene, David 53, 54
Gurr, Andrew 71

Harbage, Alfred 66, 124, 127
Haughton, William. *See* Day, John
Heilman, R.B. 27, 44, 47, 71, 130
Herford, C.H. 40
Heywood, Thomas 8; *The Four Prentices* 48, 49, 127; *If You Know Not Me You Know Nobody*: Part I 90, Part II 73-4; *The Rape of Lucrece* 83; *The Royal King and the Loyal Subject* 127; *A Woman Killed with Kindness* 78-9
History of King Leir, The 19, 29, 30, 52, 85, 111, 114
Histriomastix 37
Holinshed, Raphael 111
Hoyle, James 42-3

James, D.G. 8, 47
James, Henry 71
Johnson, Samuel 11, 16, 56
Jonson, Ben 5, 8, 13, 22, 37, 48; *The Alchemist* 67-8; *Catiline* 84; *Cynthia's Revels* 21, 37, 40, 41; *Epicoene* 25, 30, 45; *Every Man in his Humour* 37, 60-1; *Every Man out of His Humour* 37, 60-1; *Poetaster* 3, 4, 7, 8, 50; *Sejanus* 77, 83, 84, 88; *Volpone* 84-5, 90, 113-14, 132

Kempe, William 93
King Leir. See History of King Leir, The
Kirsch, Arthur C. 83
Kozintsev, Grigori 53
Kyd, Thomas 5, 39

Leech, Clifford 77
Lennox, Charlotte 108
Levin, Richard 73n, 130, 131, 135
Lewis, C.S. 18
Lewis, Matthew 'Monk' 38
London Prodigal, The 91

Lyly, John 5-8 *passim*, 21, 37
Lyons, Bridget Gellert 134

Mack, Maynard 8, 14, 23, 27-8, 34, 46, 51, 66, 92, 123
Maid's Metamorphosis, The 37, 129
Markels, Julian 122n, 129
Marks, Carol L. 47, 119
Marlowe, Christopher 5, 8, 34, 56, 107; *Doctor Faustus* 6, 49, 71-2; *Edward II* 6; *The Jew of Malta* 6, 59, 88; *Tamburlaine* 35, 49, 69, 71-2
Marston, John 5, 8, 13, 29, 34, 37, 56, 74, 113; *Antonio and Mellida* 39; *Antonio's Revenge* 21, 45-6, 69, 113; *The Dutch Courtesan* 61-2, 113, 128; *The Fawn* 50, 127; *Jack Drum's Entertainment* 37, 138; *The Malcontent* 12, 21; *Sophonisba* 13, 39-40, 44, 68, 71; *What You Will* 41, 50
Massinger, Philip 34
Maturin, Charles 38
Mehl, Dieter 42-3, 44, 127
Merry Devil of Edmonton, The 72
Middleton, Thomas 13, 37, 62, 65, 74; *A Chaste Maid in Cheapside* 25, 29-30, 50; *The Family of Love* 74; *The Phoenix* 36-7, 127; *A Trick to Catch the Old One* 62; *Your Five Gallants* 27. *See also* Dekker, Thomas
Mirandola, Pico della 121
morality plays 55, 56, 58, 79, 94-5, 105, 131, 135
moriae encomium 93-107, 117, 137
Muir, Kenneth 3, 34, 41
Mundus et Infans 59, 94, 105

narrative: and plot 47-8; importance of in Elizabethan drama 35, 36, 47-9, 54-5, 73-4, 128-9; departures from in Elizabethan and Jacobean drama 23, 36-8, 47-51, 54-5, 130-2 *passim*
Nowottny, Winifred 8, 71

Parrott, Thomas M. 68
Pico. *See* Mirandola
plot 47-8
private-theatre traditions 5-6, 7, 17, 37, 60-2, 64-5, 124, 125, 127, 132, 138
public-theatre traditions 5-6, 17, 35, 37, 60-1, 72-4, 78-9, 93-5, 109, 113-14, 119, 129, 131-2, 135, 136, 137-8

Rosenberg, John D. 67n, 120
Rowe, Nicholas 15
Rowley, Samuel 95
Rowley, William 17

Schelling, Felix E. 128
Schlegel, A.W. von 70, 76
Shakespeare, William: *All's Well That Ends Well* 7; *Antony and Cleopatra* 19, 114; *As You Like It* 6, 93, 95; *The Comedy of Errors* 43; *Cymbeline* 7, 77, 83, 115, 117; *Hamlet* 7, 11, 16, 18, 21, 49, 51-4 *passim*, 76, 109, 110, 114, 117; *Henry IV* 6, 49; *Henry VI* 6, 49; *Julius Caesar* 52
KING LEAR: character groupings in 28-9, 53, 45, 74-5, 81, 86-91, 97-99, 101-2; date of 4; departures from narrative concerns in 19-20, 21-2, 33, 51-5; emblematic patterning in 24-5, 30-2, 41-5, 96, 112-13, 122, 129, 130; extremes of action and characterization in 16, 22, 28, 30, 46-7, 51, 53, 69-70, 77-8, 81-2, 85-6, 92, 95-6, 102-3, 120-1; romance elements in 116-17; tempo of 15-16, 19, 22, 53, 77, 109-10, 134; thematic and affective emphasis on feelings in 7, 18, 22, 30, 40-1, 56-7, 66-7, 70-3, 77-80, 85-6, 92-3, 115-16, 122; use of place in 14-15, 72-3, 92
Love's Labour's Lost 6, 21, 127; *Macbeth* 11, 18, 51, 52, 76, 109, 110, 114; *Measure for Measure* 7, 127,

132; *The Merchant of Venice* 6; *A Midsummer Night's Dream* 6, 43, 93; *Othello* 16, 18-19, 21, 34, 51, 53, 70, 76, 88, 109, 110, 114, 117, 132; *Pericles* 7, 116; *Richard II* 6, 52; *The Tempest* 7, 110, 116; *Troilus and Cressida* 7; *Twelfth Night* 93, 95, 99; *The Winter's Tale* 7, 80, 110, 111, 115, 116

Sharpham, Edward 45, 132
Shaw, John 119, 137
Sheil, Richard 38
Shelley, Percy Bysshe 31, 77
Sidney, Sir Philip 46, 48, 116
Simpson, Percy and Evelyn 40
Sophocles 112
Spencer, Theodore 3
Spenser, Edmund 15, 111
Spivack, Bernard 58, 59, 66

Tarlton, Richard 93
Tate, Nahum 4, 14, 19, 21-2, 30, 108, 115
Tourneur, Cyril 125; *The Atheist's Tragedy* 69; *The Revenger's Tragedy* 56, 82-3

Tuve, Rosemond 46, 120

Valiant Welshman, The 113
Vice, the 58-60, 62, 66-7, 88, 94

Wager, William 94-5, 101, 105
Waith, Eugene M. 133
Warning for Fair Women. A 78-9, 113, 137-8
Webster, John 8, 17, 125; *The Duchess of Malfi* 69; *The White Devil* 56-7. *See also* Dekker, Thomas
Welsford, Enid 93-4, 99
Wickham, Glynne 55, 60
Wilbur, Richard 55
Wilkins, George 17, 88-9
Wilson, Harold S. 115, 116n
Wisdom of Doctor Dodypoll, The 39

Yeats, William Butler 3
Yorkshire Tragedy, A 78-9

Zitner, Sheldon P. 31